D0487913

Old English Instruments of Music

Portrait said to be Lady Mary Sidney with her Archlute (Penshurst Place)

CANON FRANCIS W. GALPIN

Old English Instruments
of Music

THEIR HISTORY AND CHARACTER

Fourth edition, revised
with supplementary notes by

THURSTON DART

King Edward Professor of Music at
King's College, University of London

METHUEN & CO LTD
11 NEW FETTER LANE · LONDON EC4

First published by Methuen & Co Ltd, 1910
Second Edition, 1921
Third Edition, Revised, 1932
Fourth Edition, Revised and reset, 1965
Printed in Great Britain by
The Shenval Press
London, Hertford and Harlow

To the Master,
Wardens, Court of Assistants
and
Livery of the Worshipful Company
of Musicians

Floruit – Floret – Florebit

Contents

CONTENTS

The verses which introduce each chapter are taken from a manuscript in the British Museum (Roy. 18 D. ii), where they are described as "The Musicall Proverbis in the Garet at the New Lodge in the Parke of Lekingfelde" (*temp*. Henry VIII), from a poem by Robert Manning of Lincolnshire (*c*. 1303), from Chaucer's *Nonne Preestes Tale* (1390) and from Sir William Leighton's *Teares and Lamentacions of a Sorrowfull Soule*, published in 1613.

List of Plates

xi

*On each plate the sizes of the instruments shown are
proportionate to their actual size, and to each other*

The pages from manuscripts are reproduced on plates 2, 3, 7, 12, 20, 21,
28, 33, 36, 38, 40, 43, 48, 51, 52, 53 by courtesy of the Trustees of the
British Museum; Corpus Christi College, Cambridge; the Warden and Fellows
of All Souls College, Oxford; the University Library, Glasgow; the Bodleian
Library, Oxford; Trinity College, Cambridge; the University Library,
Cambridge; Lambeth Palace Library; St John's College, Cambridge.

List of Illustrations in the Text

Original Preface

WHEN THE GENERAL EDITOR asked me to contribute a volume on Musical Instruments to the series of The Antiquary's Books I found myself confronted by two great difficulties: there was, first of all, the vast extent of the subject, of which mere portions have already called forth large and important works; and then there was the question whether it would be possible to put in a popular form material which should also satisfy the inquiries of the student and archaeologist. The latter requirement will explain the admission of much which might otherwise be thought unnecessary; for instance, to the ordinary reader it may seem a needless task to describe the compass, pitch, and tunings of these old-world instruments, and yet there are no details about which I have been so frequently asked, especially by those who happen to possess musical relics and desire to hear once more the voices of the past. Having a profound sympathy with such desire, I hope they will find that, although the introduction of the Staff Notation into the text has been avoided, these interesting particulars can be easily ascertained by comparing the signs used with the key given in the Appendix.

In order to deal at all adequately with so extensive a subject, it has been considered advisable to restrict it to a description of the instruments used in England and in other parts of the United Kingdom so far as they have shared our old English life; and it was thought that the end of the eighteenth century, or shortly after, would form a suitable point at which to close their history. The increasing popularity of the Pianoforte and the improvements made in the Wind Instruments rendered the last century much more modern than its immediate predecessor.

For the origin of the Musical Instruments used by our forefathers I have not hesitated to go to times most remote and to trace their wanderings westward through countries far removed from our island. But for literary and pictorial illustration I have confined myself almost entirely to English authors and English artists, and most of the medieval miniatures here reproduced are presented in this connection for the first time, as I have endeavoured to avoid the oft-repeated continental examples and to obtain photographs of musical subjects not already published.

xix

This determination added greatly to the work of preparation, but it achieved another interesting result; for by the careful collation of a large number of illuminated manuscripts of undoubted English workmanship, together with English ecclesiastical carvings of various periods, it has been possible to obtain some idea of the order in which the different forms of instruments appeared among us and of the approximate date at which they first came into use. Such details, indeed, are more than mere points in musical history: they assist the identification of the source of the manuscripts themselves; for example, I conclude that any work which, previous to the close of the fifteenth century, shows an illustration of the Transverse or Concert Flute cannot be considered as a genuine English production, because this instrument, now so well known to us, was not introduced into this country till the reign of Henry VII or his successor, though in Germany, Italy, France, and subsequently in Flanders, it had been in popular use from the thirteenth century. Another instrument which may assist in a similar way is the small Lute or Mandore, which did not appear in England till the close of the fourteenth century, although it had long been employed on the Continent. Illustrations which will enable such typical forms to be identified are here given.

The study of Musical Instruments now no longer with us is therefore necessary, not only for the musician and composer, but for the man of letters, the artist, and the chronicler of our national life; for many allusions to customs of bygone times cannot otherwise be understood, and we should be spared such a trying ordeal as we were recently subjected to by one of our leading illustrated papers, which introduced into a thirteenth-century scene a twentieth-century Mandoline with up-to-date mechanism.

To the ethnologist also such a study is invaluable, but to none does it yield so great a pleasure as to the collector. From the red-letter day when I secured my first "Serpent" and carried the evil beast home to awaken the echoes of Trinity Great Court, at one time the acquisition and now, I am thankful to say, the more economical appreciation of all kinds of musical instruments have given zest to holidays and recreation to leisure hours. To an Englishman, however, such a pursuit is at present a cause of much humiliation; for as we stand among the carefully arranged collections of the Metropolitan Museum of Art in New York, the Brussels Conservatoire of Music or of the Hochschule at Berlin, we are compelled to acknowledge that England has no such national collection, no galleries where the lover of music can trace the evolution of his favourite instrument through the long ages of the past by a graded series of typical specimens clearly explained by labels, charts, and handbooks. Have not the Board of Education one room to spare in their new and unrivalled building at South Kensington, where something more than a few selected instruments with costly decoration may greet the musician's eye and make him turn away with the thought that he evidently stands outside the Arts? The lines on which such a systematic collection might be simply and effectively arranged are set out in the Appendix.

Before concluding this long-drawn prelude I must acknowledge the thanks which I owe to those who have assisted me in the present work. They are, indeed, so many, that if any are omitted by name, it is not because my appreciation of their kindly help is less sincere. I am, however, especially beholden to Mr R. B. Armstrong, of Edinburgh, for his valuable information on the Irish Harp, and his labour and ingenuity in making the first correct reconstruction of the oldest instrument of the kind known to us; to the authorities of the British Museum, the Victoria and Albert Museum, the London Society of Antiquaries, Lambeth Palace Library, the Bodleian Library, the Cambridge University Library, the Glasgow University Library, the Advocates' Library at Edinburgh, the National Museum at Dublin, All Souls College at Oxford, Trinity College, St John's College, Corpus Christi College, Peterhouse and the Fitzwilliam Museum at Cambridge, for the willing way in which they facilitated my work of inspecting and photographing the manuscripts and works of art in their keeping; to Miss Weld, for permission to examine the famous Luttrell Psalter, now at Lulworth Castle, Dorset; to the Dean and Chapter of Westminster (through the Rev Canon Duckworth) for leave to photograph the Litlington Missal; to Sir Frederick Bridge, to whose interest in the old English instruments all owe a debt of thanks; to Dr T. L. Southgate, Master of the Worshipful Company of Musicians; to Mr A. H. Littleton, Herr C. Claudius, of Copenhagen, and the Yorkshire Philosophical Society, for illustrations of English instruments in their possession; to Miss Salvin, the late Dr Watson, Dr J. C. Cox, Mr W. Barclay Squire, Mr F. Bond, Mr S. C. Cockerell, Mr C. Goulding, to my son Mr C. J. Galpin, and others; and not least, to my wife, one of the few lutenists left, for her practical interest in the production of these pages and the labour of preparing them for the press.

I trust that the source from which each illustration has been taken will be found to be duly acknowledged; if it is not mentioned, it is to be understood that the instrument is in my own collection. Some of my statements may be challenged by musical antiquaries, but I hope they will believe that they are given as the result of due investigation, and that the objectionable system of elaborate footnotes would have been required to trace the steps by which each conclusion was reached. If my deductions are wrong, I am willing to bear correction. That further research will reveal new facts is certain, and no one will welcome more gladly than myself all contributions toward a better knowledge and appreciation of the old English instruments of music.

HATFIELD REGIS VICARAGE
HARLOW

FRANCIS W. GALPIN
(1910)

Note for the Fourth Edition

Ever since it was first published more than fifty years ago, Canon Galpin's book has remained the classic treatment of its subject. For the third edition (1932), the author revised certain details and added additional plates. But this edition, like its predecessors, has long been out of print and unobtainable; moreover, the pace of scholarly research into the history of instruments and their use has quickened during the last thirty years, partly as the result of the example furnished by Canon Galpin himself. It seemed time, therefore, to issue the book anew.

This fourth edition reproduces the text of the third edition, unaltered in its wording, but entirely reset in type. Slips of spelling and date in the text have been corrected without comment. Since the original line and halftone blocks, like much else, were destroyed during the Second World War, new blocks have been made. Wherever possible the original instruments, sources or books used by Canon Galpin have been called into use again, and his quotations checked. I am grateful to William Oxenbury for his help with this revision.

Supplementary footnotes have been added to the text wherever this seemed desirable. These are designed either to draw attention to recent research – much of it by members of the Society that bears Galpin's name – or else to suggest certain points on which he may have been misled or mistaken. Very few footnotes were necessary; this is the best tribute that could be paid to the excellence of Canon Galpin's book, and to his surefootedness in a subject he had made so peculiarly his own. Most of the authors cited in these footnotes are English or American. This is in no sense intended to slight the work of many other scholars, from many other nations. But Galpin was English, the topics he discusses are English, the bulk of his collection was sold to America more than forty years ago, and an outstanding catalogue of the collection was published for the Boston Museum of Fine Arts in 1941.

In his foreword to this catalogue Galpin wrote:

NOTE FOR THE FOURTH EDITION

"To me a musical instrument is a thing of life, something that will speak to us and reveal the hidden secrets of its sound. Therefore I made every effort to secure specimens that were playable or could be rendered so. To restore the ravages of time and replace the tale of years provided for me the greatest joy in their possession."

These were the sentiments that animated those who formed a Society to continue his work, soon after his own hand and heart were stilled in 1945. This book shows how much he did, how little seems left for others to do, and with what affection he is remembered.

KING'S COLLEGE   THURSTON DART
STRAND   (1965)
LONDON, W.C.2

Books of Reference

The preceding edition of this book included two book-lists, the first prepared for the original edition of 1910, and the second a supplementary list for the edition of 1932. Many of the books Canon Galpin listed have not stood the test of time; others have become out of date in detail; and during the last thirty years very great strides forward have been made in our knowledge of musical instruments, their history and their use. It seemed best, therefore, to replace these earlier book-lists with a completely new one. This is in no sense a bibliography – which might well run into thousands of references – but rather a choice of the twenty or so publications that will most repay the browsing reader who wants to find out more about the subject. Most of these books have their own very full bibliographies; individually and as a group they enable the vast tapestry of English instruments and their music to be viewed from a number of different directions; and most of them have illustrations either of the instruments themselves, or of the music composed for them. I have added a few words of comment on each book. Other books will be found among the footnotes to the various chapters.

The Galpin Society Journal (The Galpin Society: 1947 to date).
   The Galpin Society was formed in October 1946 with the object of bringing together all those interested in research into the history of European musical instruments. Its name commemorates the pioneer work of the late Canon Francis W. Galpin; its aims are to promote the study of the history, construction and functions of instruments of music and all cognate subjects, and to further this research by the publication of a Journal and by all other practicable means. The Journal, an occasional publication, has been issued about once a year since its inception. A very large number of its articles bear directly upon topics discussed in the present book; for convenience, its title has been abbreviated in footnotes to *GSJ*. Copies may be purchased from Eric Halfpenny, 258 Cranbrook Road, Ilford, Essex, England.

Musical Instruments through the Ages, edited by Anthony C. Baines for The Galpin Society (Penguin Books: 1961).

A symposium, by sixteen different authors, giving the most up-to-date information available. Very full bibliographies.

The New Oxford History of Music (Oxford: 1954 to date).
Another work of composite authorship, with the defects and advantages inseparable from such an undertaking. Invaluable for general background reading.

A History of Music in England, by Ernest Walker, revised and enlarged by Sir Jack Westrup (Oxford: 1952).
Long a classic, now brought fully up to date.

La Musique Instrumentale de la Renaissance (Paris, Centre National de la Recherche Scientifique: 1955).
The proceedings of a symposium held in 1954, containing more than thirty substantial studies on various aspects of sixteenth-century instrumental music by leading authorities from all over the world. In French throughout.

Woodwind Instruments and their History, by Anthony Baines (Faber: 1957).
A magnificent and authoritative study.

Bach's Orchestra, by C. S. Terry (Oxford: 1932, reprinted 1958).
Despite certain faults in the chronology of Bach's work, this remains a standard book; each instrument is discussed separately. Well illustrated.

The Stringed Instruments of the Middle Ages, by Hortense Panum, translated by Jeffrey Pulver (Reeves: no date, but about 1930).
A bit old-fashioned, but nevertheless fundamental to any study of the subject. More than 400 illustrations.

Elizabethan Music and Musical Criticism, by Morrison Comegys Boyd (University of Pennsylvania: 1940).
The most readable and perceptive general survey of the subject known to me.

Musical Instruments and their Music, by Gerald R. Hayes (Oxford: 1928 and 1930).
Intended to be a series of five volumes, but only two ever appeared: "The Treatment of Instrumental Music" and "The Viols, and other Bowed Instruments". Both are of great value, distinguished alike for the breadth of their scope and the elegance of their style.

De Muziekinstrumenten in de Nederlanden en in Italië naar hun Afbeelding in de 15e eeuwsche Kunst: hun Vorm en Ontwikkeling, by Valentin Denis (Antwerp: 1944).

A most valuable iconographic investigation of instruments depicted in fifteenth-century paintings from Italy and Flanders: in Flemish. A summary of the author's findings will be found in *GSJ*, II, pp. 32–46, in an English translation.

Musicians in English Society from Elizabeth to Charles I, by Walter L. Woodfill (Princeton University: 1953).

Based on a profound study of surviving archives, this reviews the whole field of professional music-making during this period. Indispensable, and most richly documented.

Music and Poetry in the Early Tudor Court, by John Stevens (Methuen: 1961).

Part Three ("Music at Court") gives the best available account of musicians in English Society during the period immediately preceding Woodfill's book (say, 1475 to 1550).

Roger North on Music, edited by John Wilson (Novello: 1959).

The seventeenth-century English musical scene, viewed by an enthusiastic and intelligent amateur musician of the time, who has much to say about the theory and practice of instrumental music.

English Chamber Music, by Ernst H. Meyer (Lawrence & Wishart: 1946).

Despite a somewhat doctrinaire approach, a most sympathetic and learned exposition of the surviving music, with many musical examples.

Musica Britannica (Stainer & Bell: 1951 to date).

A National Collection of masterpieces of earlier English music, from 1400 to 1830 or so, expertly edited and with important prefaces. Many volumes are devoted to instrumental music.

The Autobiography of Thomas Whythorne, edited by James M. Osborn (Oxford: 1961).

A window into Elizabethan music, opened by one of its lesser practitioners.

Music in Medieval Britain, by Frank Harrison (Routledge: 1958).

An exhaustive discussion of the period from the Norman Conquest to the Reformation, dealing almost exclusively with sacred music. With many illustrations, and more than 200 musical examples.

William Lawes, by Murray Lefkowitz (Routledge: 1960).

The most important part of Lawes' output as a composer consisted of consort music; this book gives an excellent study of its growth and development during the middle years of the seventeenth century. Many musical examples, and a useful bibliography.

The Harpsichord and Clavichord, by Raymond Russell (Faber: 1959).

Magnificently illustrated, this is the fullest and most up-to-date study of the subject, with twenty invaluable appendices. These include a new transcript of the inventory of Musical Instruments belonging to King Henry VIII; this has been used as a basis for checking Appendix 4 of Canon Galpin's book.

Ancient European Musical Instruments, by Nicholas Bessaraboff (Harvard University: 1941).

This book-list began with a Journal bearing Galpin's name; it may most appropriately end with the sumptuous catalogue of his collection, now preserved in the Boston Museum of Fine Arts, in memory of Leslie Lindsey Mason. More than 500 pages, lavishly illustrated, fully and most accurately annotated, beautifully printed.

*

The quotations from the list of Henry VIII's instruments appear in the text as quoted by Canon Galpin. A new transcription of the manuscript is printed as Appendix 4.

Chapter I

Rote and Harp

The Harpe is an instrumente of swete melodye,
Rude intelligens of the sounde conceyvethe no armonye;
But who so in that instrumente hathe no speculacion,
What restithe withyn the sounde borde hathe but smale probacion.

LEKINGFELDE PROVERB (*temp.* Henry VIII)

AMID THE CONFUSED MASS of legendary lore and heroic romance which so unfortunately obscures our accurate knowledge of the early history of the British Isles and the conditions – social and artistic – under which their inhabitants lived, one fact stands forth as well ascertained, and it is this – that the first stringed instrument recognized by them which we can consider at all worthy of "Dame Musicke and her art" took the form of a lyre, similar to but not necessarily identical with the classic forms of Greece and Rome.

The Sicilian traveller Diodorus, who lived and wrote just before the Christian era, tells us in the fifth book of his Historical Library that among the Celts were to be found certain musical composers who were called Bards, and that they accompanied their songs of praise or of invective upon instruments "like lyres" (ὀργάνων ταῖς λύραις ὁμοίων); whilst the historian Ammianus, who flourished about the year A.D. 375, carries the comparison still further, and in his fifteenth chapter describes the Bards as chanting the deeds of their illustrious men in heroic verse to the sweet strains of the lyre (*dulcibus lyrae modulis*).

To this instrument the early inhabitants of our islands gave the name of CROT or CRUIT; for in an old Gaelic legend, which describes a battle fought in Ireland between the inhabitants and a horde of piratical intruders called Fomorians, the Druid chieftain invokes his magic lyre (Crot) by the name "Coircethairchuir", which the great Irish scholar O'Curry has translated "Thou quadrangular harmonious one" – an epithet which could be applied only to some form of lyre. According to the Irish annals the battle occurred in the year 1800 B.C., but the date is not necessarily so remote. The effect of the Druid's performance was truly wonderful: the story tells

I

how, in order to discover the fate of a favourite musician, he and two comrades had penetrated into the camp of the enemy, where they found the lyre hanging in the banqueting hall. At the voice of the Druid it leaped from the wall and came to him at once, killing nine persons on its way. On it he played the three great musical strains of his nation: at the sound of the first tears filled all eyes; with the second he overcame them with uncontrollable laughter; and finally, with the third, he sent the entire host to sleep, during which the three champions made good their escape with the magic Crot.

The same name in a Latinized form is presented to us in the well-known poem of Venantius Fortunatus, who was Bishop of Poictiers about the year A.D. 600. In it he exhorts the Roman to sing to the Lyre, the Greek to the Cythara, the Briton to the Chrotta (the Latinized form of the word Crot), and the Barbarian, of whom more presently, to the Harp; and it is immaterial to our purpose whether the writer wished to confine his exhortation to his neighbours the Bretons or included also the inhabitants of our own islands; for not only was communication across the Channel frequent and close, but the peoples were practically identical in race, language and customs.

Now if it be asked from what source the ancient Britons obtained this lyre-shaped instrument, the most probable answer is, from their earlier home upon the Sumerian Plain of Western Asia. For there, in that cradle of the coming race, the existence of the lyre is proved by the actual specimens lately discovered at Ur of the Chaldees, which must certainly have been wrought three thousand years or more B.C. From this source the Greeks, and consequently the Romans, obtained it, and the Homeric Kitharis and the Celtic Crot have a common parentage. Some, it is true, would account for its presence in Ireland through the influx of the Milesians, who came from Northern Spain accompanied by a Cruitire or Crot-player; but if Irish annals are to be trusted, the instrument is mentioned in legends (such as that already described) which are connected with events certainly anterior to the arrival of these latest immigrants.

Among the northern nations of Europe the same instrument appears; in Germany it was so popular that in a manuscript of the twelfth or thirteenth century A.D., found by Abbot Gerbert in the monastery of St Blasius, it is called the *Cythara teutonica*, and is depicted as a lyre with rounded angles, slightly incurved sides and seven strings (Fig. 1). An almost identical instrument, but with five strings only and a pendent tuning-key, is also depicted by the same writer in his *De Cantu et Musica Sacra* from another manuscript found in the monastery. Unfortunately both of the originals perished in a fire which destroyed the monastic library in 1768. Similar

2

instruments are shown in Notker's Psalter of the tenth century.

Illustrations from sculptured Irish crosses of the eighth and ninth centuries are given in Plate 1; they represent the two forms of Cruit – the smaller and earlier form, resembling the lyre, and also the larger Cruit, which came into use during the seventh century, but disappeared before the more popular Clarsech or Irish Harp of the eleventh century, as described later on in this chapter.

By that time, however, the instrument was generally known on the Continent as the Hrotta, Rotta or Rotte, the second form of the name being, in fact, substituted for the word Chrotta in one of the versions of Venantius' poem just quoted; and whilst it still maintained its popularity in Ireland, where it was still called Cruit, it had in England to a great extent disappeared from practical use under the change of nationality and the advent of the more attractive Harp. For in the eighth century Gutberct, an English abbot, in a letter to his friend Lullus Archbishop of Mainz, says that he would be greatly obliged if he would send him over a musician "who can play upon the instrument (*cithara*) that we call a Rotte, because I have an instrument but I have no performer". The word Rotte, in fact, does not appear in the Anglo-Saxon language, but the word *cytere*, which is found, may have represented the instrument.

A Rotte which was in actual use at or even before this period is now preserved in the Ethnographical Museum at Berlin. It was found in the Black Forest, in the grave of a warrior, together with his sword and bow. His beloved Rotte was lying on his breast clasped by his arms; but owing to its great age, strings, pegs and bridge had all perished. It is made of oak, blackened by the lapse of centuries, and consists of a lower board about three-quarters of an inch in thickness, hollowed out throughout almost its entire length with a thin upper board or front covering the whole. Its total length is thirty inches, the width at the base barely six and three-quarter inches, and across the top bar eight inches. There were originally six strings, but no sound-holes, and two small slits on the arms held a suspending cord. An illustration of an exact facsimile of this interesting and valuable relic, with strings, pegs, and bridge added, is given on Plate 9. Another, but later, example has been disinterred in Norway, and is illustrated by Engel in his *Early History of the Violin Family*. It had seven strings, and three of the original pegs are still existing. The learned author considers that the back of the instrument is missing, but from his drawing it is evident that it is the thin front board that is lost. This Rotte, called by Scandinavian antiquaries *Straengleg*, is two feet in length, eleven inches wide, and four inches deep.

The back is convex like the shell of a tortoise. Later a bow was used.[1]

Of the tuning of the Rotte we have at present no details; but from ancient records we learn that, when the instrument was not in use, it was generally kept in a leathern bag, which was slung across the back of the itinerant performer. The tuning-key is also mentioned, and, as has been already stated, is depicted in contemporary manuscripts. As a rule no plectrum was used, but the strings of sinew or metal were touched by the fingers of the left hand. There is a fine illustration of a six-stringed Rotte in an English manuscript of the eighth century (Brit. Mus., Vesp. A. i), and of another with five strings, of the same date, but showing the reverse side of the instrument, in a Psalter belonging to Durham Cathedral. A third example of its use is found in the frontispiece of an Anglo-Saxon Psalter of the eleventh century at the University Library, Cambridge, where it is seen in the hands of Heman, while Asaph is playing on the bowed Rotte (the Crwth or Crowde), of which we shall speak in a subsequent chapter. Of these examples the first and third are reproduced in Plates 2 and 38. A Rotte with other instruments is also shown on Plate 21 from an eleventh-century apocalypse of English workmanship in the Bodleian Library, Oxford.

In English literature of the thirteenth century onwards the name is spelt Rote, but it is the same instrument. For Chaucer, after he has told us of the accomplishments of the Friar in his Canterbury pilgrimage, that

> Wel couthe he synge and pleyen on a Rote,

adds:—

> And in his harping when that he hadde sunge
> His eyen twynkled in his hed aright
> As don the starres in the frosty night.

Owing, however, to the altered spelling of the word, an unfortunate confusion has arisen between this instrument and the Rota, which is used by some of the later Latin writers to denote the Organistrum (described in a subsequent chapter) – a Viol played by the revolution of a wheel (*rota*).

Gower, in the *Confessio Amantis* (1393), spells the name Riote, and Edmund Spenser, in the *Faërie Queene*, still remembering or discerning its similarity to the instrument of classic days, describes Apollo's Lyre as "Phoebus' Rote".

In a poem by John Lydgate, entitled "Reson and Sensualite", written

---

[1] For photographs and a description of a twelfth-century Rotte found buried near Danzig in 1949, see Alicia Simon, "An Early Medieval Slav *Gesle*", *GSJ*, X, pp. 63–5.

PLATE I

1. Small Cruit or Crot, eighth century (Castledermot N. Cross)

2. Large Cruit or Crot, ninth century (Ullard Cross)

PLATE 2

Rotte and Horns, early eighth century

PLATE 3

2. Harp, early fourteenth century

1. Harp, eleventh century

PLATE 4

Clarsech or Irish Harp, early thirteenth century

about the year 1420, the following lines occur in the description of a garden concert:

> For there were Rotys of Almayne,
> And eke of Aragon and Spain.

This allusion enables us to explain a difficulty. The ordinary Rote had from five to eight strings, but we also read of Rotes furnished with seventeen strings. The author who mentions this more elaborate instrument is Guiraut de Calanson, a Provençal poet at the commencement of the thirteenth century. Now Notker the elder, who preceded him by 300 years, informs us that already players had altered the ten-stringed triangular Psaltery to suit their greater convenience, and had added to the number of the strings, giving it the barbarous name Rotte. Moreover, the Arab writer Al-shakandi tells us that in his day (1231) the Rotteh was a musical instrument which, with others, was made in Seville. From this we conclude that there were two forms of the Rote in use in the later centuries of the Middle Ages, the lyre-shaped northern form, "the Rote of Almayne", of which we have already given illustrations from English as well as from German sources, and a southern form (somewhat triangular in shape, with many more strings, backed by a sound-board similar to that of the Psaltery, but distinct from it) which was known as the "Rote of Aragon and Spain". Examples of this instrument occur in the miniatures which adorn one of the thirteenth-century manuscripts of the *Cantigas de Santa Maria* in the library of the Escorial.

It is impossible to say at what period the ordinary Rote went out of general use in this country; perhaps, even in Spenser's day, the word lingered only as a poetical fancy. It is, however, interesting to observe that one form of the Harp-Lute invented, or rather resuscitated, by Edward Light of London, at the close of the eighteenth century, was practically a revival of the ancient lyre-shaped Rote with twelve strings, seven of which passed over a short finger-board. It is illustrated on Plate 9. This instrument, which is still occasionally met with in curiosity shops and auction-rooms, was tuned as follows:

> Strings on the finger-board – c''' g'' e'' c'' b' a' g'
> Open strings – f' e' d' c' g

The pitch was a sixth lower. It was strung with gut strings, with the exception of the lowest string, which was of covered silk. The instrument was yet further improved by Wheatstone under the name of the Imperial Harp-

C

Lute. Unfortunately it gives no clue to the tuning and scale of the ancient Crot or Rote.

We pass to the HARP, and here we are treading on dangerous ground, for to the Sister Isle this instrument has for centuries stood as the emblem of her nationality. In the twelfth- or thirteenth-century manuscript, however, found by Gerbert at St Blasius, side by side with the "Cythara teutonica" or

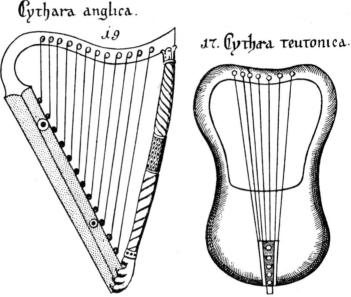

Fig. 1 Harp and Rote – 12th or 13th cent. (St Blasius)

Rote just described, we see the figure of a twelve-stringed Harp, and over it is written "Cythara anglica" (Fig. 1).

Grattan Flood, in his *History of Irish Music*, which is as full of patriotism as it is of valuable information, simply claims this illustration as that of an Irish instrument, and, whilst he acknowledges with the savant O'Curry that the Cruit was originally a form of ev*Lyre*, he nertheless calls it a small Irish *Harp*. There is no evidence, either from manuscript or sculpture, at present forthcoming, to show that the Harp, in the triangular form in which we know it, was used at all in Ireland or by the Celtic people before the end of the tenth century. That they possessed large Cruits as well as smaller forms is, as we have already said, well known, both from the allusions of Irish writers and the examples carved on the ancient crosses erected during the eighth, ninth and tenth centuries in Ireland and the west of Scotland; but these instruments were quadrangular in shape, as shown in the picture of the Cross of Ullard, in County Kilkenny, represented in Plate 1 and of which a further account is given in the Appendix (p. 210). In these large Cruits the soundboard was still placed *behind* the strings as in the smaller form from which they were evolved. An English illustration of an instrument very similar to the quadrangular Cruit will be found in the twelfth-century Psalter preserved in the Library of St John's College, Cambridge (Plate 43).

Whence, then, came this true Harp, which gradually, but effectually, supplanted the earlier lyre-shaped and quadrangular instruments? From an English, or rather a Northern source; because we can hardly say the Angles invented it, seeing they held it in common with other Scandinavian tribes, some of whom eventually settled in Ireland.

For, acknowledging, as we must, the advanced Christian civilization of Ireland and of the Celtic people in the sixth century, we cannot allow ourselves to suppose that the Bishop of Poitiers would willingly or consistently have applied to them such words as these – "Let the *Barbarian* sing to the Harp." To the good Bishop *Barbarians* meant the hordes of heathen invaders who had by this time obtained a footing in Brittany, as they had for more than a century in Britain. It was the Angle, the Saxon and the Northman who used the Harp, "the sole accompaniment of their barbarian songs", as Venantius also tells us, the bonds of kinship and community of interest binding them close together, until in the ninth century they met as rivals.

The Harp is mentioned in the greatest English epic extant, *Beowulf*, which appeared in the sixth century, and this remarkable work not only has for its subject the heroes of Scandinavia, but closely resembles in its poetic form the oldest Norse Sagas, in this respect being far superior to the earliest productions of Gothic Germany. In it we find the popularity of the Harp already established, whereas both in France and also in Germany it slowly crept into favour in later times. Whether the old Norsemen, who could put such excellent clinker-built boats on the sea, gave to the earlier Eastern Harp the front stay or pillar which is now a characteristic of the Western type, it is impossible to say. It would be no very new thing had they done so; for some of the later Greek Trigons – the triangular Harps of Asia Minor – were very similar in structure, though perhaps not in size, to the earliest Northern instruments. It may be that in their long voyages of discovery and pillage these Sons of the Sea had obtained such forms; or perhaps the placing of a stick between the two ends of the curved Eastern Harp to resist the string pressure occurred to them spontaneously. All we know is that to this instrument, however produced, they gave the name *Harpa*, or in Anglo-

Saxon *Hearpe*, from the word *harpan*, to pluck, which embodies the old Aryan root RAP, to seize or clutch. Even to this day the position of the harpist's hands suggests the claw-like action of his forefathers, who played with their long nails.

An interesting passage, bearing upon the introduction of the Harp by the English, is contained in the seventh book of *The History of the Kings of Britain*, by Geoffrey of Monmouth (1100–54). He is, it is true, writing of a time six centuries anterior to his own, but he claims to have had access to a most ancient book in the British tongue, and doubtless also incorporated in his own work many floating traditions. He informs us that when Colgrin, whose father had succeeded Hengist in the leadership of the English invaders, was besieged in York by the Britons, his brother, Boldulph, reached him with the news of reinforcements by shaving his head, and dressing like a strolling player on the Harp (*Cythara*). But on this occasion the Harp would have betrayed his nationality, so we are told he walked up and down in the British trenches showing his skill as a minstrel by playing strains of his own composition on a Lyre (*Lyra*), the Chrotta. As this was the popular instrument of the Britons, it effectually aided the disguise. Then, gradually approaching the walls of York, he was recognized by his compatriots, and drawn up by a rope into the city. An illustration of the English Harp of the tenth century, taken from a manuscript of the *Metrical Paraphrase of Genesis* by Caedmon in the Bodleian Library (Junius xi), is given in Fig. 2, and with it may be compared those of the Harp as depicted in an eleventh-century manuscript preserved in the Library of Corpus Christi College, Cambridge (Plate 3), in another of the same century at the Cambridge University Library (Plate 38), and in an early fourteenth-century manuscript in the Library of All Souls College, Oxford (Plate 3), where the royal musician is endeavouring to tune his instrument. All these illustrations are of English workmanship. Early examples by English artists are also shown in a British Museum manuscript (Harl. 603) of the tenth or eleventh century, and in eleventh-century manuscripts in the British Museum (Tib. C. vi, Ar. 60 and Claud. B. iv), and the Bodleian Library (Bodl. 352). We may perhaps warn the unwary that the Harp found in the eighth-century manuscript at the British Museum (Vesp. A. i) is on an inserted page of the thirteenth century.[1]

Early in the eleventh century Irish musicians adopted the instruments of

[1] The remains of an early medieval harp were found among the treasures of the Sutton Hoo excavations, and they are now in the British Museum, together with a reconstruction of the instrument made by Arnold Dolmetsch: see the British Museum's handbook on *The Sutton Hoo Ship Burial*.

their music-loving neighbours, but they did not take its name Hearpe, so strange to their ears: they made use of their own old word Cruit, which, as we shall presently see, came to be applied to any stringed instrument, whether Lyre, Harp, or Fiddle. Moreover, this Northern Harp, transplanted into Ireland, received under the genius and scholarly training of the minstrel schools a remarkable development. Its strings, of untanned hide or twisted horsehair, were replaced by those of metal, gold, silver or a white bronze called Findruine, materials which had probably been already used for the strings of the quadrangular Cruits.

Fig. 2 Harp – 10th cent. (Oxford)

Perhaps the earliest illustration of the Irish instrument is afforded in the carvings on the west front of Ardmore Cathedral, of about the twelfth century, reproduced in the *Journal of the Society of Antiquaries of Ireland* (Vol. XXXIII). This more elaborate Harp was called *Clarsech*, and the illustrations on Plates 4, 5, show two existing specimens. The smaller is the O'Brien Harp of the early thirteenth century, preserved in Trinity College, Dublin, and popularly, but erroneously, known as the Harp of King Brian Borumna.[1] As cleverly restored to its original form by Mr R. B. Armstrong, it shows the characteristic shape of all the earlier wire-strung Clarsechs both in Ireland and Scotland. The larger, known as the Bunworth Harp, was made by John Kelly in 1734, and is typical of the instrument at the close of its existence. Both Harps are well described and illustrated with others in Mr Armstrong's work on *The Irish and Highland Harps*. As will be seen, the front pillar was intentionally formed into a graceful curve. Through constant practice the musical skill of these Harpers elicited the admiration of all, and by them the wire-strung Harp was soon introduced into Western Scotland, where it was known as the Clarscha. On the eastern side of that country, however, the Northern or Scandinavian instrument was already in use, as

[1] This harp is now thought to have belonged to the King of Thomond (*c.* 1221).

9

shown by the carvings on ancient crosses of the ninth and tenth centuries.

Brompton, who wrote in the middle of the twelfth century, expresses his astonishment at the animated execution, the sweet and pleasing harmony, the quivering notes and intricate modulations of the Clarsaghours; whilst Giraldus Cambrensis, Archdeacon of St David's, who visited Ireland in 1183, remarks that, "Unlike that of the Britons, their playing is not slow and harsh, but lively and rapid." By Britons no doubt Giraldus meant his countrymen in Wales; for there a hair-strung Harp, adopted evidently from their English neighbours, was in use. It was called *Telyn*, a word which is generally supposed to imply something that is stretched; but O'Curry considers that it was a sort of nickname given by the Irishmen to the more feeble Welsh instruments, which they rudely called "buzzers".

From the following satirical ditty, attributed by a writer of the sixteenth century to one of the Welsh minstrels, it is evident that they were somewhat ridiculed for their Harp-playing:

> If I have my Harp, I care for no more;
> It is my treasure; I keep it in store.
> For my Harp is made of a good mare's skin,
> The strings are of horse-hair: it maketh good din.
> My song and my voice and my Harp doth agree,
> Much like the buzzing of an humble-bee:
> Yet in my country I do make pastime
> In telling of prophecy which be not in rhyme.

It may be necessary to explain that the mare's skin was employed to cover the hollow, trough-like sound-board of the instrument.

In the fourteenth century the introduction into Wales of a combined form of Irish and English Harp met with a strong resistance from the Bard Davydd ab Gwylim. His tirade is too long for quotation here in full, but it receives due notice in Jones' *Relics of the Welsh Bards* (Vol. I). From it we gather that the Harp of his forefathers, to which he clung so affectionately, was strung with strings of twisted hair, whereas the new Harp was strung with gut. His Harp had a straight pillar, that of the intruder was "bending"; the sound-board in the Welsh instrument was flat, this was "swelling". "Its noise," he continues, "is like that of a lame goose amongst the corn; a squealing, foolish Irish witch; its trunk and hoarse sound were but formed for an age-worn Saxon." How thankful the patriotic or, as some would say, prejudiced old Bard would be to know that, although the Welsh Harp resigned its hair-strings, it kept its straight pillar and flat sound-board, and, with the improvement of additional strings made in the fifteenth century, became the first chromatic Harp in Europe – a standing monument of the skill and ingenuity of the gallant Principality.

A seventeenth-century manuscript in the British Museum called *Musica neu Beroriaeth*,[1] containing, as its title-page records, music in two parts (i.e. bass and treble) for the Harp, shows us the old notation and music used for the instrument. The two outer rows of strings were tuned in unison, whilst the intermediate one gave the sharps and flats. The instrument was generally "set" in the key of *G*. The compass, of course, varied with the number of strings, but a triple-strung Harp, made in the middle of the eighteenth century by John Richards, of Llanrwst, who constructed the instrument of the famous blind Parry, has a compass of five octaves from *G'* to *g'''*. It is shown in the illustration on Plate 6. In the outer rows there are thirty-six and twenty-seven strings respectively, the lowest nine notes being single; the intermediate row has thirty-two strings, making ninety-five in all. A simpler form of this elaborate instrument seems to have been the Double Harp, described by Galilei in his *Dialogue on Ancient and Modern Music* (1581), which had a compass of four octaves and a note; but Mersenne, in his great work *Harmonicorum Libri XII* (1635), depicts a Welsh Harp with triple stringing and a compass of four octaves only. It has now given place to the Pedal Harp, invented in Bavaria about 1720 by Hochbrucker, improved by the French maker, Cousineau, and, with its double action, popularized by Erard in this country in the early years of the last century.

We have dwelt thus at length on the Irish and Welsh instruments, because we find them so frequently employed in this country side by side with the primitive form of earlier times. For the illuminated manuscripts of medieval days show that the Harp, which first came into common use in England, was a simple diatonic instrument with from eight to eighteen strings, though the usual number was eleven or thirteen. The frame was small, and generally

---

[1] A facsimile of this manuscript (B.M. Add. MS 14905) was issued by the University of Wales Press Board, Cardiff, in 1936, with a prefatory study by Henry Lewis. The manuscript is dated 1613; its title-page was provided in the late eighteenth century, and cannot be relied upon as a description of the contents. The notation is a form of tablature, not unlike the Southern Italian keyboard tablature of about the same time, in which music for the right and left hands appears respectively above and below a single horizontal line. The strings are identified by letter-names, the octave by additional symbols (as in German organ tablature), and a multiplicity of signs is used for ornaments. While no one has yet produced a satisfactory study of the manuscript, it seems clear that the strings are tuned diatonically, not chromatically, their normal tuning being the scale of G minor (one flat). E and B are mutable strings throughout; for certain special effects other strings could also be re-tuned, to form pentatonic or other gapped scales. The music is certainly not for the chromatic Welsh triple harp.

rested on the knee of the performer, though in an early fourteenth-century Psalter belonging to All Souls College, Oxford, as shown in Plate 3, it is placed on a low stool – the blue Harp-bag lying in folds around its base – a not unusual feature in the illustrations; the front pillar too was almost straight, and the cross-tree or harmonic curve but slightly bent. In many instances the performer is shown using a large tuning-key for turning the metal pins. In the later centuries of the Middle Ages gut strings seem to have been always used, though, as we have seen, the Welsh clung to the earlier hair; and, while the tuning of the instrument was purely diatonic, such semitones as were required could be formed by pressing the string against the cross-tree with the fingers of the left hand; for in the earlier examples only the right hand was used in playing, the Harp being inclined towards the right shoulder, as shown in the illustration from the Cambridge Anglo-Saxon Psalter. In an English manuscript of the late thirteenth century (Brit. Mus., Harl. 745) the player holds a large plectrum in his right hand, but this is unusual; we generally see the musician portrayed as described in *The Geste of King Horn*:

> Ant toggen o' the harpe
> With is nayles sharpe.

The early history of England abounds with allusions to this popular instrument. The story of Caedmon's inability to play the Harp when handed round after the feast, as recorded by Bede in the eighth century, shows what was expected of every educated man; and the comparative ease with which both Saxon and Dane passed from camp to camp disguised as minstrels convinces us that everywhere harpers were welcomed. According to the laws of Wales, which date principally from the twelfth century, the three things indispensable to a gentleman were "his harp, his cloak, and his chessboard". His Harp was valued at sixty pence, and its tuning-key at twelve pence, the Harps of the king and a doctor of music being twice as costly; while the three proper things for a man to have in his house were these – "a virtuous wife, his cushion in his chair, and his harp in tune". St Dunstan, as we know, was a ready performer on the Harp, as well as on other musical instruments, but St Ealdhelm, Bishop of Sherborne (705–9), appears to have found a very practical use for his talent, for it is related of him that on one occasion he entered a church to deliver a sermon and discovered that no one was present. Nothing disconcerted, he left the church, took his Harp, and, standing on a bridge hard by, soon attracted a considerable crowd by his playing. Then he delivered his sermon.

In the household payments of our Sovereigns we find frequent mention of gratuities and wages given, not only to their own harpers – whose fidelity at times proved their preservation – but to the musicians whom they met on their progresses. Among those of Edward I and his queen are the following: "To Melioro, the harper of Sir John Matravers, for playing on the harp when the King was bled, xx^{s.}" "To Walter Lovel, the harper of Chichester, whom the King found playing the harp before the tomb of St Richard vi^{s.} viii^{d.}"

Extracts such as these could be multiplied indefinitely, but the above must suffice.

It is interesting to remember that at least two kings of England were performers on the Harp, following in this respect the steps of Alfred the Great of famous memory; for in the *Issue Rolls* of the reign of Henry V and Catharine of Valois is the entry: "By the hands of William Menston was paid £8 13s 4d for two new harps purchased for King Henry and Queen Catharine." We learn from another entry that these instruments were constructed by one John Bore, of London. Henry VIII was also a harpist, and in a Psalter especially written and illuminated for him (Brit. Mus., 2 A. xvi) he is portrayed playing upon his Harp, whilst his fool, Will Somers, turns away with a grimace. This illustration is designedly placed against the opening words of Psalm liii: "The fool hath said," etc.

In the seventeenth century the wire-strung Irish Harp with its thirty to thirty-three strings became fashionable in England, probably owing to the accession of King James, for in Scotland the Clarscha, as it was then called, was in as general use as in Ireland.[1] In 1630 Martin Peerson published a volume of *Mottects or Grave Chamber Musique. Containing Songs of five parts of several sorts, some ful, and some Verse and Chorus. But all fit for Voyces and Vials, with an Organ Part; which for want of Organs, may be performed on Virginals, Base-Lute, Bandora, or Irish Harpe.* Evelyn tells us that his friend, Mr Clarke, a gentleman of Northumberland, was "the most incomparable player on the Irish Harp. Pity 'tis that it is not more in use; but indeede to play well takes up the whole man." In 1668 he heard Sir Edward Sutton play, and remarks, "He performs genteelly, but not approaching my worthy friend."

The large Irish Harp with full compass from *C* to *d'''* or *f'''* continued to be made till almost the middle of the eighteenth century when the French

[1] Some notable works for a consort of strings and Irish harp were composed by William Lawes: see Murray Lefkowitz, *William Lawes* (Routledge, 1960). One of his Fantazias for two violins, bass viol and harp or organ will be found in Ernst Meyer's *English Chamber Music* (London, 1946), pp. 271–7; others have been published by Stainer & Bell, and a substantial selection is also included in *Musica Britannica*, XXI.

Pedal Harp, with its ingenious mechanism for altering the pitch of the strings, proved its master, and relegated it, with all the simple diatonic instruments, to obscurity. About the year 1800, John Egan, of Dublin, tried to introduce a small improved Harp which is sometimes described as an Irish Harp. It had, however, but a brief popularity, and in its shape and strings of gut more closely resembled the *Cythara anglica* of bygone days than the historic emblem of the Emerald Isle.

Chapter II

Gittern and Citole

With Drumes and Fife and shrillest Shalmes,
  With Gittron and Bandore,
With the Theorba sing you psalmes,
  And Cornets evermore.

SIR WILLIAM LEIGHTON (1613)

OUR RESEARCHES INTO the history of the Rote and Harp carried us to the primitive records of the races and tribes who made their earliest settlements in Northern Europe. We have now, however, a group of instruments, broadly described as the Gittern or Guitar and the Citole or Cittern,[1] whose early history is wholly connected with Southern Europe and the Asiatic nations bordering on the eastern shores of the Mediterranean Sea, while under the same category also must fall the Mandore and Lute, which form the subject of the next chapter.

As distinguished from the Rote and Harp, they are characterized by a flat or convex body, to which is attached a neck or finger-board, and from one another they are known by the following details: in the Gittern the back of the resonating body is flat, and its vertical sides are incurved, as in the Guitar of the present day; in the Mandore and Lute the back is convex, and the outline of the body is pear-shaped in the former instrument and almost oval in the latter; whilst in the Citole we have a hybrid type, possessing a flat back like the Gittern, but a pear-shaped or oval outline, without incurvations, similar to that of the Mandore and Lute.

It has been usually supposed that the incurvation of the sides was adopted as a necessity when instruments of the Gittern class were sounded by means of a bow in place of the fingers or a plectrum. Undoubtedly, as we shall see in the case of the Rebec and Viol, the incurved form added greatly to the usefulness of the bow and the facility with which it could be brought to

---

[1] A most important study of the evolution of these instruments has been made by Emanuel Winternitz; it appears, entitled "The Survival of the Kithara and the Evolution of the Cittern", at pp. 209–14 of the Proceedings of the Joint Congress (Cambridge, 1959) of the International Association of Music Libraries and the Galpin Society. These have been published under the title *Music, Libraries and Instruments* (Hinrichsen, 1961).

bear on the strings; but the narrowing of the sides into what is technically known as a waist is seen in a tenth-century illustration of the *Cythara teutonica* or Rote, and, long before there is any trace of a bowed instrument, we find the like incurvations, as, for instance, in the bas-relief dating from before the year 1000 B.C. discovered in the old Hittite palace of Ujuk, near Sinope, in Asia Minor, and figured by MM. Periot and Chipiez in the fourth volume of their *Histoire de l'Art de l'Antiquité*. A photograph of this very interesting relic forms the frontispiece to Miss K. Schlesinger's *Precursors of the Violin Family*. The instrument there represented is very similar to a modern Guitar; it is held across the chest, the left hand stops the strings on the narrow neck, whilst in the right hand there is a plectrum. On Assyrian and Egyptian monuments, however, the oval or pear-shaped outline for the body of such instruments is the form commonly depicted.

Now it is well known that the Greeks and Romans adopted many of the instruments which they found in popular use throughout Asia Minor, although they did not admit them to the unique position of the classic lyre. To these various forms the generic name *Cithara* was given, and under that title this instrument with vertical incurved sides and flat back was brought into Southern Europe, the first name given to the Guitar in medieval times being *Guitare Latine* or *Chitarra Latina*, in order to distinguish it from the *Guitare Moresque* or *Chitarra Sarracenica* with its long neck, oval-shaped body and round back, which was afterwards known in Southern Italy as the Colascione, and is frequently depicted in the *Cantigas de Santa Maria* already mentioned.

In this way, and popularized by the troubadours and minstrels, the Guitar reached our country in the thirteenth century; the earliest illustration in a manuscript of English workmanship, which has at present come under our notice, being in the Ormesby Psalter of the late thirteenth century, now in the Bodleian Library, Oxford. The name in English literature appears in the fourteenth century as GITTERN, GETERNE, GYTTREN or GYTHORN. Philologists tell us that the "n" is superfluous, the proper form being Gitter, as we find it written in the list of the minstrels who played at the Westminster festivities of 1306; but the early French form is Guiterne, and the Italian is Chiterna or Quinterna, so in all probability the word is a contraction of Chitarrone, a large Cither; and indeed it is sometimes written Guitteron.

The Gittern when it appeared in England had four strings, usually of gut, affixed to a tail-piece, which was attached by a cord to a knob or button placed at the end of the instrument and often made most ornamental.

16

According to Michael Praetorius (1618), the strings were tuned thus: *d′ a f c* or *g′ d′ b♭ f*, the actual pitch varying with the size of the instrument. There was a bridge, as in the Violin, but the strings were plucked with a plectrum; in some cases the sound-hole was in the centre, as in the Guitar of the present day; in others, as in the Gittern held by one of the angelic musicians carved in the spandrels of the late thirteenth-century choir-arches at Lincoln Cathedral, there were small curved slits on either side of the bridge. The most curious detail, however, was that the neck – in the earlier instruments at any rate – instead of being free from the body at the back, was attached to it, or rather was one with it, the thickness of the body being extended to the peg-box and an oval-shaped hole pierced in it just behind the finger-board, through which the player's thumb passed and stopped, when necessary, the fourth string.

This is clearly shown in fourteenth-century carving at Worcester Cathedral, and in a cast now in the Architectural Museum at Westminster, which is said to have been taken from an original of the same century formerly to be seen in Westminster Abbey. It is also well depicted in the illustration on Plate 7 from an early fourteenth-century manuscript of English work (British Mus., Arundel 83). The illustration in Fig. 15 of the same date, from a manuscript at All Souls College, Oxford, shows one of the earliest English examples of the "free" neck gradually introduced from the Continent during the fourteenth century.

We are not left in any doubt as to this peculiarity, for there is still an English Gittern of the early fourteenth century in existence. It was preserved at Warwick Castle, and has been persistently described as a Violin. Tradition says that it was given by Queen Elizabeth to her favourite, the Earl of Leicester, and by the permission of the Trustees of the British Museum we are able to reproduce a photograph of this interesting and valuable relic (Plate 7). A full description will be found in Carl Engel's *Catalogue of the Musical Instruments in the South Kensington Museum* – now the Victoria and Albert Museum, where a facsimile is to be seen. It has four strings and is two feet in length; apparently in the year 1578 it underwent some restoration, as that date and the initials "I. P." are engraved on a nut at the back, which fixes the silver stud to which the tail-piece is attached. Experts in handicraft, however, are of the opinion that the exquisite and intricate carving with which the whole instrument is adorned is fourteenth-century work "about the year 1330", and it is with the Gittern of that very period that its shape and construction accord. The silver plate, covering the tuning-pegs and bearing the royal arms and those of the Earl of Leicester, as well as the silver stud and fittings mentioned above, are, of course, sixteenth-century additions. The front table or sound-board, the tail-piece, and the finger-board are later still and incorrect. When played with a bow (and there is no original bow belonging to it) it is very awkward to hold, and necessarily produces "a close sluggish tone", as stated by Sir John Hawkins in his *History of Music* (1776); but, placed as a Gittern across the chest and played with a plectrum, it will be found both convenient to hold and pleasant to hear. We trust that this unique survival of the old English Gittern will no longer be condemned to occupy, as a Violin, a false and ludicrous position.

Students of Chaucer will remember that this was the instrument with which the parish clerk serenaded the carpenter's wife with dire results to himself, when, as says the poet,

> The moone, whan it was night, ful brighte shoon
> And Absolon his Giterne hath i-take.

For, before the introduction of the Lute, the Gittern was the popular accompaniment for singing. Langland, in the *Vision of Piers Plowman*, says of himself that he was no minstrel for,

> Ich can not tabre, ne trompe, ne telle faire gestes,
> Ne fithelyn at festes, ne harpen,
> Japen ne jagelyn, ne gentillische pipe,
> Nother sailen, ne sautrien, ne singe with the giterne.

Jumping, juggling and dancing (sailen) were part of a minstrel's repertoire.

In the sixteenth century the so-called Spanish Guitar was introduced into England. Henry VIII died possessed of four Gitterons called Spanish Vialles, the Spanish *Vihuela* of that date differing from the ordinary Gittern, according to Don Luys Milan of Valencia (1536), in having six strings instead of four.

In *The Verney Memoirs* we read that about the year 1635 Lady Verney's son, whilst his father was an exile in France, was being taught to sing and play "on the Guittarr"; and her daughter Pegge was "to learn the Lute". In fact, the Guitar, which at that time was strung with five pairs of double strings, was so popular in France that in Portugal it is known to the present day as the *Viola franceza*. With the influx of French fashions into England during the seventeenth century the improved instrument, played generally with the fingers instead of a plectrum, completely eclipsed the older Gittern and in time relegated the Lute also to oblivion.

Amongst the musicians for a masque performed before King Charles II in 1674, there were four "Gittar" players who were dressed in "white rich

18

Taffety gownes and caps of gilt leather adorned with feathers". From the bills for this gay clothing, which still exist among the Lord Chamberlain's Records, it is evident that the royal tradesmen found the name of the instrument a difficulty, for it is sometimes spelt "Kittar" and at other times "Gytarrh". The five pairs of double strings gave place to the present six single strings towards the close of the eighteenth century. The earlier form is shown on Plate 10 and the first three pairs of strings were tuned to *e′ b* and *g*, and the other two pairs to *d′ d* and *a A*: the added sixth string is tuned to *E*.

In the CITOLE, which is our next subject, we have an instrument which has been much misunderstood. The name is spelt in various ways, appearing in English literature as Sytholle or Sitole, Cythol or Cytol. Dr Rimbault, in his *History of the Pianoforte*, describes it as a small rectangular Psaltery played with the fingers, deriving the word from *Cistella*, a little box; and although he gives an illustration in connection therewith, there is no reason to believe that it represents the Citole. On the contrary, we are told by Cerone, a Spanish writer who lived in Italy at the close of the sixteenth century, that the Citola was identical with the Cetera, the Cither or Cittern. The word in its original form was probably *Citharola*, "little Cither", whence the Provençal *Cithola*. To Bishop Oresme of Lisieux (14th cent.) "cithare est Cithole".

It was one of the instruments which an accomplished minstrel was expected to play; for in the *Conseils aux Jongler*, written by Guiraut de Calanson in 1210, it is stated that a Jongleur must play the Pipe and Tabor, the Citole, the Symphony, the Mandore, the Manichord, the seventeen-stringed Rote, the Harp, the Gigue, and the Psaltery with ten strings. A description of these instruments will be found in this book under their respective chapters.

The earliest illustration at present observed of the medieval Citole occurs in the title-page of a copy of the Gospels in Latin, executed for the Emperor Charlemagne in the eighth century. In the hands of adoring angels or elders before the heavenly throne are shown small instruments, stringless but with three tuning-pegs; as there are no bows we may presume that they were played with the fingers or a plectrum, although it is only right to say that in these and similar illustrations where instruments of music are being presented before the Divine Presence, the bow, even of known bowed instruments, is often omitted.

A reproduction of this interesting page is given in the third volume of

Count Bastard's *Peintures et Ornements des Manuscrits*, and with it may be compared the illustrations in an Apocalypse of English workmanship of the early eleventh century now in the Bodleian Library, Oxford (MS. 352). Here the instruments seem to have a pair of double strings and are probably meant for Rebecs (Plate 21).

The Citole appears far less frequently in English manuscripts than the Gittern: it may be that in this country it was not so popular. It is, however, mentioned by the author of the legendary *History of Fulke FitzWarine*, written in the early part of the thirteenth century, and in the English romances of the fourteenth and early fifteenth centuries, such as *Launfal*, *Lybeaus Desconus* and *The Squyr of Lowe Degre*, it is frequently named in conjunction with the Sautry of Psaltery. In the metrical *Life of Alexander*, by Adam Davie, composed in the fourteenth century, we are told of a great entertainment that:

> At the feste was trumping,
> Piping and eke taborying,
> Sytolyng and eke harpyng.

The instrument also received royal patronage, for among the payments to the minstrels who attended the Westminster Festivities in 1306, when the son of Edward I received knighthood, we find that Janyn le Citoler was given one mark; moreover, the Court Band of Edward III contained a Cyteler, and it is interesting to notice that on the front of the Minstrels' Gallery in Exeter Cathedral, erected in·the reign of this same king, we have one of the best examples of the instrument. It appears in the hands of the first musician on the left; he is plucking with a plectrum the four strings, which the old writers tell us were of wire; the string-holder is attached to the front table and acts also as a bridge; the neck is free, that is, it is not obstructed as in the Gittern, which is shown in the hands of the ninth musician; it is terminated by a little figure-head, of which more anon. Another excellent representation of the early fifteenth century occurs in the nave of Beverley Minster. Both are reproduced in Figs 3 and 4. In the sixteenth century it was known as the Cithren or Cittern, a change of name for which there seems but little reason. The final "n" may have arisen from a supposed analogy with Gittern, or from a confusion with Cithren – the plural form of the German word, in which country it was much practised.[1] This instrument, however, must be

---

[1] The final "n" is more likely to have arisen through confusion – deliberate or inadvertent – with "Cytheron", a common Elizabethan variant of Cyprian Aphrodite's "Cythera". Compare the mythological overtones of such instrument-names as "Pandora" or "Orpharion" (="Orpheus"+"Arion"), both instruments belonging to the cittern family.

carefully distinguished from the modern German Zither, which is a species of Psaltery. A Cittern is shown on Plate 55.

Though for some reason or other it had been especially associated with ecclesiastical ornament, it was destined to lose its high estate, ousted by the superior attractions of the Lute, which began to be popular in this country early in the fifteenth century. A nobleman's collection, it is true, contained

Fig. 3 Citole – 14th cent. (Exeter)   Fig. 4 Citole – 15th cent. (Beverley)

Citterns, and good Master Laneham, the favourite of the Earl of Leicester, tells us that "sometimes I foot it with dancing, now with my Gittern and else with my Cittern"; in 1556 "a faire Cyterne" was among the New Year presents made to Queen Mary, and the Elizabethan composers, such as Morley and Rosseter, used it in their Consort Lessons;[1] but it was most frequently to be found in taverns and barbers' shops, where it provided entertainment for customers when daily papers were unknown.

[1] A complete score of Morley's fascinating Consort Lessons has been published by the New York Public Library (1959), transcribed and reconstructed by Sydney Beck; the volume also includes an important introductory essay. Two of the most outstanding Lessons have also been published by Stainer & Bell (1957), edited by Thurston Dart; in the preface to this edition, it is suggested that the Treble Viol part was originally composed for violin, and that the Flute part is for tenor transverse flute, not for recorder.

The little carved head – often exceedingly grotesque – which surmounted the neck and peg-box is frequently alluded to in English literature. Forde, in his *Lovers' Melancholy* (act ii, sc. 1), writes of his lady's fair face, "Barbers shall wear thee on their Citterns", and Shakespeare, in "The Pageant of the Nine Worthies" (*Love's Labour's Lost*, act v, sc. 2), bandies the following words between the Schoolmaster Holofernes, who personates Judas, and the Lords-in-Waiting on the King:

HOL. I will not be put out of countenance.
1ST LORD. Because thou hast no face.
HOL. What is this? (*pointing to his face*).
2ND LORD. A cittern-head (*wooden and ugly*).

From Antony Holborne's *Cittharn Schoole*, published in 1597, we gather that the tuning of the instrument was as follows, *e' d' g b* – a curious arrangement, which, however, facilitated the production of certain common chords. An example of the instrument is shown in Plate 8.

In addition to the Cittern with four open notes, there were larger instruments with an increased number of strings. They do not seem to have been so popular in England as on the Continent, especially in Germany, but on the title-page of *New Citharen Lessons* (1609), by Thomas Robinson, who describes himself as a "Student in all the liberall Sciences", there is an engraving of a Cittern with additional strings like those of the English Guitar shown in Plate 8. It has seven pairs of strings on the finger-board and seven single strings by its side. This was called a "fourteen-course Cittern" because it possessed that number of open notes, and the instrument was tuned thus – *e' d' g b♭ f d G* for the strings on the finger-board, and *F E D C B♭' A' G'* for the strings at the side, which were conveyed to the peg-box over a nut placed in the mouth of a grotesque head at the top of the instrument. Robinson attributes its invention to an Italian, with alterations and improvements by himself. In England it was called the Syron.

Of the music for the Cittern, which was written or printed in the form known as tablature, an explanation will be given in the next chapter.[1]

As Sir Frederick Bridge says in his *Samuel Pepys, Lover of Musique*, the eminent diarist possibly played this instrument as well as others; for, after the landing of Charles II at Dover in 1660, by the request of the Admiral, Lord Sandwich, and with the help of the lieutenant's Cittern and two

---

[1] For more on this subject, see Thurston Dart, "The Cittern and its English Music", *GSJ*, I, pp. 46–63, and the supplementary notes in *GSJ*, II, p. 31 and V, p. 43. From the List of Sources at the end of the article it will be seen that Playford had already published two books containing cittern music before the appearance of *Musick's Delight* in 1666.

candlesticks with money in them for cymbals, "we made barbers music, with which my Lord was well pleased". In 1666 Playford, by publishing his *Musick's Delight on the Cittern*, tried to refine its use, preferring the use of the fingers to that of the plectrum; but, like the other wire-strung instruments which we now proceed to describe, it had had its day and yielded to the popularity of the English Guitar of the eighteenth century.

For besides the Cittern there were several instruments of the same class in use in England during the sixteenth and seventeenth centuries. The Pandore[1] (Pandora or Bandore), which with Treble and Bass Viols, Lute, Cittern, and Recorder, had a part in the Consort Lessons of Morley and Rosseter, was very popular in Queen Elizabeth's reign, and is said to have been invented by one John Rose, a citizen of London, in the year 1560. At any rate, in Gascoigne's tragedy *Jocasta*, produced in 1566, "Bandores" are named among the various instruments employed to accompany the dumb-shows which preceded each act. A beautifully decorated specimen is in the possession of Lord Tollemache, and is well illustrated in Hipkins and Gibb's *Musical Instruments, Historic, Rare, and Unique*. The outline is waved or festooned; the string-holder, which is attached like that of the Cittern to the front table, is straight: it has pegs for ten strings, arranged in five pairs; on the ribs or sides are carved the words *Cymbalum Decachordum*, and within is the label –

> Johannes Rosa Londoni fecit.
> In Bridewell the 27th of July 1580.

It is said to have been given to Sir Lionel Tollemache by Queen Elizabeth, as a memento of a visit to Helmingham Hall. In a book printed for William Barley, entitled *A new booke of Tabliture* ... (1596), a similarly shaped instrument with six pairs of strings is figured and described under the usual name Bandore, a corruption of Pandore, which in its turn takes its title, though not its structure, from an Asiatic instrument called Pandoura or Tanboura. A Pandore is shown in Plate 55.

Another wire-strung instrument of a kindred nature was the Orpharion,[1] so named after the mythical Orpheus. It possessed seven pairs of strings, but the string-holder was placed on the front table slantwise, thus shortening the length of the upper strings. The frets, pieces of gut or metal placed across the finger-board to mark the division of the scale and to increase the

---

[1] See Donald Gill's exhaustive treatment, "The Orpharion and Bandora", *GSJ*, XIII, pp. 14–25; see also Thurston Dart, "La pandore", *Le Luth et sa Musique* (Paris, C.N.R.S.: 1958), pp. 225–9.

vibration of the strings when stopped by the fingers, were arranged, of course, to meet this curious position of the string-holder or bridge. In the Claudius Collection of Musical Instruments at Copenhagen there is a fine English specimen of this instrument bearing the maker's label –

Francis Palmer. Anno 1617.

By the courtesy of the Curator we give a photographic illustration of it on Plate 8.

The Orphion, invented by Thomas Pilkington, who was born in 1625, must have differed in some way from the earlier Orpharion.[1]

Another very similar form was called the Penorcon, and is mentioned and figured by Praetorius in his *Syntagma Musicum* (1618). It had nine pairs of strings, and therefore, in the illustrations given by the learned author of the Orpharion and Penorcon, the names should be transposed. Yet another instrument of the Cittern class was the Poliphant or Polyphon, on which, we are told, the Virgin Queen was most proficient. Its outline was still more fantastic, somewhat resembling the later Harp-Lute, and an illustration is given in *The Academy of Armory*, written by Randle Holme in the seventeenth century (Brit. Mus., Harl. 2034), who allots it from twenty-five to forty strings. It was invented by Daniel Farrant, son of the organist of St George's Chapel, Windsor, and afterwards one of the Court Musicians, together with another wire-strung instrument called the Stump, of which no further particulars are now known. There is little doubt but that the small differences of detail between some of these kindred forms were frequently lost sight of and the names constantly interchanged. Additional improvements were also made from time to time – for instance, the strings of Rose's instrument had but five open tones, while those of the Pandore, for which Morley wrote in 1599, had six open notes and were tuned to $a e c G D C$; but the Pandore described and figured by Robert Fludd in his *Historia utriusque cosmi* (1617) had seven open notes tuned to $a e c G D C G'$, with two frets on the neck and four on the front table; and he says that it sounded the Bass, the Tenor or the Counter-tenor, whereas the smaller Cittern was used for the Tenor, Counter-tenor and Alto. An example of the Pandore or Bandore with seven pairs of strings is given in Plate 8.[2]

[1] This is all rather muddled: Francis Pilkington (*c.* 1570 – *c.* 1638), composer, singer and lutenist, seems to have had a special liking for the Orpharion, and its name appears on the title-page of his book of lute-songs (1605). His last published work, *The Second set of Madrigals* (1624), includes a pavan for the orpharion by his patron, the Earl of Derby. Francis's brother, or nephew, Thomas, was a musician to Queen Henrietta Maria (see Wood's *Fasti Oxonienses*, I, 269), and was born in about 1605.

[2] Galpin erred in his reference to the illustration of the Bandora in Fludd's treatise, which shows the correct number of eleven frets on the neck and four over the table.

In 1599 was published a new book of Tablature containing *Sundrie easie and familiar Instructions, showing how to attaine the knowledge to guide and dispose the hand to play on sundrie Instruments, as the Lute, Orpharion and Pandora . . . collected out of the best Authors professing the Practice of these Instruments*, and they are mentioned in several other musical publications of the first half of the seventeenth century; but we have failed to find any publication for the Poliphant or Penorcon under their proper names. All these instruments were played not with a plectrum but with the fingers, and Barley's book tells us that they must be "easily drawn over the strings, not suddenly griped or sharpelie stroken as the Lute is; for if yee should doo so, then the wire strings would clash or jarre together, the one against the other, which would be a cause that the sound would be harsh and unpleasant; therefore it is meet that you observe the difference of the stroke".

Drayton, in his *Polyolbion* (1613), alludes to the Cittern and Pandore as of "the sterner wiry chord", and in an earlier work (1590) bids the praises of the Virgin Queen be

> Set to the Cornet and the Flute,
> The Orpharion and the Lute.

Heywood, in his *Fair Maid of the Exchange*, compares a lady's hair to "Bandora Wyres", which were of yellow brass: and Mace, in his *Musick's Monument* (1676),[1] classed Bandores, Auferions, and Citterns as instruments strung with "wyar strings": while Lord Bacon tells us that the deeper-toned strings were "wreathed", that is, covered with finer wire.

In the Inventory of the Goods and Chattels of Sir Thomas Kytson of Hengrave Hall, Suffolk, who died in 1602, amongst the many musical instruments he possessed there is the following item, "one Bandore and a Sitherne with a dooble case", which shows that the two instruments were commonly used together, the former for accompaniment, the latter for melody. The Bandore is mentioned by Mr Pepys, who notes in his *Diary* under the date October 15, 1662, that when he was staying at the Bear Inn at Cambridge, "I could hardly sleep but waked very early, and when it was time did call Will, and we rose: and Musique, with a Bandore for the Base, did give me a levett." The singers who made this "waking music" or levett were supported by the chords of the Bandore.

As has already been said, the advent of the English Guitar in the eighteenth

---

[1] A facsimile edition of *Musick's Monument*, to be accompanied in due course by a second volume of commentary and transcriptions, was issued by the C.N.R.S., Paris, in 1958; the edition is by Jean Jacquot and André Souris.

century caused the disappearance of Bandores, Poliphants, and similar wire-strung instruments, or rather, it supplanted them; for, owing to the use of the fingers instead of the plectrum, the English Guitar, though smaller, could be used for accompanying the voice as well as for solo performance. Its six open notes, produced by four double strings for the higher and two single strings for the lower, were tuned somewhat like the old Bandore, namely to $g'\,e'\,c'\,g\,e\,c$.

The instrument, which had a decorative appearance, is frequently depicted in the portraiture of the eighteenth century, as, for instance, in the picture of the Hon. Mrs Charles Yorke, by Sir Joshua Reynolds, and in one of Zoffany's family groups. It was made in various sizes, two of the smaller "to be managed by young ladies from seven to ten years of age, the other by ladies of ten and upwards". In 1760 the prices varied from $1\frac{1}{2}$ guineas to 6 or 7 guineas. In Rees' *Cyclopaedia* (1819) Dr Burney thus writes of it: "The common Guitar used in England has frequently had fits of favour in this country. About fifty years ago its vogue was so great among all ranks of people as nearly to break all the Harpsichord and Spinet makers, and indeed the Harpsichord masters themselves. All the ladies disposed of their Harpsichords at auctions for one-third of their price, or exchanged them for Guitars, till old Kirkman, the Harpsichord maker, . . . purchased some cheap Guitars and made a present of several to girls in milliners' shops and to ballad singers in the streets, whom he had taught to accompany themselves with a few chords and triplets, which soon made the ladies ashamed of their frivolous and vulgar taste and return to the Harpsichord."

This craze probably accounts for the large number of specimens of the English Guitar (Cetra or Citra, as it was sometimes called) which appear in the auction rooms and curiosity shops of the present day. On the later eighteenth-century instruments Preston's improved apparatus for tuning by means of a watch-key is generally found, and in some cases a mechanical device for sounding the strings is attached. In its earlier form this consisted of little buttons or keys placed at the side of the instrument, one button for each set of strings, which either forced small points against the wires and plucked them as in the Spinet, or else projected hammers through the central sound-hole and struck the strings as in the Pianoforte; but a more approved apparatus consisted of a small box, furnished with six keys and six hammers, which was affixed to the Guitar just over the bridge, and struck the wires passing beneath them. Patents were also taken out for the addition of Trumpet, Harp, Hautboy, and Cremona stops, but they did not succeed in perpetuating the use of the instrument. Examples, however, of the keyed Guitar, or Pianoforte Guitar as it was called, are sometimes still to be met with.

Early in the nineteenth century both it and the simpler form disappeared in favour of the easier "Spanish" Guitar, but an attempt was made a few years ago to revive the English instrument under the name of the "Portuguese" Guitar. As a relic of an historic past the English Guitar would repay study and practice; unfortunately the instruction books issued in the halcyon days of its popularity are out of print and unattainable. Mr R. B. Armstrong has therefore done good service in reprinting one of the most important of them in his *English and Irish Instruments*, where full details of the stringing and fingering of the English Guitar will be found, with specimens of the music both for solo performance and vocal accompaniment. The illustrations on Plates 8 and 9 show an English Guitar, with double peg-box for additional Bass strings, made in 1757 by Remerius Liessem, a celebrated London maker; an English Guitar by Lucas, of Golden Square, London, with the patent tuning apparatus; and an eighteenth-century instrument to which has been attached Smith's Patent Box, making it a keyed Guitar. An instrument produced by Edward Light, of London, at the close of the eighteenth century, and called the Harp-guitar, was tuned like the English Guitar, with one or two additional Bass strings for G and F; all the eight strings, which were of gut and covered silk, sounded a sixth lower in actual pitch. It is occasionally to be seen in the sale-rooms, and, with the Harp-lute and other kindred instruments, has been well described by Mr Armstrong in the work just mentioned.

Chapter III

Mandore and Lute

He that is a perfyte musicion
Perceyvithe the Lute tewnes and the goode proporcion;
In myddest of the body the stringis sowndith best,
For, stoppide in the freytis, they abyde the pynnes wrest.

LEKINGFELDE PROVERB (*temp.* Henry VIII)

STRINGED INSTRUMENTS WITH convex bodies, though now built up of strips of wood or ivory, are eminently characteristic of those used by the Oriental races, and are reminiscent of the time when the body or resonator consisted of a simple gourd or half-gourd covered with skin. In fact, all our musical instruments of this form, such as the Rebec and the Mandoline, as well as the Lute and Mandore, are traceable to the Persian, Arabic and Moorish influences of the Middle Ages; in some instances, through Greece and Italy at an early date, at a later period through Spain, and later still by the contact of Western Europeans with the Saracens on the eastern shores of the Mediterranean.

The first European Lutes had but four strings of gut, tuned to the same notes as the Gittern; but in the thirteenth century the number had already been increased, until in the elaborate instruments of the seventeenth century there were twenty-six or thirty strings to be carefully tuned and regulated, so that it was said, with perhaps a certain amount of truth, that if a lutenist had attained the age of eighty, you might be sure that he had spent sixty years of that time in tuning his instrument.

The smallest kind of Lute was called the Lutina or Mandura, a corruption of the name Pandoura or Tanboura, given to an Eastern representative of the same class. In a manuscript of the eleventh century, preserved in the National Library at Madrid, the instrument is shown with the long neck, which marks the Oriental Tanboura of the present day, and as it is depicted in the sculptures of the Assyrian palaces and the wall paintings of Egyptian temples. Its true representative in our own time is the Colascione of Southern Italy.[1]

[1] For a valuable discussion of early lute-types, both long and short in neck, see Laurence Picken, "The Origin of the Short Lute", *GSJ*, VIII, pp. 32–42.

PLATE 5

Clarsech or Irish Minstrel Harp, by John Kelly, 1734

PLATE 6

Welsh Harp, by John Richards, *c.* 1750

PLATE 7

1. Gittern, early fourteenth century

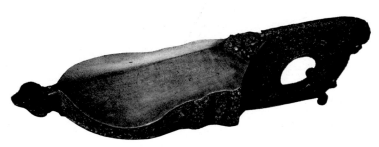

2. Gittern, *c.* 1330

PLATE 8

1. Cittern by John Preston (working 1734–70). 2. Large English Guitar by R. Liessem, 1757. 3. Bandore, facsimile based on the dimensions and drawings in Praetorius and the Talbot MS. 4. Orpharion by Francis Palmer, 1617

The MANDORA or MANDORE, which we find in the hands of the Jongleurs of the twelfth and thirteenth centuries, was a more compact instrument with a shorter neck. It was in general use in Spain, in Italy, and in Southern France in the thirteenth century, and appears in Flanders early in the fourteenth; but, so far as we are aware, there is no illustration of it in an undisputed English work before the year 1400, except in the Missal of Abbot Nicholas de Litlington, written in 1384, and now in the library of the Dean and Chapter of Westminster, of which great Abbey Litlington was at one time the head. The instrument there represented is shown in Fig. 5. The crozier of William of Wykeham, on the crook of which the Mandore also appears, is probably earlier than this; but the enamel plaques, whereon are depicted a variety of musical instruments, are of French origin, made, it may be, at Montpellier.

Fig. 5 Mandore – late 14th cent. (Westminster)

In our country the Citole and Gittern with their flat backs were evidently preferred, and their popularity continued in England when on the Continent the Mandore and Lute with their gut strings and rounded backs had already superseded them.

Early illustrations of the small Lute with four strings occur in the Chapterhouse at Westminster among the fifteenth-century wall-pictures painted by an Englishman, John of Northampton, a monk of Westminster. Here, too, will be seen an early example of the large Lute, and another instance occurs among the carvings in the nave of Beverley Minster. The illustration in Plate 53 is taken from an early fifteenth-century manuscript of English workmanship (Brit. Mus., 1. E. ix).

In the sixteenth century the Mandore, so popular in France, is found, with the larger Lute, in Scotland. An interesting collection of melodies for the "Mandwr", as it is termed, is preserved in the Advocates' Library at Edinburgh. From this manuscript, formerly the property of Sir John Skene, Dauney, in 1838, produced his *Ancient Scotish Melodies.* The tuning of the instrument, which then had five sets of strings, is given thus:

29

$g''\ d''\ a'\ f'\ c'$; and it is evident from the style of the music that the fingers as well as a plectrum were used. A second tuning, $g''\ c''\ g'\ c'\ g$, is called in the manuscript the "old tune of the Lutt". The actual pitch and number of strings varied with the size of the Mandore, which was usually about twenty inches long.

At this period there was another small instrument called by Praetorius *Mandürichen* or *Pandurina*, which could be conveniently carried under the cloak; this form still survives in the Mandoline, though the gut strings have in most cases been superseded by those of wire, and the instrument is played with a plectrum. A Flemish Mandore or Lutina and a Pandurina are shown in Plate 10.

Many years ago, in a Venetian warehouse, we came across an old Lute-case. On opening it, a fine seventeenth-century Lute, richly inlaid with ivory, met our gaze. Lifting it out, a small compartment was discovered behind the rest for its neck, containing a little Mandore in exactly the same style. These instruments were, no doubt, intended for use together, the smaller for the melody and the larger for the accompaniment. In one of the seventeenth-century MSS at the British Museum (Sloane 1021) will be found a *Galliarda Anglica* for Mandore and Lute (*Testudo minor* and *Testudo major*).[1]

Of the larger instrument, to which the name LUTE is usually restricted, it is possible to speak in fuller detail; in fact, there is so much to be said, that only a summary of its history and excellencies can here be given. To it the hero sang his tale of chivalry, the mother hummed her lullaby, the lover urged his pleading, and the maiden gave her answer. By such associations as these, the Lute was endeared to old and young alike, and was certainly the most attractive, as it was also the most difficult, of all the stringed instruments of the sixteenth and seventeenth centuries. The name is derived from the Arabic words *El Oud* – the instrument of wood – and it is mentioned as being used in Persia in the seventh century under that name. Its distinguishing features are the large pear-shaped or oval body, which is much deeper and fuller than in the Mandore, and the head or peg-box, which is turned back in some cases almost at a right angle to the neck and finger-board, as shown in the illustrations which accompany one of the thirteenth-century manuscripts of the *Cantigas de Santa Maria*, preserved in the library of the Escorial, and reproduced by Don Juan Riaño in his *Notes on Early Spanish Music*.

This curious device, which is also to be found in the Mandore, is said to

[1] This duet is more probably for lute and bass lute.

have been adopted in order that the strings might have a firmer bearing on the nut or bar, over which they are stretched before passing on to the finger-board. It is more probable, however, that it was made for the performer's convenience, as, owing to the length of the neck, some forms of the Oriental Lute are extremely awkward to hold. The illustration of an existing specimen dated 1593 is given in Plate 10, and will show the typical shape of

Fig. 6 Lute – late 15th cent. (British Museum)

the Lute in Western Europe during the sixteenth century. It will be remembered that the English Gittern possessed a similarly recurved peg-box, though, in that case, the head was attached to and supported by the body of the instrument.

The large Lute does not appear in paintings or carvings of English workmanship till the fifteenth century, when it is shown with four strings – probably four pairs of strings – as in the wall-paintings of the Chapter-house at Westminster, already mentioned, in the window of the Priory Church at Malvern, erected by Henry VII in memory of his son Arthur, and in the late fifteenth-century manuscript (Brit. Mus., Harl. 2838), as depicted in Fig. 6. On the Minstrels' Pillar at St Mary's Church, Beverley,

31

it appears with five pairs of strings. It is mentioned, however, in the four-teenth century, among the list of instruments upon which the musicians attending the Westminster Feast performed, for Janin le Lutour received forty shillings – the only lutenist of the seventy-five minstrels present. Another early mention of it in England occurs in the Hosteller's Accounts of Durham Priory, under the year 1361-2, as follows: "In uno viro ludenti in uno loyt et uxori cantanti apud Bewrpayr"; which doggerel Latin informs us of a payment made to a man who played the Lute, and to his wife, who sang before the monks when recreating themselves at their manor of Beaurepair. Lydgate also, in an unpublished poem quoted in the Romance of *Sir Degrevant*, issued by the Camden Society, speaks of "Lutys" as being with "Rubibis" (of which hereafter) and "Geterns" more fit for "estatys" (that is noblemen's houses) than for "taverns". In the sixteenth century, however, the Lute was everywhere practised and admired (Plate 56).

Henry VIII, as well as his daughters Mary and Elizabeth, was an ad-mirable lutenist, and they all maintained Luteplayers at high salaries in their households. We find Alfonso d'Este sending as a present to the King in 1517 a "Cythara eius generis quos (!) in Italiâ leutos vocant". During this period the ordinary or Treble Lute had five pairs of strings with one single string called *chanterelle* for the highest note in the tuning. As they were all of gut, and the smaller, or "minnikins", were very fragile and easily broken, a gift of Lute strings was one of the most useful presents which could be made to a player – even Queen Elizabeth did not disdain to accept them. The instrument was usually "set" to the following notes, *a' e' b g d A*, the actual pitch varying with the size and strength of the Lute and the character of the music.[1] By the end of the century a seventh pair was added, giving a whole tone below the sixth pair, and in time there were attached five more diatonic bass strings, either double or single, in order to increase the down-ward compass of the instrument. In the latter half of the seventeenth century the French tuning of the Lute, which was that most generally esteemed, was

---

[1] The recognized tuning for the lute in sixteenth-century England appears to have been *g' d' a f c G*, the three lowest courses being strung in octaves. By the end of the century the octave stringing had been abandoned, but many players seem to have liked to use a seventh course tuned to *D*. (See Donald Gill, "The Elizabethan Lute", *GSJ*, XII, pp. 60-2.) From about 1625 onwards the new "French" lute became increasingly fashion-able, largely due to the influence of the elder Gaultier; its preferred tuning was *f' d' a f d A*, with five diapasons descending diatonically below this. For additional material on the lute in England see *The Lute Society Journal* (1956 to date); David Lumsden, "The Sources of English Lute Music (1540-1620)", *GSJ*, VI, pp. 14-22; Thurston Dart, "Miss Elizabeth Burwell's Instruction Book for the Lute", *GSJ*, XI, pp. 3-62; and *Le Luth et sa Musique* (C.N.R.S., Paris, 1958). Note that the top string of the Theorboe was usually tuned to *g* (not *g'*, as on p. 33), by reason of the greater stop-length of the instrument.

g′ e′ c′ a e B on the finger-board and *A G F E D C* for the strings at the side, which were called Diapasons and were not stopped by the fingers. Regarding the actual pitch, the eighth string on a full-sized Lute generally corresponded to Bass *G*, as here shown. To facilitate the tuning and arrangement of so many strings an additional peg-box was fixed at the top of the neck, either by the side of that already existing or as an extension of it. In this way were formed the Archlute, a long unwieldy instrument chiefly used in orchestral performances, and the Theorboe, a smaller Tenor Lute employed as an accompaniment to the voice. The Theorboe was tuned as follows, *g′ d′ a f c G* for the strings on the finger-board and *F E D C B′ A′ G′* for those at the side, the sixth (as here) or the seventh string generally corresponding to Bass *G* in actual pitch. An interesting and perfect example, dated 1619, is shown in Plate 10.

The Archlute, in its largest form, was called the Chitarrone; it was over six feet high, and the enormous length of its neck gave additional sonority to the deep bass strings or Diapasons (Plate 10).

The portrait of Lady Mary Sidney, mother of Sir Philip Sidney, at Penshurst Place in Kent, shows such an instrument, which she is supporting by her right hand, the lower end resting on the floor. The picture is reproduced as our frontispiece by the kind permission of the Right Hon. Lord de L'Isle.[1]

The Theorboe is said to have taken its name from a Signor Tiorba, who introduced it to the public; but Thomas Mace, in his *Musick's Monument* – that *locus classicus* of English Lute-playing published in 1676 – says that it was only the old English Lute revived. Among the seventeenth-century pocket-book notes of Dr Plume, preserved in manuscript in his library at Maldon, there is the following entry: "Inigo Jones first brought the Theorboe into England after the Popish Conspiracy in 1605. At Dover it was thought some engine brought from Popish countries to destroy the King, and he and it were sent up to the Council Table" of the Star Chamber.

Lutes, however, of various sizes to correspond with the pitch of the voices had already been made; for in the Inventory of Sir Thomas Kytson's effects made in 1603 there are mentioned "one great base lute and a meane lute", also "one trebble lute and a meane lute"; and in 1607, at Campion's Masque in honour of Lord Hay's marriage, there were in the orchestra "3 lutes, 2 meane lutes and a base lute".

---

[1] The sitter's costume defines a date of *c.* 1610 for the portrait; since Lady Mary died in 1586, the identification cannot be correct.

It is a melancholy fact that the instrument which played so worthy a part in the musical world of the sixteenth and seventeenth centuries is now so rare and so little known that many people imagine that it was "blown like a flute". Even in 1676 Mace had to lament the signs of its waning popularity, for thus he addresses his beloved instrument:

> What makes Thee so Sad, my Noble Friend,
> As if Thou wert (with sorrows) near Thy End?
> What is the cause, my Dear-Renowned-Lute,
> That art of late so Silent and so Mute?
> Thou seldom dost in Publick now appear,
> Thou art too Melancholly grown I fear.

To him the Lute replies:

> What need you ask These Questions why 'tis so?
> Since 'tis too obvious for All men to know.
> The World is grown so Slight; full of New Fangles,
> And takes their Chief Delight in Jingle-Jangles:
> With Fiddle-Noises; Pipes of Bartholomew,
> Like those which Country-Wives buy, Gay and New,
> To please their Little Children when they Cry:
> This makes me sit and Sigh thus Mournfully.

The intricacies and niceties of Lute-playing are carefully and curiously described by this enthusiastic musician. We are introduced to the various graces beloved of the lutenist – the Back-fall, the Elevation, the Relish (single and double), the Slide, the Springer, the Sting, the Tutt, the Rake, and many others. In the transcription of a Lute lesson given on page 39 an attempt has been made to represent some of them. Of the Shake, as performed by Mace and much admired, he says that he attributes it to the fact that he had occasion to break both his arms, so his answer to would-be imitators was this: "They must first Break their Arms, as I have done; and so, possibly . . . (by Practice) they may get My manner of Shake". He tells us that for the Lute's body, which should be of a dark black reddish colour with nine "ribs", the best wood is Air-wood (The Oriental Plane), and next our English Maple: "Ebony and Ivory . . . (though most costly, and taking to a common Eye) are the worst." The front table should be made of the straight-grained finest sort of fir called Cullincliff[1] but sometimes "Cyprus" is very good. "Venice Lutes" were most highly esteemed, and those by Laux Maler, a German maker of the early sixteenth century, were much prized, King Charles I giving £100 for one by this master. A Lute of his workmanship is in the

---

[1] *i.e.*, "Cologne-cleft".

Victoria and Albert Museum, but has unfortunately been altered into a form of Guitar, as many of these instruments were in later days. A specimen in its original condition is preserved in the Frischmuth Collection at the University Museum, Philadelphia, USA. It has five pairs of strings, nine ribs, and the peg-box placed at a right angle to the neck. Mace also recommends that the Lute, when not in a good warm case, should be put "into a Bed, that is constantly used, between the Rug and Blanket; . . . only to be excepted, That no Person be so inconsiderate, as to Tumble down upon the Bed whilst the Lute is There; For I have known several Good Lutes spoil'd with such a Trick". Three sorts of strings were used – Minnikins for the higher notes, Venice Catlins for the middle, and Lyons for the Basses. Twenty shillings per annum he gives as an ordinary charge for strings, and so refutes the common theory that "one had as good keep a Horse as a Lute for Cost". From the *Lord Chamberlain's Records* we find, however, that the usual annual allowance for such strings during the seventeenth century was £5, and the same allowance was granted to the Court Musicians for Harp and Bass Viol strings. In 1688 a year's bill for "Catleens" amounted to £1.

Our author also explains the proper method of "fretting" the instrument. "Fret" is the name given to the cross ridges on the neck of Lutes, Viols, Citterns, Guitars, etc., which, while they mark the place for stopping the string with the finger for any particular note, add to its tone and resonance by keeping the string from touching the finger-board too closely. In the wire-strung instruments, as in the Mandoline of our own day, they were usually made of metal or ivory; but on the Viols and Lutes they were of cat-gut tightly stretched and tied round the neck. As they occasionally slipped or broke, a new "fret" had to be put on; this replacement was merely a matter of manual skill and did not necessitate musical knowledge or ability to play the instrument. Hence Hamlet is represented by Shakespeare as saying to Guildenstern, who has failed to make him respond to his will, "though you can *fret* me, you cannot play upon me". The word is derived from the old French *ferretté* "banded with iron or other metal".

As regards the price of the Lute, the £100 paid by Charles I was of course an unusual sum. From the *Household Expense Books* of the Tudor sovereigns we take the following extracts:

1495. To Hugh Denes for a lewte, xiii[s.] iiii[d.]
1501. For a lewte for my Ladye Margaret, xiii[s.] iiii[d.]
1531. Paied to Arthur the lewter for a lewte for the Duke of Richmond, xx[s.]

In reckoning the present value of these or similar payments it should be borne in mind that during the fifteenth century and the first half of the sixteenth century the purchasing power of money was ten or twelve times greater than in our own day.[1] During the second half of that century, however, its value rapidly fell, until at the opening of the seventeenth century it was only a third of what it had been.

In 1590 an old Lute, the property of a member of St John's College, Cambridge, realized but one shilling. In 1610 two Lutes for Prince Henry cost £33 6s 8d, but the usual price in the seventeenth century – as shown by the instruments purchased for the King's music – was from £10 to £15 for a Lute and from £14 to £20 for a Theorboe. James Masters, a Fellow Commoner of Trinity College, Cambridge, in the year 1640 commenced his studies on the instrument, and his account for six months was as follows:

1646, Dec. 7.	For borrowing a lute one month, iiiˢ·
1646/47, Feb. 19.	For a lute with a case to it, ii¹¹· xˢ·
	For two dozen of small strings, iiiˢ·
1647, May 7.	For learning one month on the lute, xˢ·
June 29.	For fretting my lute, iˢ·

The office of Lutenist to the Chapel Royal, established early in the eighteenth century and valued at £41 10s per annum, continued to be held until 1846, but for the last eighty years at least as a sinecure, the instrument itself having disappeared; for the English Guitar and, towards the end of the eighteenth century, the Harp-Lute and the Harp-Lute-Guitar had taken its place in popular estimation.

The Harp-Lute has already been described in the first chapter and is figured in Plate 9. The English Guitar, of which details were given at the end of the second chapter, is also there depicted; and the Harp-Lute-Guitar, which was tuned thus *g″ e″ c″ b′ a′ g′ f′ e′ d′ c′ g*, sounding a sixth or seventh lower, is shown just below it. The British Lute-Harp, afterwards called the Dital Harp, though it somewhat resembled the Harp-Lute in shape, was played upon with both hands, the semitones being obtained by keyed mechanism pressed by the finger, whence its name. It was produced by Light in 1816, and a most interesting account of its development is given by Mr R. B. Armstrong in his *English and Irish Instruments*.

Specimens of the true Lute are now very rare and valuable, and though they are generally relegated to museums and artists' studios, the instrument has lately been revived, and an awakened interest will probably enable us to hear it more frequently as an accompaniment to the voice or in "consort" with its old-world *confrères*.

[1] A more realistic factor for the purchasing power of money then and now (1964) would be between thirty and forty.

PLATE 9

1. Rotte, fifth–eighth centuries. 2. English Guitar by Lucas, eighteenth century.
3 Keyed Guitar, early nineteenth century. 4. Harp-lute by E. Light, *c.* 1810.
5. Harp-lute-guitar by E. Light, *c.* 1800

PLATE 10

1. Mandore or Lutina, eighteenth century. 2. Pandurina by M. A. Bergonzi, 1756. 3. Lute by Sixtus Rauwolf, 1593. 4. Theorboe by Mathys Hofman, 1719. 5. Archlute or Chitarrone, Italian, seventeenth century. 6. Guitar by Champion, *c.* 1800

In the domain of literature it is only natural that the Lute should fill an important part. Shakespeare, as already noted, frequently gives it a place in his plays, the actual instrument being introduced upon the stage in *Julius Caesar* (a terminological inexactitude), and with more propriety in the play of *Henry VIII*, when Queen Catherine's maid sings the charming song commencing "Orpheus with his Lute", to dispel her Royal Mistress's sadness. In the *Taming of the Shrew* (act ii. sc. 1) there is the amusing description of an encounter between Katherine the Shrew and her pretended music-master Hortensio, who complains to her father of the violent treatment he has received in these words:

> I did but tell her she mistook her frets,
> And bowed her hand to teach her fingering,
> When, with a most impatient, devilish spirit,
> "Frets, call you these?" quoth she, "I'll fume with them,"
> And, with that word she struck me on the head,
> And through the instrument my pate made way;
> And there I stood amazèd for a while,
> As on a pillory, looking through the lute,
> While she did call me rascal fiddler
> And twangling Jack, with twenty such vile terms,
> As had she studied to misuse me so.

The technical term "fret", already explained, here affords the dramatist the opportunity of another play on the word.

In a poem written to commemorate the entry of Queen Anne of Denmark into the Scotch capital in 1590 we are told:

> Sum on Lutys did play and sing
> Of instruments the onely King.

And the following extract from an old play about 1670 entitled *The Humorists* shows the use of the Theorboe as an accompaniment, though already beginning to give way to the Guitar:

DRYBOLE. My melodious pipes are a little obstructed; but to serve you, I will chant forth incontinently. But, Madam, I want a Theorbo to pitch my voice.
LADY LOVEYOUTH. Will not a Gittar serve?

Mr Pepys, of course, played both the Lute and Theorboe, while his fellow-diarist and contemporary Evelyn, on hearing Dr Walgrave, physician to the Duke and Duchess of York, accompany a song with his Theorboe-Lute, writes: "He performed beyond imagination, and is doubtless one of the greatest masters in Europe on that charming instrument." In saying this he was but maintaining the prestige which our English lutenists for more than a century had already enjoyed, owing to the skill of such able musicians as John Dowland, Robert Johnson and Dr John Wilson.

As an example of the music so much admired by our forefathers we append an extract from Thomas Mace's book, from which quotations have already been freely made. It is entitled *My Mistress*, and had a peculiar fascination

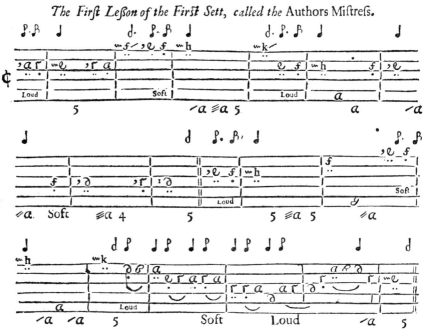

Fig. 7 Lute Music by Thomas Mace (*Musick's Monument*, 1676)

for the author and composer from the fact that it was written by him when engaged to his future wife and absent from her. The rest of the story shall be told in his own quaint style.

"After I was Married, and had brought My Wife Home, to Cambridge; It so fell out, that one Rainy Morning I stay'd within; and in My Chamber, My Wife, and I, were all alone; She Intent upon Her Needle-Works, and I Playing upon my Lute, at the Table by Her; She sat very Still, and Quiet, Listning to All I Play'd, without a Word a Long Time, till at last, I hapned to Play This Lesson; which, so soon as I had once Play'd, She Earnestly desired Me to Play It again; For, said She, That shall be Called, My Lesson."

To this the Lutenist answered, "It may very properly be call'd Your Lesson; For when I Compos'd It, You were wholly in My Fancy, and the Chief Object, and Ruler of My Thoughts."

After this pretty domestic incident the air was always known by his pupils as "Mrs Mace".

~~~ = *vibrato*   = *appoggiatura*   = *mordent*

an 8 below a note (or clef) means '8va bassa'

(*Transcription by Thurston Dart*)

It is very simple, as will be seen in the reproduction of the original (Fig. 7) and its transcription into Staff Notation given above; nor does it in any way represent the elaborate and florid compositions which were the delight of skilled lutenists such as Mace himself; but it affords a clear and well-defined example of the way in which music for the Lute and other instruments was written in the sixteenth and seventeenth centuries according to a system called Tablature, of which, as an appropriate conclusion to this chapter, we give a short explanation.

In the case of the stringed instruments, such as the Lute, Viol, Cittern, etc., the signs used denoted the particular "fret" on which, or rather just behind which, the finger of the player was to be placed; in the wind instruments they denoted the holes to be covered, as seen in the Flageolet music reproduced in Fig. 27. In the example of Lute Tablature the lines do not represent a stave as might at first be thought, but they signify the strings of the instrument. In the Tablature for the Cittern, with but four pairs of open strings, four such lines are used; in the Lute music, because the sixteenth-century instruments usually had six pairs of strings – or five pairs and a single string – six lines are employed in the Tablature. When additional strings were attached to extend the compass in the Bass they were marked by the signs a', a'', a''', 4, 5, 6, etc., placed below the bottom line. The "frets" are shown by letters, "a" being the open string resting on the nut, "b" the first fret, "c" the second, and so on up to "k", the ninth and last fret. The time is denoted by a signature placed at the commencement of the piece and the length or the time value of each note by musical characters placed above the fret letters, it being understood that the duration of all succeeding notes is to be the same until contradicted by another sign. The various graces and relishes are expressed by marks placed to the left of the fret letter, and the dots immediately below the letters show which finger of the right hand is to be used for plucking the string. In the ordinary Lute music these latter signs were usually omitted. Here the uppermost line represents the highest string, but in Italian Lute Tablature this order was reversed and it represented the lowest string. In Viol Tablature the "bowing" was marked by straight lines equivalent to slurs. The Spanish Guitar and even the Violin had their music at one time written in this manner, and Tablatures for the Organ and Clavichord are to be found in the compositions of the sixteenth and seventeenth centuries. The system was probably copied from the signs used for the vocal music in the Middle Ages, and has now, for instrumental purposes, completely disappeared, though for singers it is still continued after an improved method in the Tonic Sol-fa. The music for many of the Chinese instruments is also written in similar curious and (to the uninitiated) mystic signs. Notation by numbers has also been advocated, and was used in Spain for the Lute; but as Mr Abdy Williams, in his *Story of Notation*, so truly says, "What was required was a universal notation, suitable for all instruments, which should show the intervals, not the frets and strings; and this was found in the rapidly developing vocal staff notation." It is the general use of this system which has placed instrumental music, as well as vocal, within the reach of all, and makes it so desirable that in the elementary schools of our country the staff notation – combined perhaps at first with the Tonic Sol-fa – should be, without exception, thoroughly taught.

Chapter IV

Psaltery and Dulcimer

Yn Harpe, yn Thabour, and Symphan gle
Wurschepe God, yn Troumpes, and Sautre;
Yn Cordys, an Organes and Bellis ryngyng,
Yn al these, wurschepe ye hevene kyng.

ROBERT MANNYNG (*c*. 1303)

IN THE PSALTERY AND DULCIMER we have yet a third type of medieval stringed instruments sounded without the use of a bow. The characteristic feature is that of a rectangular or triangular case, forming the sound-box, across which are stretched strings of metal, but sometimes of gut, as in the Turkish Kanoon, which appeared in Western Europe as the *Canon*. There is no finger-board or neck as with the Lute, nor is there any means of altering the pitch of the strings except by turning the tuning-pins, which are placed in a row on one side of the instrument, and to which the strings are attached.

The two forms differ in one important point: in the Psaltery the strings are set in vibration by being plucked with the fingers or with a plectrum, whilst in the Dulcimer they are struck with two light hammers or rods of wood; and for this reason the Psaltery is the parent of the keyboard instruments known as the Virginal, Spinet and Harpsichord, whilst the Dulcimer has given us the Pianoforte.

In dealing with the history of these instruments the following curious fact presents itself: that whereas illustrations, allusions to and descriptions of the Psaltery are unusually frequent and circumstantial, the early history of the Dulcimer, though it shows itself distinctly towards the close of the Middle Ages, is shrouded in obscurity. In fact, the earliest reliable illustration of the latter instrument, which we have yet noticed, occurs on a carved ivory book-cover of Byzantine workmanship in the British Museum (Egerton 1139), said to have been made for Queen Melissenda, wife of Foulques, Count of Anjou and King of Jerusalem, about the middle of the twelfth century. With it are depicted a Rebec, a Harp, a quadrangular Psaltery or Cruit and a Viol with incurved sides.

42

So alike, however, are the two instruments in every respect except in the manner of playing, and so easily could the long *plectra* employed by the performer on the horizontal form of Psaltery (as shown, for instance, in the illustration on Plate 20, taken from a late twelfth-century manuscript) be used for *striking* the strings as well as for plucking them, that in all probability the earlier Dulcimers are included under the general name of Psaltery. As it is, Mersenne, in his treatise *Harmonicorum Libri XII*, calls the Dulcimer the Psalterium, and speaks of the small rod used for striking the strings as a *plectrum*; similar instances will be found in later writers also. In France during the eighteenth century the Psalterion was certainly a Dulcimer.

That the transition between the two instruments is easy is shown by the action of an itinerant musician whom we met a few years ago: he had transformed his Dulcimer into a Psaltery by the simple process of changing the strings to a somewhat smaller gauge and plucking them with the fingernails of both hands, as the instrument rested on a low stand before him. The effect was decidedly good, and, as the soft part of the hands was easily used for damping the strings and shortening their excessive vibration, the chords, as they were played, were distinct and harmonious. When treating, then, of the Psaltery, it is quite possible that we are considering at the same time the earliest forms of the Dulcimer.

The origin of the Psaltery is undoubtedly Asiatic; as the Santir it is known at the present day in Persia and India, and as the Kin and Koto in China and Japan. The European name, however, was given to it by the Greeks from the "twitching" or "plucking" of the strings. Under this term they doubtless included forms which might be more correctly classed with the Lyre and Cithara, the strings being plucked on both sides; in fact, old as the Psaltery is, we fail to find on the sculptured slabs and frescoed walls of the more ancient nations any representation of the characteristic details of the instruments. The so-called Assyrian Psalteries are in reality small Trigons or triangular Harps with "free" strings, i.e. played on both sides, and of the Assyrian Dulcimer we will speak later. Yet the simple expedient of stretching chords across a hollow box or cavity must have suggested itself at a very early period in the history of man; for the fable of the tortoise-shell found by Hermes, who, as he touched the dried sinews lying across the empty carapace, drew forth the pleasing sound of music, shows us the beginnings, not of the Lyre type of instrument, as has generally been supposed, but of the Psaltery. Indeed, in Eastern Asia, where examples of the true Harp are practically unknown, the Psaltery type is quite a common as well as an ancient

43

form. The instrument, known perhaps to the Jews as the Nebel, which, as Josephus tells us, had twelve sounds and was plucked with the fingers, passed into Greece and Italy with other Oriental importations. From its association with Biblical tradition it appealed strongly to the early Christians, and throughout the first half of the Middle Ages the Psaltery was especially favoured by ecclesiastics, but it must be remembered that the Psalms did not derive their title from the Psaltery, for the old Greek word *Psalmos*, which originally meant the sound of the Lyre or a song accompanied by the Lyre, was even in classical times used for any strain of music vocal or instrumental.

The medieval Psaltery was constructed in two principal shapes. The earlier, as far as Europe is concerned, appears to have been triangular. The player generally placed it across his breast for performance, the point of the triangle turned downwards, so that the broad base was easily supported between the arms, and the hands left free to strike the strings. A modification of this shape appears in the eleventh century when the sharp corners were flattened, and gradually the instrument, assuming a trapeze form with a more fantastic outline, was known in Italy as the "strumento di porco", from its supposed likeness to the face of a pig. This form is shown in the illustration on Plate 52, taken from a late thirteenth-century manuscript (Brit. Mus., Add. 35166) of English workmanship. The instrument is held in an inverted position as being offered before the heavenly throne. Sometimes it was placed on the lap during performance, as depicted in the early fifteenth-century manuscript illustrated in Plate 53 and in the carvings at Manchester Cathedral (Fig. 9); so sings the poet in the old Romance of *Eger and Grime*:

> the Ladye lovesome of hew & hyde
> sett her downe by his bed side,
> shee layd a sowter upon her knee,
> & theron shee playd full love somlye.

On the other hand it was often made in the shape of a right-angled triangle, and was held in an upright position. In the seventeenth and eighteenth centuries this was known in Germany as the *Spitzharfe*, the Pointed Harp or David's Harp (Plate 13), and usually had strings on both sides of the sound-board. About the year 1800 Edward Light brought before the British public a very similar instrument under the name Diplo-Kithara. It had twenty-three strings of wire on either side, those on the right for the melody, those on the left for accompaniment. A fine specimen is in the Dublin National Museum (Plate 13).

The other form of the instrument was rectangular and resembled a shield; but the shape appears to have been unnecessarily awkward, and it disappeared from general use in England in the fourteenth century, though it existed longer on the Continent, and is still seen in one form of Dulcimer. Held in an upright position, it is named and figured in an eleventh-century manuscript of English work (Brit. Mus., Tib. C. vi), reproduced in Plate 12.

Of the tuning of the Psaltery we have no ancient account, but in the sixteenth century the writer Martin Agricola, in his *Musica Instrumentalis* (1528), describes and figures a triangular Psaltery of twenty-five single strings with a diatonic compass of three octaves and three notes from F to bb''; the illustrations, however, of earlier instruments show only from eight to twenty strings. Mersenne's Psalterium, already mentioned as identical with the Dulcimer, has but thirteen double strings and a compass of an octave and four notes from c to g', with one pair of bass strings tuned to G.

As the instrument was especially favoured by the clergy, as well as in later days by roving troubadours and wandering minstrels, allusions to it in literature are unusually frequent. The Psaltery was as popular an accompaniment to the voice as the Harp and the Gittern. In a poem of the twelfth century describing the Coronation Feast of King Arthur, "psalterys and monochords" appear in the musical part of the entertainment. Nicholas, Chaucer's "poore scholar", solaced himself with its music:

> And al above ther lay a gay sautrie
> On which he made, a-nyghtes, melodie,
> So swetely, that all the chambre rong,
> And Angelus ad Virginem he song.

But the Oxford clerk, who was devoted to his books and studies, loved Aristotle better "than robes riche, or fidel or sautre". Amongst the minstrels who attended the Westminster Feast (1306) were several Psaltery players, as, for instance, "Gillotin le Sautreur", who received forty shillings, and "Janyn le Sautreur de Mons. de Percy", who was paid one mark. Guillot le Psalteron was the Queen's minstrel.

The instrument, however, lost its position in England during the sixteenth century, owing not merely to the popularity of the Dulcimer, but to the superiority of its own offspring, the Virginal and Harpsichord. In a list of musical instruments used in this country about the year 1663 (Brit. Mus., Sloane 1326) it no longer appears, but in remote places it probably still retained its hold, for in a description of English instruments of music

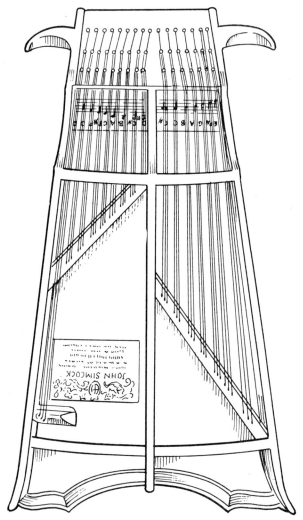

Fig. 8 Bell Harp (*c.* 1700), showing the position in which
it is held by the player

given at the close of the seventeenth century a sketch of a rectangular
Psaltery is called a Shepherd's Harp (Brit. Mus., Harl. 2027), and in an
Essex farmhouse we discovered a trapeze-shaped Psaltery with eight single
strings dated 1789. It is illustrated in Plate 11.

The Psaltery is still commonly used in Spain and also in the Canary
Isles. In recent years a child's instrument, sometimes called the Prince of

Wales' Harp, has gained a certain degree of popularity, and as the Erato Harp,[1] with elaborate mechanism for damping certain strings, has received public recognition. They have only brought once more into practical use the "gay sautrie" of bygone days.

Mention must also be made of another form of Psaltery produced about the year 1700 by John Simcock, of Bath, and called the Bell Harp, either in honour of the captain of his regiment or, more probably, from the manner of using the instrument and the effect it produced. Tans'ur, in his *Elements of Musick* (1767), says: "Its form is like a bell and kept swinging whilst played on, whose strings are struck by each Thumb, being armed with a split quill, whalebone or thin horn, which, when artfully managed, affords tolerable good harmony." The instrument generally had sixteen triple strings tuned as follows:

$$\text{For the right thumb} - d''' \; c\sharp''' \; b'' \; a'' \; g'' \; f\sharp'' \; e'' \; d'' \; d'$$
$$\text{For the left thumb} - c\sharp'' \; c\natural'' \; b' \; a' \; g' \; f\sharp' \; e'.$$

An illustration of one of the original instruments is given in Fig. 8, but some later Bell Harps have as many as twenty-four open notes.

Of the special characteristics of the DULCIMER as distinct from the Psaltery we have already spoken. The name is supposed to be a modification of the words *Dulce Melos* or *Douce-melle*, an appellation given to a "sweet-toned" stringed instrument used in France in the fourteenth and fifteenth centuries, and which possessed in the succeeding century a keyboard variety of the clavichord type described in a subsequent chapter. Although it was recognized in Spain in the fourteenth century as the Dulcemel, no Psaltery struck with sticks is shown among the very many musical instruments which illustrate the Escorial manuscript of the *Cantigas de Santa Maria* executed in the previous century. In England the word first appears in a poem written about the year 1400 called *The Squyr of Lowe Degre*. We quote the passage in full, beginning at line 1069, as it mentions many instruments to which allusion has been or will be made:

> There was myrth & melody
> With harpe getron and sautry
> with rote ribible and clokarde
> with pypes organs & bumbarde
> with other mynstrelles them amonge

[1] This appears to be a fancy name for what is more commonly known as the "auto-harp" – a form of zither with a built-in mechanism for filtering out common chords by means of damping certain strings.

with sytolphe and with sautry songe
with fydle recorde and Dowcemere
with trompette & with claryon clere
with dulcet pipes of many cordes.[1]

Furthermore, when Prince Edward was entertained at Coventry in 1474 he was greeted, we are told, with "the ministrelsie of harpe and dowsemeris"; and at a pageant given in Westminster Hall in 1502 a ladies' orchestra of twelve performers "made music on clarycordis, dulsymers, clarysymballs and such other".

Nor are we without illustrations of the Dulcimer of this period, for among the carved representations of angelic musicians in the roof of the nave of Manchester Cathedral, which was erected between the years 1465 and 1468, not only is there a performer on a twenty-stringed Psaltery, but another on a fifteen-stringed Dulcimer, which he strikes with two small hammers. Both are illustrated in Figs. 9 and 10. Moreover, in the Psalter prepared and illuminated for King Henry VIII (Brit. Mus., 2 A. xvi) a group of musicians is depicted with a Harp, Dulcimer, Trumpet, Pipe and Tabor. Perhaps the "Dulsacordis" mentioned in *The Houlgate* (or "Owl"), a poem written in Scotland in 1543, also represents the Dulcimer. Mr Pepys has passed his approval on this instrument, for under the date May 14, 1662, he writes: "Here (i.e. at the puppet play in Covent Garden), among the fiddles, I first saw a dulcimer played on with sticks, knocking of the strings, and is very pretty."

The common scale of the old English Dulcimer was undoubtedly diatonic; from the illustration given in Plate 11, which shows the Dulcimer with the long continuous bridges characteristic of the earlier form, and not the separate studs or bridges which mark the English instrument of the last century and the modern European instruments of today, it will be seen that there are fourteen sets of strings, consisting of four in each set. The three longest and deepest in tone pass over the right-hand bridge and under that on the left: they are tuned to *d, e* and *f♯*. The other eleven strings pass over the left-hand bridge, and are playable on either side of it; to the right they give the following notes – *g a b c' d' e' f♯' g' a' b' c''*; if struck on the left, they sound *d' e' f♯' g' a' b' c♯'' d'' e'' f♯'' g''*. Music in the key of *D* with closely related keys can therefore be easily performed on it.

In the thirteenth century to some form of Psaltery the name *Cembalo* or Cymbal was given apparently because the resonance of its strings resembled

---

[1] The last line should almost certainly read "with dulcet pipes and manycordes [i.e., clavichords]". See Chapter VII.

the bell-chimes, called Cymbals, which, as we shall explain in a later chapter, were so popular in all European countries at that time. The name is interesting because one of the earliest kinds of keyboard instruments was called the Clavicymbal – the Italian Clavicembalo or Keyed Psaltery. The large Dulcimer, used in Hungarian Bands at the present time, is known by the Magyar musicians as the *zimbalom*, and the fact that the Italians call the Dulcimer the German Psaltery (*Salterio tedesco*) seems to imply that the use of little sticks or hammers first became popular in that country.

A few words must here be said upon an ancient work of art which has proved, we fear, a fruitful source of error. It has been the custom with many

Fig. 9 Psaltery – 15th cent.   Fig. 10 Dulcimer – 15th cent.
(Manchester Cathedral)   (Manchester Cathedral)

writers on musical subjects of recent date to refer the use of the Dulcimer to the days of the great Assyrian kingdom six or seven centuries before the Christian era. The example on which the theory is based, and which is unique, is supposed to be shown in a bas-relief preserved in the British Museum and known as the "Procession of King Assurbanipal". An illustration of it was given by Engel in his *Music of the Most Ancient Nations*, though he candidly acknowledges that if the instrument ever were playable the representation on the slab must be faulty. And it is faulty, but not through the sculptor's mistake; the fact is, the stone has been badly cracked, the fissure extending right through the farther end of the musical instrument; owing to the damage done, the stone flaked off on either side of the crack, and some thoughtless restorer has patched up the damaged portion with the evident desire to give continuity to the representation on the slab in

49

its present position. The part which has rendered the explanation of the instrument so difficult and misleading is by a "later hand" – the hand of an English workman – and there is nothing in the original part of the sculpture which would suggest its being anything else but one of those Trigons or triangular Harps which so frequently occur in these Assyrian bas-reliefs. Being on a late slab, the instrument is shown with a fuller and deeper sound-board, but, as its smaller predecessors, it is held vertically and played, like the ancient Lyre and modern Nubian Kissar,[1] on both sides of the strings with a plectrum in one hand together with the fingers of the other hand. It must, of course, be remembered that the English translators of the Bible had not this stone before them when they placed the Dulcimer among King Nebuchadnezzar's large orchestra in the plains of Dura. The word in the original is *symphonia*, which is far more likely to have meant the bag-pipe. Our translators, however, did the best they could to mark the grandeur of the music used on this occasion, and as the exact explanation of Assyrian instruments was beyond them, as in many details it is still beyond us, they gave us a list of representative English instruments used in their own day: for the "cornet, flute, harp, sackbut, psaltery and dulcimer" we should probably read "the horn, pipe, lyre, harp, psaltery and bagpipe".

There is yet another name given to the Dulcimer which will introduce to our notice a curious instrument formerly used in Ireland, Scotland and England, and called the Timpan or Tiompan. We meet with the word in Irish records as early as the eighth century at least, and we are told that St Dunstan, when weary of his work, used to play not only on his harp but "in timphano". Moreover, Giraldus Cambrensis, known to his twelfth-century contemporaries as Gerald Barry, Archdeacon of St David's, records that the Irish people used more especially as their musical instruments the *Cithara* and *Tympanum*, and that the Scotch made use of the *Cithara*, *Tympanum* and *Chorus*, of which last-named instrument more will be said in the next chapter. Now it has generally been supposed that in all these cases the *Tympanum* was the Drum: but here we surely have the Latinized form of the Irish word *timpan:* for whatever untutored savages may do, it is unlikely that St Dunstan, who had, moreover, been trained by Irish teachers, would solace his weary body and brain by playing on the Drum. What, then, was this *Timpan*?

Professor O'Curry, in his lectures on the *Manners and Customs of the Irish*, has probably collected all obtainable references from Irish literature of the early centuries with respect to this instrument. His researches clearly

[1] Etymologically linked with Greek "Kithara", Irish "Cruit", etc.

prove that the Timpan was first of all a *stringed* instrument and, therefore, not a Drum: that it was played with the finger-nails or with a quill plectrum; that its strings, which were of wire, were affixed to metal tuning-pins, and that in later days a rod or stick instead of the fingers or plectrum was used upon the strings. The learned Professor goes so far as to suggest a bow, but this is extremely doubtful, and he admits that the passage on which he founds his idea is very late and obscure. From a Glossary written by Cormac about the year 900 we gather further particulars: the instrument was made of sally or sallow wood, and the tone of its bronze strings was soft and sweet. Elsewhere we are told that it was not so powerful as the Cruit, and although it was sometimes called the *Benn-Crot*, the pointed or triangular Cruit, it was considered inferior to and of later date than the Cruit proper; tradition, too, gave it an Eastern origin. It seems very probable that this once popular *Timpan* was a form of Psaltery "plucked with a quill", in later days becoming a Dulcimer "struck with a rod". The difficulty underlying this identification is that mention is made of three strings only, but as we are informed at the same time that the tympanist could perform in the three great Musical Strains or Keys, of which some details are given in the first chapter, it is probable – unless, indeed, the instrument were of the Citole or Lute type – that the "three strings" are but a figurative allusion to its powers in this respect. In some cases it certainly had more than this number, for we are told that the treble strings were of silver and the bass strings of "white bronze". Some would have us believe that it was identical with the *Organistrum* or hurdy-gurdy, which is impossible, or that the tympanist was after all only a "conductor of the music". The most probable explanation, however, is the one already suggested, that it was a form of Psaltery either triangular, as implied by the name *Benn-Crot*, or with an up-curved head, as shown on an instrument carved on the late tenth-century cross of Durrow, King's County, Ireland, illustrated by Miss Stokes in her description of *The High Crosses of Castledermot and Durrow*, and in an Irish manuscript of the ninth century (Brit. Mus., Vit. F. xi) figured by Engel in his *History of Musical Instruments*. A pointed quadrangular instrument appears on the tenth-century Cross of Abbot Muiredach at Monasterboice, Co. Louth, and closely resembles the ancient Baltic Psaltery called *Kantele* shown on Plate 13. The latter instrument is now, however, played horizontally across the knees; originally it had but five strings. An ancient chronicle also relates that the Irish monks of the great Monastery of St Gall in Switzerland played on the *Cithara* and the *Psalterium*; and in the illustrations which adorn an early thirteenth-century manuscript of Giraldus' works preserved in the

British Museum (13 B. viii) the figure of a Psaltery player accompanies the description of the popular instruments of Ireland. As regards the derivation of the name, the Irish writer Cormac, previously mentioned, considered that it came from two Irish words meaning "soft" and "bronze"; Grattan Flood, in his *Story of the Harp*, thinks that it was because the body of the instrument was shaped like a Drum (*tympanum*). If neither of these derivations be accepted, we think that since the player was frequently described in olden days as *striking* the strings even when the plectrum was used, the instrument may have been called *tympanum* for that reason, but the mention of the use of the fingers or a quill plectrum is against its having been a true Dulcimer in its earliest days. Towards the close of the Middle Ages the word *tympanum* or *tympane* was certainly used for the Dulcimer as well as for the Drum: in France it is called Tympanon at the present day.

An allusion to the Timpan will be found in English literature in a thirteenth-century version of Layamon's *Romance of Brut*, where it is mentioned among the musical instruments played by the accomplished King Blaethgabreat:

> . . . . ne cude na mon swa muchel of song.
> of harpe & of salterium. of fidel & of coriun.
> of timpe & of lure.

By comparison with the original French poem of Brut, written by Wace, we find that all these are intended to be stringed instruments. In the earlier work the word Timpe does not appear, but Rote is used, and Notker too, in his late tenth-century translation of the 149th Psalm, gives Rotte as the equivalent of Timpanum; for, as we have stated in a previous chapter, on the Continent the Rote was considered one of the several forms of Psaltery.

The AEOLIAN HARP is an amphibious instrument which seems to resist definite classification. Furnished with strings and sounded by wind, it has been variously described as an Organ or as a Harp, but as in its best known form it closely resembles the Psaltery, we place it for our present purpose under that class, although its strings are neither plucked nor struck, the action of the wind more nearly representing the use of the bow as described in the next chapter.

The reader is probably aware that the effect of a current of air on a tightened string is to set it in motion, and, as the strength of the current is increased, to cause the string to divide its vibrating length into certain well-defined sections, which produce the regular series of harmonic notes explained in a subsequent chapter on the Horn. If, in addition to a single

PLATE II

1. Psaltery, dated 1789

2. Aeolian or Wind Harp

3. Dulcimer with Hammers

PLATE 12

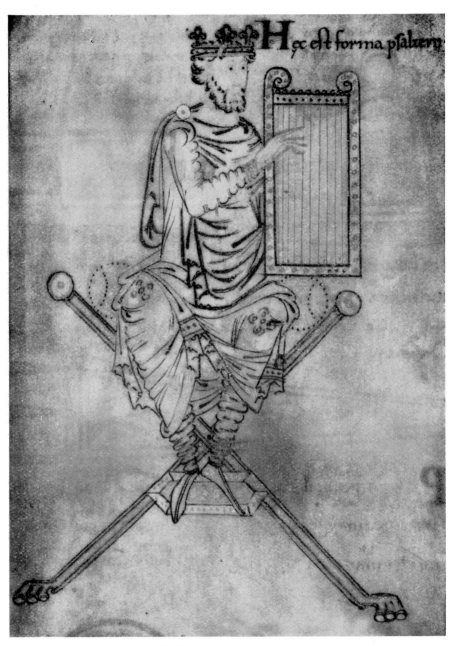

Psaltery, eleventh century

string, others are stretched by its side and tuned to the same note, as the wind pressure varies on each string concords are produced. This is the principle of the Aeolian Harp.

The ordinary instrument usually consists of a rectangular box about three feet in length, five cr six inches in width and three or four inches deep; the gut strings, ten or twelve in number, pass over two bridges resting on the long sound-board, which is pierced with holes; they are tightened by small pins inserted in one end of the instrument, and are generally tuned to G. Over the strings is placed a second board which directs and increases the wind pressure when the Harp is set in the draught of a window. In Plate 11 this board is removed.

The sounds, as they rise and fall, speak of languid ease tinged with regretful sadness, and James Thomson appropriately chose the Aeolian Harp as the musical instrument of his *Castle of Indolence* (1746). For it required no effort,

> But sidelong, to the gently-waving Wind,
> To lay the well-tun'd Instrument relin'd;
> From which, with airy flying Fingers light,
> Beyond each mortal Touch the most refin'd,
> The God of Winds drew Sounds of deep Delight:
> Whence, with just Cause, the Harp of Aeolus it hight.

Coleridge also, in his poem on the instrument (1795), tells of

> And that simplest Lute,
> Placed length-ways in the clasping casement, hark!
> How by the desultory breeze caressed,
> . . . .
> It pours such sweet upbraiding.

Although the scientist Kircher, in his *Musurgia Universalis*, published in 1650, regarded it as a new invention, the effect of the wind on tightened strings has been known and recognized from the earliest times and by nations most remote. The Chinese have their wind-harps and kite-bows, the Japanese their grotesque dragons fitted with vibrating cords. The traditions of India and Ceylon speak of harmonious sounds moved by the wind, and Jewish Rabbis tell us that David's harp hummed as at night it hung suspended over his couch, which shows that the patriarch appreciated fresh air; while the ingenious Archbishop Dunstan in the tenth century gained the unenviable name of a sorcerer by constructing an Aeolian Harp which played when placed against a crevice in a wall. As it certainly was not safe in the

F

Middle Ages to dabble in so black an art, the magic Harp appears to have been laid aside; it was left for Pope to introduce it once more to the English public in the eighteenth century under an improved form. Our own too practical age has, however, no place or time for sentiment; so Nature herself has transformed the telegraph wires of busy men into grand Aeolian Harps, and plays on them the ceaseless music of the breeze.

Chapter V

Crowd, Rebec and Viol

With Vialles and Recorders sing
   The praises of the Lord;
With Crouncorns musicke laud the King
   Of Kings with one accord.

SIR WILLIAM LEIGHTON (1613)

UNDER THESE TYPES are presented to us the stringed instruments played with a bow; and foremost we place THE CROWD, not because it is necessarily the earliest instrument so played – for the Fiddle-bow is certainly not of European origin – but because it is peculiarly associated with our own country and is closely connected with the story of the Cruit or Rote told in our first chapter. The word Crowd is an Anglicized form of the Welsh word Crwth, which is, in its turn, derived from the old Irish Crot or Cruit. In medieval Latin it appears as *Chorus*, a name which is sometimes given to a primitive form of bagpipe. An eleventh-century manuscript written in England (Brit. Mus., Tib. C. vi) gives an illustration of the Chorus, and tells us that it was made of wood and had four strings. Aimeric de Peyrac, an author of the early fourteenth century, states that it had double strings:

> Quidam Choros consonantes
> Duplicem chordam perstridentes,

and the *Promptuarium Parvulorum* of a century later gives, as the Latin equivalent of Crowde, *Chorus* or *Corus*, while a player on the Crowde is a *Corista*.

It is necessary to explain this in detail, as the word by which Giraldus Cambrensis at the end of the twelfth century describes one of the favourite instruments of the Scotch and Welsh has been frequently misunderstood. In Scotland, he says, there were three instruments in use, *Cythara, Tympanum* and *Chorus*, whilst in Wales there were the *Cythara, Tibiae* and *Chorus*. Most writers have taken for granted that the Chorus, in the case of Scotland, was the Bagpipe, because at the present day it is so popular in that

55

country. But, as will presently be shown, there is a great doubt whether the Bagpipe was used at all in Scotland before the thirteenth century, Dr Duncan Fraser's patriotic advocacy for its antiquity notwithstanding; whilst, in the case of Wales, we have no record to show that it was at any time a popular or a national instrument. The Chorus in both cases was unquestionably the small Cruit or Crwth as distinct from the larger instrument bearing that name; and whatever may have been the development in Giraldus' day among the Scotch and Welsh, in Ireland and England it was already played with a bow. For in an Anglo-Saxon Psalter of the early part of the eleventh century, now in the University Library at Cambridge, the bowed Cruit is seen in the hands of Asaph. As will be observed from the illustration (Plate 38, enlarged in Fig. 11), it was played at the shoulder and had four strings, but no finger-board: on the opposite side is Heman playing on the ordinary Cruit or Rote. On Church Island, Lough Corrane, in Ireland, there is an ancient sculpture of the twelfth century which represents a musician performing with a bow on a six-stringed Cruit, also placed on the shoulder and without a finger-board. An illustration will be found in the *Journal of the Royal Society of Antiquaries of Ireland* (1908). In Ruhlmann's *Die Geschichte der Bogeninstrumente* there is a fine representation of three performers on bowed Cruits; the instruments are of different sizes, the smallest, with two strings only, being held at the shoulder, the next size on the knee and the largest across the knees, somewhat after the manner of a bass Viol; the strings of the last two are not shown. There is no finger-board to either of them. The original of this interesting group is to be found in the eleventh-century Prayer Book of the Archduke Leopold of Austria, which is now preserved in a monastery near Vienna. The earliest representation of a Cruit with a finger-board is seen in a late thirteenth-century manuscript of English workmanship in the British Museum (Add. 35166), which is reproduced in Plate 52. We can attach but little importance to the so-called bowed Cruit shown in the Latin Bible of Charles le Chauve (ninth century), for in the original there are neither strings nor bow, and the outline of the instrument is wholly fantastic. Nor does the sculpture on the Durrow Cross (*c.* 1000), illustrated by Miss Stokes, depict anything more than a lyre-shaped Cruit played with the fingers.

Far more interesting and circumstantial is Mr Heron Allen's discovery of the seal of Roger Wade the Crowder, attached to a deed dated 1316. The seal, which is illustrated in Miss Racster's *Chats on Violins*, shows a four-stringed Cruit or Crowd with the bridge placed slantwise between the sound-holes; by its side is a short thick bow. The Crowd carved on one of the choir seats at Worcester Cathedral, and dating from the year 1397, more closely resembles the form of the instrument which was used on the Continent where it was known as the bowed Rotte. A very similar instrument is seen in the early fifteenth-century carvings which decorate the roof of the nave of St Mary's Church, Shrewsbury. A photograph of this example is given in Fig. 12. As will be observed it has four strings, and is held at the shoulder. In the Chapter-house at Westminster, among the paintings executed at the same date by Brother John of Northampton, there

Fig. 11 Crowd – early 11th cent.
(Cambridge)

Fig. 12 Crowd – early 15th cent.
(Shrewsbury)

are several well-defined specimens of the Crowd: these, when in use, are represented as being held at or on the knee.

Of the tuning of this four-stringed Crowd we have no record; probably, as Peyrac states, the strings were arranged in two pairs, like the early Viols, a fourth apart; but during the fifteenth century two more strings were added to the Welsh form of the instrument, probably the two which were placed off the finger-board, and they were either plucked by the thumb of the left hand or used in the same way as the Drones or Bourdon strings of the early Viols. In the eighteenth century the six-stringed instrument was tuned thus – d'' d' c' c'' (on the finger-board) and g' g (off the finger-board). This arrangement, together with the flat bridge of the instrument, suggests

57

that it was used for accompaniment rather than for melody. An old manuscript (Brit. Mus., Add. 14939) containing instructions for the Welsh Crwth or Crowd informs us that on it were played "the four principal chords" and the twenty-four musical "measures", which were merely a repetition of the tonic and dominant chords in a set order. To facilitate the production of these chords the bridge was set slantwise. In 1801 Bingley, during his tour in North Wales, met a Crwth player who played the national melodies with the following tuning – *b'' b' e'' e'* (on the finger-board) and *a' a* (off the finger-board). There is every reason to believe, however, that the strings on the finger-board were in reality tuned an octave lower than Bingley states: for the length of the string on the Crwth is the same as that on the Viola, and a writer of the middle of the eighteenth century describes the instrument as "a sort of Tenor Fiddle, now almost out of date".

From personal researches made among the peasantry of Wales it is evident that the use of the Crwth was continued at least till the middle of the last century. The story is told of one James Green, shoemaker, of Bronygarth, who died in 1855, that on the way to a festive gathering he encountered in a narrow lane an infuriated bull; hastily climbing into a tree he hoped to escape the attack, but the animal, determined not to lose his man, took up a position beneath the branches. The little shoemaker, though grateful enough for his safety, regretfully thought of the merry evening he had lost; so at last he determined to try the effect of music on the expectant beast. Taking his Crwth out of his bag, he struck up a favourite air. To his surprise the animal turned and fled. "Stop, stop!" cried James, his wounded pride quite overcoming his fears, "I'll change the tune." It was, however, too late, and for the first time the music of the last of the Crwth players had failed to please.

Genuine specimens of the instrument are now very rare, though probably some might still be found in the out-of-the-way parts of the Principality. There is an original specimen in the Victoria and Albert Museum dated 1742, and another in the Corporation Museum at Warrington, but lacking bridge, tail-piece and finger-board. The two examples in the Museum of the Conservatoire at Brussels are both reproductions. The Crwth here shown on Plate 14 was made in the last century by Owain Tyddwr, of Dolgelly, an old man who remembered the instrument as it was in his younger days, and took great pleasure in its reconstruction. It has a flat back, and one foot of the bridge passes through the sound-hole and forms the sound-post, a peculiar survival which is also to be seen in the modern Greek *Lyra*, a form of Rebec illustrated in Plate 16. A Crwth exhibited at Bangor about the year

1860 had only a small hole on the left-hand side of the finger-board sufficiently large to allow the thumb to pluck the two open strings.

In the earlier English literature we find the word Crowd appearing as
Choron, Corron or Coriun, as in the passage from Layamon's *Brut*, quoted
in the course of the last chapter. It there occurs in conjunction with, but
distinct from, the "fithele", a frequent combination, of which another
instance is afforded in the early romance *Lybeaus Desconus* – a title which is in
reality a transcript of the French *Le Beau desconnus*, or the "Fair Unknown",
where we are told of Trandelayn that

> Myche he couthe of game,
> With sytole sautrye yn same
> Harpe fydele and crouthe.

But in later literature the name is used, as the word Crwth is used today by
the Welsh, for any bowed instrument and more especially the three-stringed
Rebec, the *Crwth trithant* of Wales.

Palsgrave in 1530 explained the Crowd as a "Rebecq", and a certain
John Hogan, in the year 1537, was reprimanded for "singing lewd ballads
with a crowd or fyddyll".

At the Westminster Feast in 1306 eight Crowders or Crouthers were
present besides Vilours. Amongst them were two Crowders of the Earl of
Gloucester. The young Prince, crowned the next year as Edward II, in
whose honour the feast was held, was a patron of the instrument, for his
father had requested the Abbot of Shrewsbury to send him a famous
musician from his own household, "who should teach the Prince of Wales'
Rhymer the minstrelys of the Crowdy". Even in the middle of the last
century among the peasants of Southern England the word, at any rate,
still survived; for "Samuel were crowdin' very fitly until his string broked".

Now, whereas in the Crowd we observe the adaptation of the Oriental
Fiddle-bow to the Keltic Cruit or Crwth, in THE REBEC we have a bowed
instrument imported into Europe entirely from the East. Many attempts, it is
true, have been made to prove that the use of the bow was known in the
classical days of Greece and Rome, but the word *plectrum* will bear no such
translation. With the spread of Arabic influence the bow came westward;
for apparently its use was first recognized in India, evolved, it may be, from
the primitive way of playing on the Monochords or Musical Bows, which are
still to be found in that country, as they are also amongst the native races of
Africa.

The shape of the Rebec is characteristic of its Eastern home, for, like the early Lutes, it is pear-shaped in outline with a short neck and a sound-box which is convex or rounded at the back. Two Rebecs are shown on Plate 16; the specimen from modern Greece closely resembles the medieval instrument, and the Italian Rebec represents the later form. They are both, however, constructed from a single block of wood, with a thin flat board glued on the hollowed-out body.

The Rebec first appears in Europe under the name *Lyra*, which is still given to it in Greece, by which route it probably entered our continent. It is mentioned in German literature of the eighth century, and illustrations of the tenth and later centuries show it with one string only (Fig. 13). In the eleventh century, however, a form is seen with three strings or with two sets of double strings; it is so presented to us in an Apocalypse produced in England during the first half of that century, and now in the Bodleian Library at Oxford (Bodl. 352). It is reproduced in Plate 21. A similar instrument is shown in the hands of the English gleeman in a manuscript of the same century in the British Musuem (Tiberius C. vi). This example has been frequently engraved and forms one of the stock illustrations of works on musical instruments.

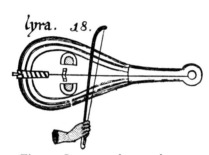

Fig. 13 Lyra – 12th or 13th cent.
(St Blasius)

A Rebec of the twelfth century is well depicted in the Norman carving in the crypt of Canterbury Cathedral, as given in Plate 15; in the page of the late twelfth-century Psalter now in the University Library, Glasgow, shown on Plate 20, the Rebec will also be seen in the hands of the musician on the left.

In that century a larger instrument of the same class also appears in this country; it was called the RUBEBE, or Rybybe as it is written in the *Promptuarium Parvulorum*. It differed not only in size but also in shape and construction, the body being oval in outline with a distinct neck, i.e. not in one piece with the body; it could be played either at the shoulder or between the knees. It came to England from Southern Europe, having been evolved from the Arabian *Rebaba*, and, under Moorish influence, had been in use in Spain from the tenth century.

The Rybybe is well portrayed among the Norman carvings of the twelfth century which adorn the south doorway of Barfreston Church in Kent

PLATE 13

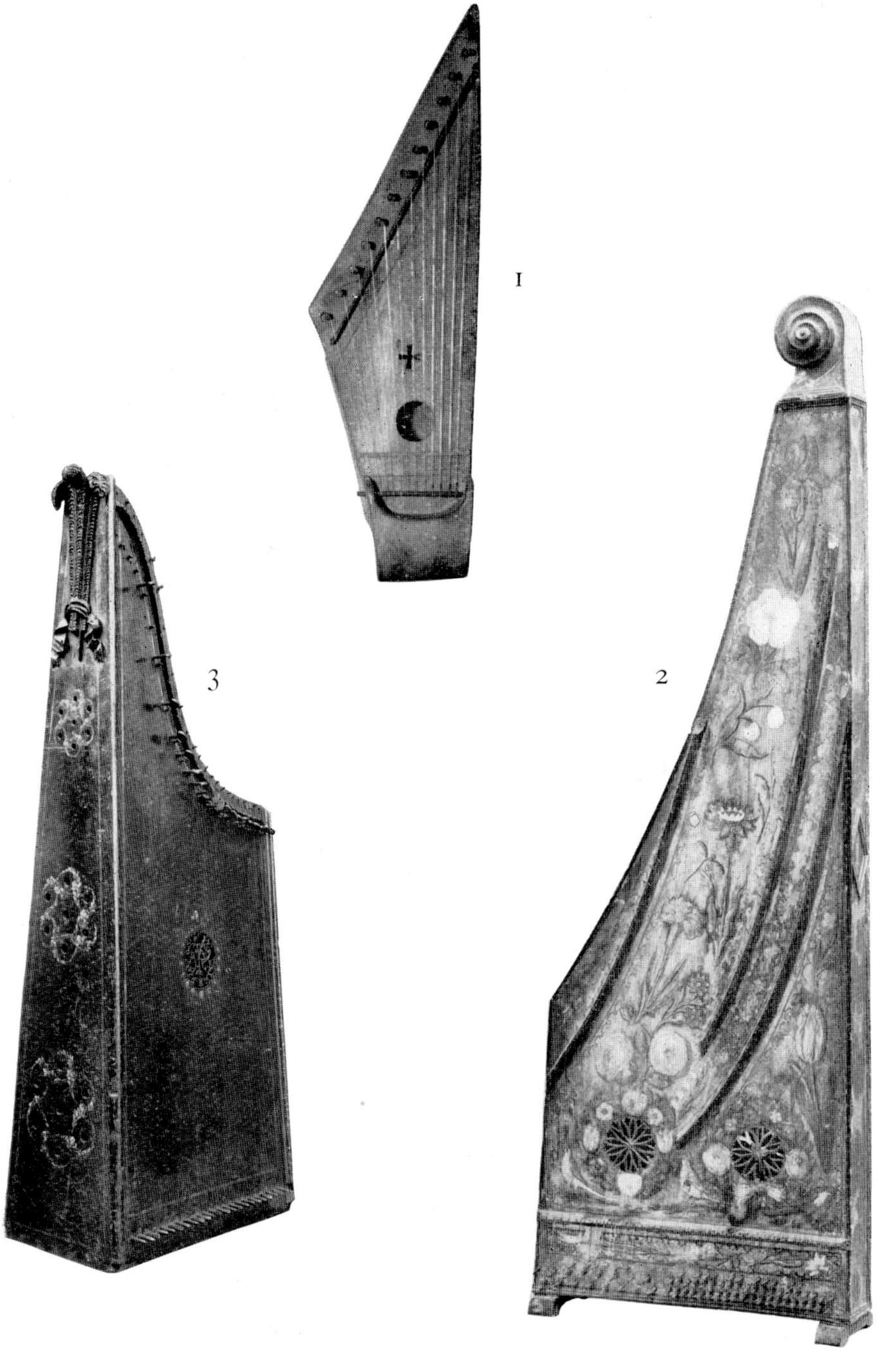

1. Kantele, Lithuania or Finland, nineteenth century.
2. Spitzharfe, seventeenth century. 3. Diplo-Kithara by E. Light, *c.* 1800

PLATE 14

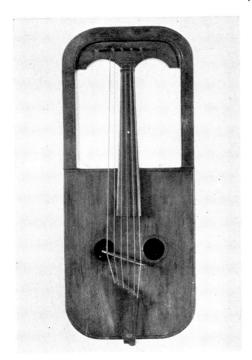

1. The Crwth

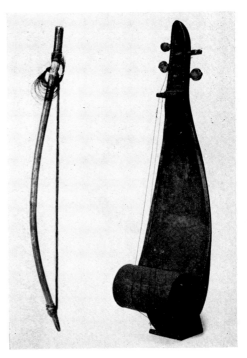

2. The Humstrum

PLATE 15

2. Rybybe, twelfth century (St Mary's, Barfreston)

1. Rebec, twelfth century (Canterbury Cathedral)

PLATE 16

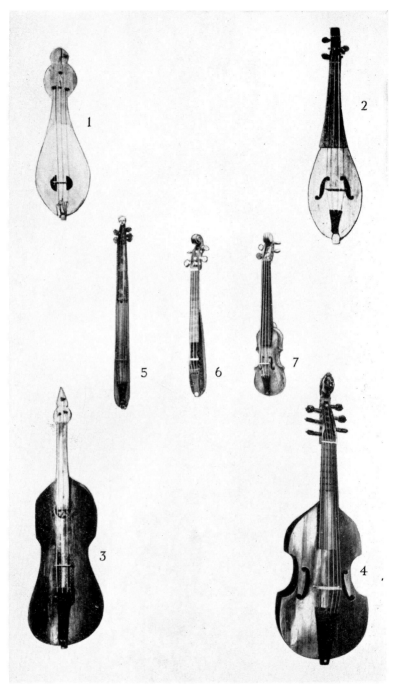

1. Lyra or Greek Rebec. 2. Rebec, reproduction of seventeenth century type.
3. Husla or Wendish Fiddle. 4. Treble Viol by Henry Jaye. 5. Kit.
6. Kit, *c.* 1700, Italian. 7. Kit, 1753, German

(Plate 15). In a crude form it appears in a late thirteenth-century manuscript (Brit. Mus., Add. 35166), as shown in Plate 52, where it is held in the musician's lap, and is both unplayable and unplayed. In a far more charming manner it appears (in Fig. 14) in the hands of the English lady who, with her sister musician on the Gittern (illustrated by her side), adorn the early fourteenth-century manuscript preserved at All Souls College, Oxford.

Fig. 14 Rybybe – early 14th cent.
(Oxford)

Fig. 15 Gittern – early 14th cent.
(Oxford)

Here, as will be noted, it is played at the shoulder. The Rybybe and Viol were both of them popular with the minstrels and troubadours. On the Continent they were often included under the one name Vielle.

As to the tuning of the Rybybe we are well informed; for Jerome of Moravia, who lived about the year 1260, has given us detailed instructions for its fingering. The two pairs of strings were tuned in fifths g and c and the compass was an octave and one note. In the late thirteenth-century Bodleian manuscript (Douce 139) there is a dance tune, transcribed in

Stainer's *Early Bodleian Music,* which, from its compass and character, was no doubt originally played on this instrument.[1]

From the word Rubebe, the other form of the name, the smaller Lyra received in Italy the name of Rubecchino or Rebecchino, whence the title Rebec; it was probably tuned in fifths like the Rybybe, but an octave higher, for we are told by Aimeric de Peyrac, that it accorded with the women's voices. By a re-arrangement of its stringing (probably through Arabic influence by way of Italy or Spain) and the use of three single strings, tuned to c'' g' c', the compass was increased and the three-stringed Rebec, its notes ranging from c' to g'', became the popular "small fiddle" of the later Middle Ages. In Germany it was known as the Geige and in France as the Gigue, whence it is believed our word "jig" is derived as the name of the dance for which this instrument provided the melody. The smallest form was called in England the Kit. In an old play written in 1510, entitled *The Interlude of the Four Elements*, a performer exclaims:

> This daunce wold do mych better yet
> If we had a Kyt or Taberet.

In the *Christen State of Matrimony* (1543) reference is made to the riotous proceedings which sometimes took place at weddings in those days. "They come," the writer says, "with a great noise of Harpes, Lutes, Kyttes, Basens and Drommes, wherewyth they Trouble the whole church: and even as they come, so do they go, in shameful pompe and vaine wantonesse." The Basens were probably Cymbals, which were at a later day known as "clash pans". The Kit, which Drayton places with the Gittern as belonging to the wandering fiddlers, ultimately took the shape and outline of the Violin, but in an attenuated form for the coat-pocket, and continued to be employed by the dancing masters until the middle of the last century. Three Kits of the seventeenth and eighteenth centuries are shown on Plate 16. The name is said to be a playful allusion to the popular idea that the larger instrument was strung with *catgut*. The French name was *Poche*, the Italian *Sordino* from the softness of the tone.

The use of the Rebec in England is referred to by Sagudino, the Venetian Ambassador, who, in his description of a banquet given by King Henry VIII to the Flemish envoys in 1517, tells us that during the dinner there were boys on a stage in the centre of the hall, some of whom sang and others

---

[1] Many other transcriptions of this tune have been made; see Gustav Reese, *Music in the Middle Ages*, Chapter VIII, for a complete list. The tune could have been played on many medieval instruments other than the Rybybe.

played "on the flute, rebeck and virginalls, making the sweetest melody".[1] In the royal band there were at that time three rebeck players, and the office, at any rate in name, was maintained by King Henry's three children and successors. In 1531 "for a Rebbecke for great Guillim" as much as twenty shillings was paid. But towards the end of the century the instrument fell into disrepute, and when Queen Mary returned to Scotland from France in 1560 she was serenaded on her arrival at the capital by "wretched violins and little rebecs, of which", says the chronicler, Brantôme, "there is no scarcity in this country". In England it became associated with the taverns and with rustic revelry. Shakespeare's wedding players in *Romeo and Juliet* (act iv), Hugh Rebeck, Simon Catling, and James Soundpost, all received their names from the strings and parts of an instrument with which they, as well as the dramatist, were familiar. Milton, in his *Areopagitica* (1644), mentions the Bagpipe and Rebec as popular in the villages, while the Lute, Violin and Guitar were played in the towns. It was to this "small Rubible" that, as he played, Absolon, Chaucer's parish clerk, could skip and dance in twenty manners:

> after the scole of Oxenforde tho,
> and with his legges casten to and fro.

Oxford has always been to the fore in fashions, and perhaps the clerk had learned his art from the parson, an Oxford man.

As regards the larger Rybybe, it was merged into the Viol even before the Middle Ages closed. Lydgate alludes to it at the end of the fourteenth century together with the "fythel" as more for "estatys than taverns".

No English specimen either of the Rybybe or the Rebec is known, though the latter may have existed in rural parts till the early part of the last century; at any rate, a somewhat degenerate form was at that time to be found in Dorsetshire under the name of the Humstrum. As will be seen from the illustration on Plate 14, the hollowed sound-box has been replaced by a tin canister, and the strings, four in number, are of wire. William Barnes, the Dorset poet, has immortalized it in the poem which bears its name:

> But now a bow do never screäpe
> A humstrum, any where all round:
> An' zome can't tell a humstrum's sheäpe,
> An' never heärd his jinglèn sound.

Ritson, in his *Observations on the Minstrels*, speaks of a man who, about the

---

[1] These instrument-names have been translated from the Italian terms used by Sagudino in his despatches to the Venetian Signory, terms that would appear to denote "recorder", "rebeck" and "harpsichord".

year 1800, was to be seen in the streets of London playing upon an instrument composed of a canister and string, which he called a Humstrum. Bonnel Thornton, in his *Burlesque Ode on St Cecilia's Day*, confuses the Humstrum with the Hurdy-gurdy. He tells us that it was sometimes called the Bladder and String; this, however, was a Monochord, known on the Continent as the

Fig. 16 Viol – early 12th cent. (Cambridge)

Bumbass. One-string Humstrums (*c.* 1500) are depicted at Thaxted Church, Essex, and Adderbury Church, Oxfordshire.

The third type of bowed instrument is THE VIOL. We purposely refrain from using the word Fiddle in this connection, because, although it is derived from the same source as the word Viol, it has been applied indiscriminately in this country to all bowed instruments, whereas the Viol is distinct, both in shape and stringing, from the Crowd, the Rybybe, and the Rebec.

The original word seems to have been found in the Low Latin of the ninth century as *Fidula*, a contraction of *Fidicula* – the little stringed instrument. This was corrupted into *Vitula* and *Viola*, whence the words Viol and

64

Vielle; whereas the old German Viedel and the English Fithele are more like the original form. Of the last word a fifteenth-century English vocabulary gives *Viella* as the Latin equivalent; but there is no proof at present forthcoming that the ninth-century *Fidula* was played with a bow.

The Viol shows the adaptation of the bow to that Guitar-shaped instrument which, centuries before the Christian era, was in use in Oriental countries, as already stated. To what place or nation we should ascribe the first step in this direction still remains a matter of doubt; but Miss K. Schlesinger's recent researches show with much probability that it was initiated by the dwellers on the eastern shores of the Mediterranean and not by Western Europeans as has been hitherto stated. In a Greek manuscript (Brit. Mus., Add. 19352) illuminated by Theodore of Caesarea in 1066, a Viol is depicted with incurved sides and a well-formed head with eight pegs inserted in the side as in the Oriental and later European instruments. This is nearly a century earlier than any example known in Europe. The earliest illustration of this instrument with which we have met in the work of a European artist is that given in Fig. 16, from a manuscript of the Commentary of St Jerome on the books of the Bible written at Canterbury, bought for Rochester Cathedral and now in the library of Trinity College, Cambridge (O.4.7). Its date is early in the twelfth century. With it should be compared the specimen of the Husla or Wendish Fiddle shown on Plate 16, which is evidently a lingering relic of the past, having like its predecessors of seven or eight centuries ago three strings, slit-like sound-holes, incurved sides, and a flat back; but embryo corners will be noticed in the upper part of the incurvations. It is interesting to observe that in 1817 Francis Chanot, of Paris, reverted to the original outline of the twelfth century to secure with other improvements a finer quality of tone. The above-mentioned writer, in her comprehensive work entitled *The Precursors of the Violin Family*, gives a sketch of a similar Viol from an Anglo-Norman manuscript of the middle of the twelfth century in the British Museum (Nero C. iv). The sculptures which once adorned the twelfth-century cloister of the Abbey of Bocherville also show the characteristic shape of the instrument.[1]

Another illustration from the hands of an English draughtsman occurs in

[1] Much new evidence concerning the early development of the lute-guitar-fiddle family has come to light since Canon Galpin wrote, and it seems probable that the earliest use of the bow may be ascribed to the nomadic tribes of Central Asia; see, among other studies, Michael Prynne, "Angelic Musicians from Central Asia", *GSJ*, VII, pp. 54–5, and VIII, pl. VIII. The use of the bow on the *fretted* instruments of the guitar family – whence the development of the viols – may not have taken place before the middle years of the fifteenth century; see Thurston Dart, "The Viols", in *Musical Instruments through the Ages* (Penguin Books, 1961), pp. 184–90.

the Psalter preserved at the University Library, Glasgow, which is considered to be of Yorkshire origin and to date about the year 1170. It is reproduced in Plate 20. In the English illuminations of the thirteenth century it frequently appears and was often held between the knees. As to its tuning and scale Jerome of Moravia gives us minute information. According to him it had, in the middle of the thirteenth century, four strings and a Bourdon string, though English illustrations usually show but three strings. The Viol player, however, among the three minstrels who support a bracket in Beverley Minster (not the more familiar figures in St Mary's Church), holds an instrument in which the five strings are clearly shown and also an elaborate tailpiece. The carving is probably of the thirteenth century. It was a more elaborate and deeper-toned instrument than the Rybybe, and the open strings represented the following notes: *d' d' g G* with *d* as a Bourdon, or *g' d' g G* with *d* as a Bourdon, or *c' c' d G* with *G* as a Bourdon, leaving the performer great option as to tuning. The shifting of the hand on the finger-board was not at this early period recognized, so there must have been many missing notes in the scale of the instrument.

In the early literature of our country the Viol is generally termed the Fithele, Fydel or, as Chaucer writes it, Fithul; but in the list of the musicians at Westminster in 1306 Vilours and Vidulators are mentioned. It is not, however, until the first part of the sixteenth century that the French word is thoroughly naturalized. In 1526 the King's music contained "2 vialls" as well as "3 rebeckes", and in King Henry's *Privy Purse Expenses* is the following entry under the year 1532: "Paied to iii of the Vyalls for their lyvery cotes at xxii[s]. vi[d]. apece . . . iii[li]. vii[s]. vi[d]." In 1538 there were six Vyalls and the following year as many as eight in the royal band. In the Court of Scotland payments were made in the year 1538 to "the four menstralis that playe upon the Veolis".

This instrument however, which became so popular in Fancies and Consorts, was an improvement on the earlier form; for in the fifteenth century the Italians had altered the flowing outline of the Viol by the addition of corners or angles, somewhat similar to those of the Violin but not so pronounced;[1] the Bourdon string, which had been placed by the side of the finger-board, was now placed upon it, and could be stopped by the fingers in the same way as the other four strings. Early in the sixteenth century a sixth

---

[1] The variety of outline given to stringed instruments during the years from 1475 to 1625 or so was very considerable; see the books of Hayes & Denis cited in the Books of Reference. In this development it would seem that all the countries of Europe played a part, perhaps even those of New Spain across the Atlantic; the extent to which the Italians led the way is very hard to determine.

string was added, and on the Treble Viol the following tuning was adopted – *d″ a′ e′ c′ g d* – the Bass being an octave lower in pitch and the Mean, or Tenor, instrument a fourth or fifth below the Treble. It is interesting to observe that Gerle in his *Musica Teutsch* (1532), when giving directions to Viol players on the use of the bow, says "it must be rubbed with Colfanium or with English Rosin which you can get at the apothecary's".

Furnished with frets like the Lute, the Viols were studied by the greatest masters of music. Owing to the depth of their sides and the flatness of the back the sound was soft and slightly reedy or nasal, but very penetrating. Thomas Mace, who praises the "generous Viol" equally with his favourite Lute, names Aldred, Jaye, Smith, Bolles and Ross as amongst the most celebrated English makers during the later part of the sixteenth century and the opening years of the seventeenth. A perfect and unique specimen of Jaye's work is shown on Plate 17; it is a Bass Viol, called by the Italians the *Viola da Gamba* because it was held between the legs, dated 1611 and signed "Henrie Jaye in Southwarke".[1] It shows what excellent workmen the English makers were, "no better in the world", says Mace, and their masterpieces must frequently have been found in the houses of their wealthy and noble patrons. At this very time in the Globe Theatre, hard by Jaye's workshop, Shakespeare was telling in *Twelfth Night* the virtues of Sir Andrew Aguecheek, "for he plays o' the Viol de gamboys". We have recently seen in a well-known auction room a fantastically shaped Bass Viol of small size, of which, however, only the back, sides and carved head were original, with the label "Henrie Jaye, dwelling in Southwarke 1610". This is the earliest date we have observed for this famous maker. A Treble Viol signed by him in 1632 is shown on Plate 16; but the head is by a later hand. The family continued to maintain their position as Viol and Violin makers for nearly two centuries. Viols were played between or on the knees.

As showing the value of these instruments at the beginning of the seventeenth century we give the following extracts from the Privy Purse accounts of Henry Prince of Wales:

1610. Vyolles twoe greate . . . . xl[li.]
Vyolles viz. one sett for the Kinge . . . . xl[li.]
One other sett and a base Vyoll for the Prince. . xxxii[li.]

In the Accompt Book of Trinity College, Cambridge, we find the item:

1595. For a sett of new Vialles . . . . . . xiii[li.]
For viall strings and mending ye College Instruments xii[s.]

[1] This Bass Viol is now in the collection of the Gemeente Museum, The Hague.

A "sett" or "chest" of Viols generally consisted of six instruments, viz. two Trebles, two Tenors and two Basses, all truly and proportionately suited. The smaller Viols disappeared in this country at the close of the seventeenth century, but the Bass Viol held its own for nearly another hundred years, when it at last yielded to the Violoncello. Henry Purcell detested the Viol[1] and wrote a three-part Round to the following words which he presented to John Gostling, Master of Arts, a famous bass singer of Canterbury and an enthusiastic performer on the Bass Viol:

> Of all the instruments that are,
> None with the Viol can compare:
> Mark how the strings their order keep
> With a whet, whet, whet, and a sweep, sweep, sweep.
> But above all it still abounds
> With a zingle, zingle, zing, and a zit, zan, zounds.

Only those who have heard the instrument played and marked the efforts of the performer to obtain as many notes as possible with one sweep of the bow can appreciate the effect of this jingling rhyme. A slightly smaller form of Bass Viol was known as the Division Viol,[2] and upon it were played those variations or divisions on a ground bass or simple theme, which became so popular towards the end of the seventeenth century. A yet smaller-sized Viol was called the Lyra Viol,[2] and on it full chords were played after the manner of and from the same tablature as the Lute. Mace, in 1676, does not consider a press of Viols complete without three full-sized Lyra-Viols, which in Consort would stand as second Trebles and could be used also for Divisions. The Lyra or Lero Viol was introduced to the English public shortly after the year 1600 by Daniel Farrant, a Viol-player in the King's Music under James I. In 1605 Tobias Hume published *Ayres . . . for two Leero Viols, and also for the Leero Viole with two Treble Viols, or two with the Treble; lastly for the Leero Viole to play alone,* and in 1609 lessons for it were published by Alfonso Ferrabosco with introductory lines by Ben Jonson. Metal strings were added to some instruments, which, running through a

---

[1] This seems mere tittle-tattle; among the more outstanding works Purcell composed for the Bass Viol are the twenty-two trio-sonatas for two violins, bass viol and organ continuo, the trio-sonata in G minor for violin, bass viol and organ continuo, and the incomparable Fantasias and In Nomines (see volume XXXI of the Purcell Society Edition: London 1959. See also Thurston Dart, "Purcell's Chamber Music", *Proceedings of the Royal Musical Association*, 85th Session, pp. 81–93).

[2] A lithographic facsimile of the second edition of Christopher Simpson's classic book, *The Division-Viol*, was published by Curwen in 1955. A facsimile of *Musick's Recreation on the Viol, Lyra-Way* (Playford, 1682) was published by Hinrichsen in 1960. Further samples of music for Division and Lyra Viols will be found in volumes IX and XXI of *Musica Britannica*.

PLATE 17

Bass Viol or Viola da Gamba by Henry Jaye of
Southwark, 1611

PLATE 18

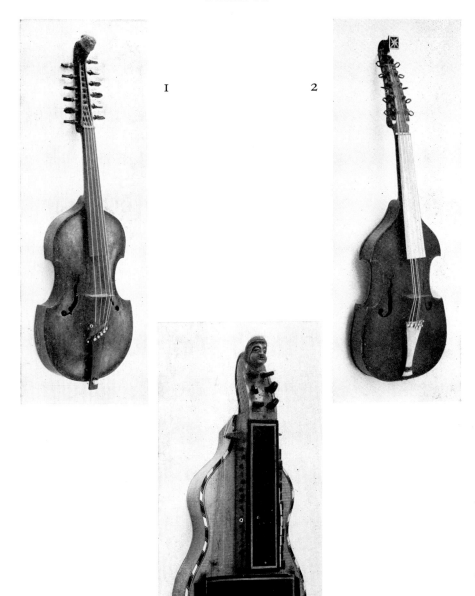

1. Viola d'Amore ascribed to Joachim Tielke, Hamburg, 1670
2. Sultana or Cither-Viol by T. Perry, Irish, 1794
3. Hurdy-Gurdy or Vielle à Roue by Louvet, French, eighteenth century

hollow passage beneath the finger-board and over a little bridge about half an inch in height, were not stopped with the fingers or touched by the hand, but vibrated in sympathy with the sounds of the gut strings. Bacon, in his *Sylva Sylvarum*, alludes to this peculiarity of the English Lyra-Viol: "It was devised that a Viol should have a lay of wire strings below, as close to the belly as a lute, and then the strings of guts mounted upon a bridge as in ordinary Viols: to the end that by this means, the upper strings strucken should make the lower resound by sympathy, and so make the music the better." The Italian Lyra was a larger and more elaborate instrument of the same kind but without the sympathetic strings, and though played with a bow it was often classed with the Lutes.[1]

Praetorius, in 1618, mentions his special feature of the English Viols, Playford, however, in his *Musick's Recreation on the Viol Lyra-way* (1656); writes: "Of this sort of Viols I have seen many: but time and disuse has set them aside."[2] He gives the tuning "Lyra-way" to the following intervals (irrespective of pitch), *e′ b g d G D*, but in Tobias Hume's Book of Ayres, already mentioned, the Leero Viol is tuned like the Bandora to *e′ b g d A G*. Though the English players of the latter part of the seventeenth century thus dispensed with the sympathetic strings, they were adopted on the Continent, and produced the Viola d'Amore and also the Baryton, for which Haydn wrote so many solos.[3] Even at the end of the eighteenth century the English origin of the sympathetic wires was not forgotten, for Leopold Mozart calls a small Viol so strung "The English Violet". Viols were also fitted with wire strings for the bow instead of gut, and, in 1679, Evelyn mentions the sweetness and novelty of such an instrument, illustrated in Plate 18, as he heard it played by a German musician. It is now represented in that country by the Streich Zither, and, through a very mistaken identification, was called the Psaltery by our forefathers; examples of the Psaltery, Sultana or Cither-Viol, made by Thomas Perry, of Dublin, in the second half of the eighteenth century, are not infrequently to be seen. A specimen dated 1794 appears on the same Plate. It is strung with five pairs of wire

---

[1] The Lyra da Gamba – a somewhat freak instrument in use between 1560 and 1630 or thereabouts – was designed to provide chords for continuo work. See Praetorius and Mersenne for illustrations and details; see also Gerald Hayes, *The Viols, and Other Bowed Instruments* (London, 1930), pp. 144 ff.

[2] See footnote to preceding paragraph. Many different tunings were in use for the Lyra Viol: see Hayes, *op. cit.*, pp. 125 ff.

[3] Haydn appears to have written mainly duos and trios for the Baryton; see Anthony van Hoboken's Catalogue of Haydn's music (Schott, 1957: vol. I), Groups X to XIV, and the new Haydn Society edition.

strings, two of steel, two of brass, and one pair of covered wire, and was probably tuned to the notes c'' g' e' (♮ or ♭) c' g. An English Viola d'Amore by Nathaniel Cross of Piccadilly, made about the year 1700, is in the Musik-historisk Museum at Copenhagen. It has the usual shape of the English Viols, but beneath the seven melody strings there are seven sympathetic wires.

Of the Violin, as also of the Pianoforte in a later chapter, we do not propose to give either an adequate or detailed history. Books such as Sandys and Foster's *History of the Violin* (1864) or Heron Allen's *Violinmaking* (1884) will give complete information on this wide subject from an English stand-point.

The instrument appears in England in the sixteenth century, for in the Tragedy of *Gorboduc*, performed before Queen Elizabeth in 1561, "the Musicke of Violenze" preceded the first act in which "wildmen clad in leaves" appeared. But Violins, as distinct from "Vialls", had already been included in the King's Music; and at the time of Henry the Eighth's death they were played by six Italians from Venice, Milan and Cremona, who are described, in 1555, as the "Violons".

Although the Violin received thus early the patronage of royalty, it was not regarded with favour by the English musicians of the period. It was more often found in the country revels and rustic festivities, where it added life and merriment to the dance.

Drayton, in one of his songs written in praise of Queen Elizabeth about the year 1590, bids his countrymen "tune the Tabor and the Pipe to the sweet Violons", and in his *Fairy Wedding* he thus addresses the musicians:

> Violins, strike up aloud,
> Ply the Gittern, scour the Crowd.

Anthony Wood, moreover, tells us that before the Restoration the gentle-men who attended music parties played on Viols, "for they esteemed a Violin to be an instrument only belonging to a common fiddler, and could not endure that it should come among them, for feare of making their meetings to be vaine and fidling". The tone of the Violin was too brilliant and powerful for the quiet-voiced Viols. Thomas Mace, who passionately clung to the music of earlier days, calls them "Scoulding Violins", which when they "run over some Coranto, Sarabande, or Brawle . . . or suchlike stuff . . . be fit to make a Man's Ears Glow and fill his brains full of Frisks, etc., than to Season and Sober his Mind or Elevate his Affection to Goodness". Playford, in his *Introduction to the Skill of Music* (1660), describes the Treble Violin as "a cheerful and spritely instrument and much practised of late". He recommends a beginner who has an incorrect ear to place six frets on the finger-board like the Viol. This enabled the player to reach bb'' and possibly c''', the whole tone above, which at that time was considered the upward limit of its compass. The Tenor Violin is larger, he tells us, and tuned a fifth lower to a' d' g c, like the Viola of the present day. The Bass Violin was tuned, according to him, g c F Bb', a whole tone below the Violoncello.

In 1572 a treble Violin cost Sir Thomas Kytson, of Hengrave Hall, twenty shillings, and he died possessed of a "borded chest with six violenns"; but the prices of instruments for the royal band during the seventeenth century varied from £6 to £12 for a Treble Violin, £6 or £7 for a Tenor and £8 to £12 for a Bass. These averages should be multiplied three and a half times to represent present value.[1] The masterpieces of the Italian makers were already esteemed, and in 1638 a Cremona Violin was bought for £12 "to play to the organ"; in 1675 a Cremona Tenor Violin, bought for His Majesty's service, cost £16; thirteen years earlier, however, Banister had received £40 for two Cremona Violins purchased for the same purpose. So gradually the Violin worked its way to prominence, but it was with the reign of the Merry Monarch, and his fondness for French fancies and fashions, that it became fairly established as the leading instrument. His "four-and-twenty fiddlers all of a row", copied from the Court orchestra of Louis XIII, played before His Majesty during meals, "being more airée and brisk than Viols". The band consisted of six Treble, six Counter-Tenor, six Tenor, and six Bass Violins – the Treble and Counter-Tenor instruments being identical, like our First and Second Violins. That inveterate critic, Samuel Pepys, though he did not appreciate the new style, acknowledged that the players were carefully trained and kept excellent time; in fact, he himself was a performer, going "at night to my Viallin" and spending his morning in fiddling "until it is time to go to the Office". Even Mace, in 1676, suggests that to the press or chest of Viols be added "a Pair of Violins, to be in Readiness for any Extraordinary Jolly or Jocund Consort-Occasion"; but, if so, he warns his readers to strengthen the Bass with a "Pair of Lusty Full-Sciz'd Theorboes".

Both Violins and Violoncellos were made in this country soon after the Restoration by such well-known men as Urquhart, Pamphilon, Rayman and Barak Norman, the latter also making Bass Viols which were justly celebrated; and the advent of German musicians in the eighteenth century served to give additional popularity to the more brilliant and resonant type of bowed instrument, so that the only member of the old Viol family now left

[1] Once again, a more realistic factor (1964) would be ten or twelve.

to us is the Double Bass, which is still frequently made with the flat back and sloping shoulders of its departed predecessors.[1]

Before we close this chapter there is one other bowed instrument to which allusion should be made, and it has been reserved till last because, though in construction the most primitive of all, it does not appear to have been used in this country until the seventeenth century. It was known as the TROMBA MARINA or Trumpet Marine, and, according to the description given in an English manuscript of the latter part of that century (Brit. Mus., Harl. 2034), it was "a long hollow instrument about two yards and a half or three yards high. It hath only one thick gut string which is played upon with a long bow or Bass-Viol stick at the head of it, a little below the winding hole. The string is wound up by a key set on a square pin and is fastened to an iron wheel with notches on for a catch to fall in. The fore part is even and smooth, but the back part is made with five or six angles and is open at the bottom, in which are fixed four wiers which are screwed up to the same musicall height as the great gut string is. The wiers give an echo to the great string, when it is played on, to admiration."

This might well be considered an accurate description of the instrument which Mr Pepys heard in 1667 and noticed "a whole concert of chords together at the end of a pause" – an effect caused by the wire sympathetic strings, but a secret which the performer, Monsieur Prin, would not divulge to his inquisitive admirer. A similar instrument is shown on Plate 19. It has fifty sympathetic strings inside, and was kept for many years in an old farmhouse in Cheshire.

Neither of the descriptions quoted, however, mentions the characteristic part of the Trumpet Marine, which is the trembling or shaking bridge over which the long string passes. The arm-like extension vibrates on an ivory plate or on the natural wood and causes the harmonic notes, which, by the light touch of the thumb, are the only sounds used, to give a loud and strident tone, and, as Pepys says, "it do so far outdo a trumpet as nothing more". As the seventeenth-century writer states, the bow is drawn across the string *just below the upper nut* and the string is touched *between the bowing point and the vibrating bridge*. This feature is depicted in Plate 19. In 1674 a concert of four Trumpets Marine was heard in London and the instrument became popular for a while, as is shown by the following advertisement in a publisher's list of 1699: "*A Second Book for the new instrument called the Mock Trumpet: containing a variety of Trumpet tunes, ayres, marches, and Minuets,*

[1] But see Eric Halfpenny, "A Note on the Genealogy of the Double Bass", *GSJ*, I, pp. 41–5.

made purposely for that instrument with Instructions for Learners; also several first and second Trebles for Two trumpets."[1] Its special characteristics were investigated by scientists, and the results of the experiments published in the *Transactions of the Philosophical Society* for 1692.

The earlier history of the instrument is peculiar. It was originally simply a bowed Monochord either used as a Drone Bass or stopped by the fingers like a Double Bass. In such a form it was a favourite with the wandering minstrels and jongleurs, surviving in the Bumbass still used in Germany, and in the Basse de Flandres and Bladder and String which were used in the Netherlands and in England during the eighteenth century and perhaps later. In order to extend the scale, other and shorter strings were added and Dichords and Trichords were formed.[2]

In the latter half of the fifteenth century, however, the curious trembling bridge appeared, and we consider that this alteration in the instrument, by which the trumpet tone was produced in the harmonic notes, was either due to the famous French trumpeter of the period named Marin or Maurin or the instrument so formed was named in his honour. We are well aware that several other explanations of the words *Tromba Marina* have been given: some would have us believe that they stand for *Tromba Mariana* – the trumpet of the Virgin – because the instrument was used in the convents by the nuns, whence it is sometimes called the Nun's Fiddle or *Nonnengeige*. Others tell us that it was employed on the ships at sea to signal to passing vessels, surely a most original use for the one gut string. The late Mr E. J. Payne thought that it took its name from its similarity to a speaking trumpet used by Italian sailors, but as the date of its invention coincides with that of Marin's fame, the use of his name for this trumpet-like instrument seems to us a natural explanation of the much-debated words.

The sounds produced by the instrument are, of course, those of the natural harmonic series described in a later chapter. The open string can be tuned to Bb', $C\ D\ E$ or even $F\natural$: if tuned to C the sounds usually employed are $c\ g\ c'\ e'\ g'\ c''\ d''\ e''\ f''\ g''\ a''$. In a manuscript copy of a Sonata for the Trumpet Marine composed by Don Lorenzo de Castro in the seventeenth century, and now before us, florid passages in quick time are written for the sounds from c' to a'': there are four movements, a *Toccata, Allegro, Aria,*

[1] The "Mock Trumpet" was not a Trumpet Marine but an early form of clarinet or chalumeau: see Thurston Dart, "The Mock Trumpet", *GSJ*, VI, pp. 35–40.

[2] During the fifteenth century a treble form of the instrument appears to have been fairly common, the so-called *Trumscheit* – perhaps intended to reproduce the sound of a trumpet, in spite of the opposition of ecclesiastical authority to instruments of this kind. A carefully-painted example is to be seen in van Eyck's incomparable "Adoration of the Lamb".

and *Menuetto*.[1] By Glareanus in his *Dodecachordon* (1547), Praetorius in his *Syntagma* (1618), Mersenne in his treatise *Harmonicorum Libri XII* (1635), the instrument is carefully described, and Molière's allusion to it in *Le Bourgeois Gentilhomme* is well known. In English literature Shadwell has immortalized it in his play of *The Miser* (1672), for that money-loving man includes in his security for an advance to a needy client "a Bolonia lute, a Roman archlute, two gittars, a Cremona violin, one lyra viol, one viol de gambo and a trump marin".

In the year 1742 Monsieur Jean-Baptiste Prin, the performer mentioned on page 72, composed *Une Mémoire sur la Trompette Marine*, which has been published in the *Bulletin Français de la Société Internationale de Musique*, Vol. IV, 1908. It is full of interesting details, explaining the sympathetic strings and the use of a regulator (*guidon*) for the vibrating bridge. His wonderful performances had evidently met with great success and his favourite instrument together with his music books were bequeathed to the *Académie des Beaux-Arts* at Lyon: unfortunately everything has disappeared except two books. The very aged Professor knew that the *Mémoire* would be his swan-song, for he says, "J'aime avec tendresse cet instrument et c'est avec douleur que je le vois pour ainsi dire mourir avec moi."

---

[1] Further music for Trumpet Marine may be found among the works of the minor Swiss composer Johann Melchior Gletle.

Chapter VI

Organistrum and Symphony

Praise Him upon the Claricoales,
The Lute and Simfonie;
With Dulsemers and the Regalls,
Sweet Sittrons melody.

SIR WILLIAM LEIGHTON (1613)

ANY ARE THE ATTEMPTS which have been made to replace the action of the bow and the stopping of the fingers on instruments of the Viol and Violin class by artificial mechanism. The Nuremberg Geigenwerk, invented by Hans Hayden and described, with an illustration, by Praetorius in his *Syntagma Musicum* (1618), by means of five or six wheels, covered with rosined parchment and turned by a foot-pedal, set the metal strings of the instrument in vibration as they were drawn down on the revolving circumferences by the action of the keys, which were ranged in front as in the ordinary harpsichord. An instrument of the same kind, dated 1625, but with gut strings, was exhibited at the Madrid Fine Arts Exhibition in 1892. It was used formerly in Toledo Cathedral during Holy Week, and the effect is said to have been that of a string quartet. Probably it would hardly have gained a more appreciative notice from the critical Mr Pepys than he expressed in his *Diary* under the date October 5, 1664, in the following words: "To the Music Meeting at the Post Office (London), where I was once before. And hither anon come all the Gresham College and a great deal of noble company: and the new instrument was brought called the Arched Viall, when being tuned with Lute strings and played on with Kees like an organ, a piece of parchment is always kept moving: and the strings, which by the Kees are pressed down upon it, are grated in imitation of a bow by the parchment: and so it is intended to resemble several Vialls played on with one bow, but so basely and so harshly that it will never do. But after three hours' stay, it could not be fixed in tune and so they were fain to go to some other musique of instruments."

Under the same date Evelyn records: "To our Society (i.e. the Royal) there was brought a new invented instrument of music, being a harpsichord with gut strings, sounding like a Concert of Viols with an organ, made vocal by a wheel and zone of parchment that rubbed horizontally against the strings." He is a more merciful critic than his companion. The Lyrichord, patented by Roger Plenius, the London Harpsichord-maker, in 1741, with its gut and wire strings, was another of these instruments sounded by rotating wheels and generally called in England "wheel cymbals" to distinguish them from the Harpsichord or Clavicymbal.[1] In Walker's Celestina of 1772, although keys were used, the bow was worked by the hand: Isaac Mott in his Sostenente Piano of 1817 employed rollers acting on silk threads which communicated the vibration to the strings. These are some of the attempts which have been made in this country, and many more have been made abroad, one of the latest and most successful being the Electric Pianoforte of Herr Kuhmayer, shown at the Vienna Musical Exhibition (1892), in which, by a system of electric magnets, an endless bow of fine leather is drawn down on the string required.

All these so-called inventions, however, are but attempts to improve an instrument which from the tenth century to our own day has been in constant and popular use. THE ORGANISTRUM, for such was its name at first, is undoubtedly derived from the Monochord, a simple contrivance for ascertaining the intervals of the musical scale by a series of movable bridges. Its single string was plucked by the finger or a small plectrum; and the instrument is shown on the knees of the uppermost musician depicted on the twelfth-century Psalter of English workmanship at St John's College, Cambridge, and reproduced on Plate 43.

This instrument of the skilled musician is thus mentioned in the Lekingfelde Proverbs:

> Many a swete refreet the musycion dothe synge,
> Whiche is litill conceyvide of light herynge;
> For whos sownde is applyede allway to discorde
> Can never deserve the tewnes of a trew Monacorde.

The advent of the bow, however, into Western Europe naturally suggested its use on the Monochord, as, by its means, the sound of the required note could be indefinitely prolonged. Devices too were adopted for shifting the movable bridges more readily and, when the bow itself was superseded by a well-rosined wheel, revolving beneath the string as it was turned by a

---

[1] For more about the Dutch instrument-maker Plenius and his instruments, see Eric Halfpenny, "The Lyrichord", *GSJ*, III, pp. 46–9; Alan Curtis, "Dutch Harpsichord Makers", *Tijdschrift van de Vereniging voor Nederlandse Muziekgeschiedenis*, Deel XIX, pp. 56–60.

handle at one end of the box-like instrument, we have the Organistrum. It made its appearance in the ninth or tenth century, for it is described by Odo of Cluny, who died in 942, in his tract *Quomodo organistrum construatur* or "How to make an Organistrum". From this short treatise, which has been printed by Gerbert in his *Scriptores Ecclesiastici* (Vol. IV), we learn that the compass was the diatonic octave from *c* to *c'* with the addition of the *b♭*. Gerbert also, in his *De Cantu et Musica Sacra*, reproduces an illustration of an instrument which agrees in the main with Odo's treatise, and, for this reason, it has often been given as the type of the Organistrum in use in the tenth century; but it is the work of a much later scribe, and Gerbert, who wrote in the eighteenth century, places it at about 500 years before his own day.

We have, unfortunately, no data at present which will enable us to decide whether the use of the wheel preceded that of the mechanism for stopping the strings or vice versa. Both systems appear separately in instruments of later times. The illustrations given by Praetorius in the work already mentioned, and carvings yet earlier, present to us the form of the ordinary Viol with its usual finger-board, but with a wheel instead of the bow. On the other hand, in the old German *Schlüsselfiedel* and the Swedish *Nyckelharpa* still in use, the strings are stopped by mechanical means, but sounded by means of the ordinary bow. Odo, indeed, mentions both the little wheel (*rotulus*) and the contrivances for stopping the strings, which he calls *plectra*.

The first reliable illustrations of the Organistrum date from the twelfth century; for the Norman carvings of the ancient cloisters of the Abbey of Bocherville (now preserved in the museum at Rouen) in which the instrument appears, were wrought shortly before the year 1200 and not when the abbey was built in the eleventh century, as frequently stated. Here and in carvings and illuminations of the same period it is shown as having a long body with incurvations at the sides and a neck from which the ends of the stopping apparatus point upwards towards one of the performers; for at this early stage in its history two executants were required, the one to turn the handle which moved the wheel and the other to manipulate the strings. The Organistrum was about five feet in length, and the incurvations, retained, it may be, from its former use as a simple bowed instrument, afforded also a convenient method of supporting it securely by the knees. In the twelfth and thirteenth centuries the strings were three in number, and it has been thought that the two outer strings were tuned in octaves and the other at the interval of a fifth or fourth below the higher string. The stopping mechanism, as contemporary illustrations show us, consisted of small rods placed beneath the strings, each bearing a low flat bridge; the ends of the rods, which appeared outside the case, were *turned* by the performer, and thus the various bridges were brought to bear on all the three strings together at any required point. This is clearly seen in the illustration given by Gerbert from the manuscript formerly at St Blasius' monastery and shown in Fig. 19A.

The general appearance of the instrument at this time will be observed in the illumination from a late thirteenth-century Psalter of English work preserved in the University Library at Glasgow and reproduced on Plate 20; also in that in Fig. 17 from Abbot de Lindesey's Psalter, illuminated by an English artist between the years 1220 and 1222, which is now the property of the Society of Antiquaries of London.

Fig. 17 Organistrum – early 13th cent.
(Lindesey Psalter)

As with the Monochord, so with the Organistrum, for Church purposes it was greatly esteemed. For on it could not only the ecclesiastical tones be produced with fair exactness, but owing to the intervals of its three strings the much-beloved *Organum*, with its succession of consecutive fourths, fifths, and octaves, could be played with accuracy and ease. Many are the treatises extant by monastic musicians detailing the method of setting out the scale of its notes with the mathematical precision of the old Pythagorean school.

But with the introduction of the small portative organ and the improvements made on the larger instruments the poor Organistrum left the church and cloister, and found itself, under a new name and in an attenuated form, in the hands of the wandering minstrels and the country folk.

Owing to the crude chords produced by its strings, it was thenceforth known as THE SYMPHONY, a title which was given to it apparently towards the end of the twelfth century; but the older name was long remembered, for the celebrated theorist John de Muris, in the fourteenth century, speaks of it as the "*Symphonia* or *Organistrum*".

In the French poetry of the thirteenth century it appears as the "chifonie", a form of the word symphony which is still retained in some parts of that country, though the name by which it has become more generally known is the "Vielle à roue" or the Viol with a wheel; but since the minstrel's Vielle, played with a bow, became merged into the Violin, the instrument has been called simply the Vielle. In Germany the Latin name Lyra, given in bygone days to bowed instruments as well as to other stringed forms, was generally qualified in this case by some such adjective as "rusticana" or "pagana", and survives in the titles "Bauernleyer", Peasant's Lyre, "Drehleyer", Crank Lyre, or "Radleier", Wheel Lyre. The epithet "Lyra Mendicorum" betrays sufficiently the beggarly purposes to which it has been put since its downfall.

Fig. 18 Symphony – 14th cent.
(Luttrell Psalter)

In our own country the name Symphony was continued for several centuries. For instance, in a Cornish drama of the early fourteenth century "recorders and symphony" are mentioned as among the instruments of King David's minstrels: later in the same century Wycliffe, in his translation of the Parable of the Prodigal Son, says of the elder brother that, "whan he cam neere, he herde a symphonie and a crowde"; whilst in the fifteenth-century vocabularies the word appears constantly. In the *Pastyme of Pleasure* (1506) it is called "Cymphan". We then nearly lose sight of it, until in the eighteenth century it reappears as the Hurdy-Gurdy, a word which a slang dictionary of 1864 would have us believe means the instrument "girded on the loins" (called *hurdies* in the north), but more probably is only a descriptive title derived from the monotonous droning sound of the instrument. Bonnel Thornton, in his *Burlesque Ode on St Cecilia's Day*, written in 1763, applied the same name to the Humstrum or Bladder and String previously described, which he concludes was generally performed on "at Funerals and on serious Occasions". It is now rarely heard, though in the hands of an expert Savoyard or Italian performer it is by no means so depressing in its effect as the modern name would lead us to suppose.

We must, however, retrace our steps and speak of the interesting and important alterations which attended the evolution of the Symphony from the

79

Organistrum in the twelfth century. Originally, as we have seen, it was a large instrument requiring the combined efforts of two performers; but, as the Symphony, it was reduced to half its original size or even less, becoming, in fact, a treble instead of a tenor instrument. Owing to this alteration it was rendered more portable and could be easily controlled by one player. At first the stopping mechanism remained much the same, the ends of the movable rods projecting upwards from the case, as seen in the illustrations taken from the Luttrell Psalter, written by an English hand about the year 1330 (Fig. 18 and Plate 48), and in the late thirteenth-century manuscript (Brit. Mus., Add. 35166) from which illustrations are reproduced in Plate 52.

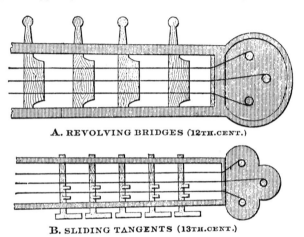

A. REVOLVING BRIDGES (12TH.CENT.)

B. SLIDING TANGENTS (13TH.CENT.)

Fig. 19 Organistrum and Symphony Actions

The internal mechanism, however, was no longer that of a turning rod and revolving bridge, but a small tangent or upright point of wood, inserted into a *sliding* rod, which was pulled against the string or strings in the same way as the primitive slides of the organs were drawn out. It was not long before it was discovered that by reversing the mechanism and *pressing* the rods in, greater facility of performance was secured; for, on withdrawing the finger, the rod with its tangent or tangents fell forward again and the strings were free. A very early example of this form of action occurs in the Psalter belonging to the Duke of Rutland and is illustrated on Plate 44. The Symphony player is depicted as being accompanied by the organ, which had at this date become its successful rival in all Church music (*c.* 1270).

A diagram of this later action will be found in Fig. 19B. It is in use on the Hurdy-Gurdy and on the Swedish Nyckelharpa to the present day, and seems to have suggested the mechanism of the earliest stringed instrument with a keyboard of balanced keys, namely the Clavichord, described in the next chapter.

In the fourteenth century the four-stringed Symphony appears, and the middle strings, tuned in unison or in octaves, were probably controlled by the tangents for the melody, while the outer strings vibrated freely, as "drones" or "bourdons", for the Bagpipe drone had appeared in the previous century. In this form it is figured by Sebastian Virdung, the writer of the earliest practical instruction book for musical instruments extant, known as *Musica getutscht* and issued in 1511 at Basle;[1] but later on in the same century other Bourdons were added, as will be seen in the fine specimen of the instrument formerly belonging to Catherine de Medici and now preserved in the Victoria and Albert Museum.

As regards the compass of the Symphony it seems to have been usually confined to a scale of ten diatonic notes; and, when in the sixteenth century the complete number of chromatic intervals was added, the additional rods and tangents required were placed as a second and lower row in front of the first. In the eighteenth century the Vielle was as popular as the Musette in the *Fêtes champêtres* of the French Court, and its compass included two complete octaves from *g'* to *g'''*. In the instruction books issued during that period we find explicit directions for the tuning of the four open strings or drones, which were respectively called the *Trumpet* (a copper string), the *Mouche* (gut) and the two *Bourdons* (wire covered). If the two melody strings were tuned to *g'*, the *Trumpet* was tuned to *c'* or *d'*, the *Mouche* to *g* and the *Bourdons* to *G* and *c* or *G* and *d*. An instrument of the eighteenth century, thus tuned, is shown on Plate 18. Sympathetic strings were also added sometimes to increase vibration; in fact, the number of open strings seems to have been left to the discretion and whim of the performer.

Whilst the Viol shape was perhaps one of the most popular forms of the Symphony, the rectangular shape, recalling the outline of the old Monochord, is not infrequently met with in medieval illumination and sculpture and is certainly earlier. It will be seen in many of the illustrations to which reference has been already made. In France the Lute shape was at one time greatly in vogue, as it was considered that its resonance was greater than that of the more usual Viol form.

It is important to remember that the old English Rote, described in the first chapter, was not a Symphony or Hurdy-Gurdy, but a form of Lyre.

---

[1] A facsimile of this important book was issued by Bärenreiter in 1931, with a preface by Leo Schrade.

Many lexicographers, such as Webster, Johnson, Nares, Halliwell and others, have given the Latin *rota*, a wheel, as the origin of the word Rote: and, as the wheel is a very evident part of the Hurdy-Gurdy, the identification of the two instruments seemed complete. Unfortunately the "Symphony and the Rote" are mentioned side by side in English literature, and were quite distinct.

Nor can we suppose that this instrument was the old Irish Timpan, as has been suggested in the fifth volume of *The Ossianic Society's Papers*. For much as the Hurdy-Gurdy may interest us through its lineal descent from a highly esteemed ancestor, its strains are hardly conducive to sleep as were those of the Timpan, nor could we conscientiously describe its sounds as "sweeter than all music under heaven". Yet the illustration reproduced on Plate 21, which is taken from an old *Bestiarium*, or Book of Beasts, written in England in the early part of the fourteenth century, and now in the British Museum (Sloane 3544), shows us that the music of the Symphony was attractive to some creatures – fishes, for instance, *qui ad symphoniam gregatim conveniunt*, as the writer says. In Sandys and Forster's *History of the Violin* many details with respect to the effect of music on animals are noted, and we have all met with the dog who hurriedly departs when the Violin is taken out of its case. In the early part of the eighteenth century a French scientist, Marville, gave the result of some experiments made with a Trumpet Marine – the Monochord described at the end of the last chapter. Upon hearing the sound a dog sat on his hind legs and fixed his eyes steadily on the player; an ass, meanwhile, went on eating thistles with absolute indifference. Cows stopped and looked a little, but passed on. Poultry gave no attention, but the smaller birds tried their best to sing it down. Owing to its trumpet-like tones, a horse seemed attracted and interested, whilst a cat paid no heed at all to the musician's efforts. We are also told that a prisoner in the Bastille, who was allowed the use of his Lute, noticed that the mice came out of their holes and the spiders descended from their webs when he began to play. Our own experience is that a cat, which was frightened at the sounds of a Flute and of a Trombone but lulled by the strains of a Fiddle, was irresistibly attracted and evidently pleased with the skirl of a Bagpipe. As it was a Persian cat, could it have retained a lingering recollection of the reed instruments so characteristic of its Oriental home?

The learned Athanasius Kircher, in the ninth book of his *Musurgia* (1650), informs us with all the seriousness of a scientific man that, having read in the works of his predecessors of the strange effect which the material, of which the strings of instruments were made, exercised upon animals, he prepared with some trouble and expense two instruments, each fitted with several strings, but in the one case with wolf-strings and in the other with those of sheep. He caused the first to be played inside a sheepfold, but unfortunately it did not frighten the animals as it should have done, being wolf. Then he had them played both together, but there was no jarring or breaking of the strings owing to the antipathy of the animals from whose intestines they had been made. So he came to the conclusion that there was nothing in it, and that he would believe no statement henceforth unless he had put it to the test.

John Playford, in the Preface to his *Introduction to the Skill of Musick* (1661), tells us of a much more likely incident which he witnessed when he was travelling near Royston, in Herts. He met a herd of stags, about twenty, upon the road, following a Bagpipe and a Violin, "which, while the music played they went forward, when it ceased they all stood still; and in this manner they were brought out of Yorkshire to Hampton Court". It is this knowledge of the influence of music upon the animal world which has led herdsmen from time immemorial to construct those simple instruments of which Chaucer sings, whose sounds might not only solace their own lonely hours, but calm and cheer their grazing flocks:

> Pipes made of grene corne
> As have thes little Herdegroomes
> That kepin Beastes in the broomes.

Not being piscatorially inclined, we leave for others the experiment of the fishes and the Hurdy-Gurdy.

Chapter VII

Clavichord and Virginal[1]

A slac strynge in a Virgynall soundithe not aright;
It dothe abyde no wrastinge, it is so louse and light.
The sounde borde crasede forsith the instrumente
Throw mysgovernaunce to make notis whiche was not his intent.

LEKINGFELDE PROVERB (*temp.* Henry VIII)

THE THIRTEENTH CENTURY has been aptly described as the century of great men, great thoughts, and great deeds; even in the more obscure domain of Music and the gradual development of Musical Instruments it was fraught with great consequences. For whilst Masters of Polyphony were perfecting their system of measured music by the varied forms of note and cadence, and Adam de la Halle with his companion troubadours were penning their secular songs in three-part harmony, close attention was also being given to the one detail which more than anything else has popularized and extended the practice and enjoyment of the Divine Art, namely the introduction of the keyboard. Invention it can hardly be called, when we remember that two centuries before the Christian era the Greek musicians ran their fingers over the keyboard of their Water Organs, and, as the poet Claudian of the fourth century A.D. tells us when he witnessed the performances of the Roman players of his own day, "with light touch, drew forth mighty sounds". The discovery at Carthage of an earthenware facsimile of such a keyboard instrument and fragments of others has shown that this was no mere flight of fancy. Associated, however, as these organs were with the orgies of gladiatorial contests and the wantonness of theatrical displays, they were banned by the early Christian Church, and the keys were forgotten, their utility lost sight of, until in the opening years of the thirteenth century the little pneumatic organs received those

---

[1] Important contributions to the history of stringed keyboard instruments in England will be found in Donald Boalch, *Makers of the Harpsichord and Clavichord 1440 to 1840* (Oxford, 1956) and Raymond Russell, *The Harpsichord and Clavichord* (Faber, 1959); Russell's book has a particularly important and ample bibliography. For more about the classical and early medieval organ, see Willi Apel, "Early History of the Organ", *Speculum*, vol. XXIII, no. 2 (April 1948), pp. 191–216.

PLATE 19

Trumpet Marine, an ecclesiastical instrument, seventeenth century, played by the author

PLATE 20

Musical instruments of the late twelfth century: chime-bells, harp, rebec, viol, recorder, pan-pipes, organistrum, psaltery and handbell

button-like excrescences which formed the basis of a medieval keyboard.

Now it was evident to the men of that day that what had been done for the organ could also be done for the stringed instruments; and, as a beginning, to the *Organistrum* were adapted little "tangents" instead of revolving bridges as described in the last chapter, which, while they gave greater facility in performance, suggested also the simple mechanism of the earliest stringed instrument with balanced keys, known as the MANICHORD or CLAVICHORD. For, if the melody-string of the present-day Hurdy-Gurdy – the humble descendant of the Organistrum – be sufficiently tightened, an air can be played upon it by the sharp impact of the tangents alone, without turning the wheel by which the strings are usually set in motion. And such a tangent placed at the further end of a balanced key forms the whole mechanism of the Clavichord; by its sharp impact it not only marks off the length of string required for a particular note, but also sets the string in vibration with sufficient power to give a sweet sympathetic sound of short duration, the vibration of the superfluous part of the string being deadened or damped by a strip of soft cloth. The mechanism, known technically as the action, is shown in Fig. 24.

But with such tangents arranged in a row beneath a *single* string, it was found that only one note at a time could be played; and so the inventors of the Clavichord took several strings of equal length and, by placing tangents – two, three or four – under each string, they were able to obtain the meagre harmony which the practice of their day demanded.[1] Once, however, the principle was adopted, its extension was merely a matter of time; but it is somewhat remarkable that four centuries were to elapse before the number of strings was so increased that each tangent could have its own string; yet so it was, and the *fretted* Clavichord, as the instrument with more than one tangent to a string was called, remained in popular use till the days of Sebastian Bach, the *fret-free* principle – or "one tangent one string" – being generally attributed to Faber of Crailsheim, in Saxony, about 1720; but in the late Dr Watson's Collection at Manchester there is a fret-free Clavichord by J. W. Gruneberg of Alt Brandenburg, dated 1700, evidently altered however at a later time.

To the thirteenth century, then, we may refer the invention of the first *stringed* instrument furnished with a practical keyboard. Its name Manichord – the hand-played string – by which it was always known in Italy,

[1] The existence of a "monochord with several strings" has been successfully disputed by Walter Nef, "The Polychord", *GSJ*, IV, pp. 20–4. An up-to-date discussion of the early history of the clavichord will be found at pp. 68–73 of *Musical Instruments through the Ages* (Penguin Books, 1961).

Spain and France, is so closely similar to the word Monochord that much confusion has arisen between the two. Probably Guiraut de Calanson, the Provençal poet of the first part of the thirteenth century, gives us the earliest instance of the name in his list of musical instruments, on which an accomplished jongleur should be able to perform. His "Manichorda una corda" may indeed have been identical with the one-stringed instrument played with a bow which at a later date was called the Trumpet Marine, as explained in a previous chapter; but it is quite possible that at that time tangents and keys had already been applied to a simple Monochord. The word *Clavicordium* first appears in 1404 in some old German rules for the Minnesingers; and under the same title it was known in England; for in Caxton's translation of the Romance of *Geoffrey de la Tour* issued in 1483 we read that a young man in the garb of a minstrel came to the castle on a feast day: "he cam and salewed the lordes and ladys, and when he had done to them reverence, Syre Geoffrey called hym before hym and demanded hym where hys Vyell or Clavycordes were and that he should make hys craft. And the young man answered, 'Syre, I cannot medle therewith.' 'Haa,' seyd the knight, 'I cannot byleve it; for ye be contrefaytted, and clothed lyke a mynstrell.' " Evidently he was considered a questionable character.

In the following century the *clavycordes* or *paire of clavycordes*, according to the common expression of the time explained in a subsequent chapter, are frequently mentioned. The following extracts are from the *Privy Purse Expenses* of Henry VII:

> 1502. Jan. 7. To one that sett the Kings cleyvecords, xiii[s.] iv[d.]
> 1504. March 6. For a paire of clavycords, x[s.]

And another from those of his queen, Elizabeth of York:

> 1502. Aug. 19. To Hugh Denys for money by him delivered to a strangier that gave the Quene a paire of clavycordes, iiii[li.]

Second-hand instruments were cheap, according to the Inventory of John Post, late the King's servant:

> 1525. In ye garret over ye great chamber an old payre clavycords: val. viii[d.]

In the Lekingfelde Proverbs of the time of Henry VIII, and in Hawes' *Pastyme of Pleasure*, 1506, we find the spelling "claricorde". Some have thought that this denotes a different instrument, perhaps of the Dulcimer kind, but it is probably only a mistaken transcript of the original word, of which we have another instance in the name "clarysymbal" for "clavysymbal" for we are told that when King James IV of Scotland was paying his addresses to Margaret, daughter of Henry VII, "he beganne before hyr to play of the clarycordes and after of the lute, which pleased hyr varey much". Upon the same instruments she afterwards played, and we have already seen that the English royal family were "clavycorde" players, and withal good judges and exponents of the art. In fact, in the Lekingfelde Proverb both forms of spelling are thus given:

He that fyngerithe well the keyes of the Clavicordis makithe a goode songe,
For in the meane is the melodye with a rest longe:
If the tewnys be not plesant to hym that hath no skyll,
Yet no lac to the claricorde, for he doith his goode will.

The common name for the instrument in Scotland was "monocordis", a corruption of the French "manicordes". Thus, in the *High Treasurer's Accounts* for the year 1497, there is this entry: "To John Hert, for bearing a pare of monocordis of the Kinges fra Abirdene to Strivelin, ix^s."

In *A Treatise betwene Trowthe and Enformacion*, made by William Cornishe in the Fleet Prison during the year 1504, there is an interesting stanza on the Claricorde which shows that the player tuned the few strings of his instrument to the proper pitch and consonance before performance:

The Clarricord hath a evynly kynde;
As the wyre is wrested hye and lowe,
So tunyth it to the player's mynde,
For as it is wrested so must it nedes showe.
As by this reson ye may well knowe
An instrument mystunyd shall hurt a trew songe,
Yet blame not the claricord, the wrester doth wrong.

That the process of tuning would not be either difficult or laborious may be gathered from a fifteenth-century illustration of the instrument – one of the earliest in existence, another being in the Weimar *Wunderbuch* of about the middle of the same century. The English example occurs in the hands of a winged figure carved in wood and placed in the finely decorated roof of the nave of St Mary's Church, Shrewsbury, constructed during the first half of the century. The instrument is rectangular in shape, with nine keys and six strings; the latter were probably arranged in pairs as in the Lute, three tangents being beneath each pair of strings, which were perhaps of wire, though possibly of gut. A reproduction from a photograph of this unique example will be seen in Fig. 20. At first, as in this instance, the strings were all the same length, but in the sixteenth century separate bridges (as in the

Monochord) were introduced to shorten the length of the higher strings. In Italy and France these survived till the middle of the seventeenth century, but in Germany the instrument had already been fitted with a continuous and curved bridge before the year 1600. An illustration of the more primitive form is shown on Plate 22. This instrument was made by Onesto Tosi, of Genoa, in the year 1568, and there are as many as four tangents striking on the same pair of strings. The "dampers", consisting of strips of cloth, will be noticed on the left-hand side of the case.

In England the Clavichord was not in so great request as the Virginal and Spinet; in fact, no old example of English make is known unless it be the small well-preserved specimen once in the possession of a Master of the Worshipful Company of Musicians, Dr T. L. Southgate; it is said to be by Peter Hicks, and dates, as its keyboard and construction show, from about the year 1700. Now in the Victoria and Albert Museum, it is illustrated in Plate 22, where the long curved bridge will be noted. On the analogy of "Harpsicon" for "Harpsichord", it is very probable that the seventeenth-century "Claricon" represented a Clavichord. In 1663 we find from the *Lord Chamberlain's Records* that John Hingeston, Keeper and Repairer of His Majesty's organs, was paid for mending a "claricon", as well as "Her Majesty's harpsichord that stands in her own chamber".

In a list of instruments used about that date (Brit. Mus., Sloane 1326) the "Clarichord" is placed with the "stringed instruments of Rapps or Gutts". The keyboard variety of the *Doucemelle*, mentioned already in connection with the Dulcimer, was probably a form of Clavichord with wooden instead of metal tangents, or some other device, such as gut strings, to render its tone peculiarly sweet. M. Bottée de Toulmon, in his *Dissertation sur les Instruments de Musique employés au Moyen Age*, described it as a Pianoforte; but this view is not borne out by the words of the manuscript, attributed to the fifteenth century, on which he based his theory, nor has it been generally accepted.[1]

When the Pianoforte actually arrived – in the early part of the eighteenth century – it proved the successful rival of the Clavichord as of the other keyboard instruments; and although the tangent principle held its own till the end of that century in Germany (and in Norway and Sweden still later), the instrument may be said to have remained in abeyance until the last decade of the nineteenth century, when some Clavichords were again made

[1] A facsimile edition of this manuscript (Paris, Bibliothèque Nationale, Fonds latin 7295) was issued in 1932, edited by le Cerf and Labande; the most recent discussion of its contents will be found in Cecil Clutton, "Arnault's MS", *GSJ*, V, pp. 3–8.

in London on the *unfretted* principle, for the performance of works by the old masters, and have since been multiplied.

Closely associated in history with the tangent Clavichord is a group of keyboard instruments, which, under various shapes and names, such as CLAVICYMBAL, VIRGINAL, SPINET, and HARPSICHORD, present, in their action, a common principle. In all of them the sound is produced by means of a small point, either of metal, as in the earliest forms, or of leather or quill in the later examples, which is attached to an upright slip of wood called a "jack" and plucks the string as it passes it when the further end of the balanced key, on which the "jack" rests, is depressed by the finger. As it returns, a movable tongue of wood into which the striking-point is inserted allows the quill or leather point to repass the string without repeating the stroke. This tongue of wood is kept in position for each upstroke by a light spring at the back. The action is shown in Fig. 23.

As this is the characteristic principle of the Virginal, Spinet, and other like instruments, a protest should be made against the ignorant practice of giving the name Spinet to the small square or rectangular pianos of the late eighteenth and early nineteenth centuries. We admit that it is not wholly the fault of our modern curiosity dealers; for the name was occasionally given to such pianos in the eighteenth century; for instance, John Shybli's advertisement in the *New York Gazette* (1774) tells us that he had for sale "one neat Chamber Organ, one hammer Spinet, and one common Spinet". But the name is misapplied when hammers are present, as this mechanism stamps the instrument at once as of the Piano type, while in the same way the rising "jack" and plucking-point place it in the group now under consideration.

The date of the invention of this form of keyboard instrument and the name and nationality of the inventor are at present lost to us. It probably appeared after the Clavichord and in the fourteenth century, its progenitor evidently being the plucked Psaltery described in a previous chapter. According to Scaliger (b. 1484), the metal "points" or "plectra" were exchanged for quills towards the close of the fifteenth century, and from this fact the instrument was called the "Spinet", the quill point resembling a thorn or fishbone. Before this, however, the instrument, perhaps in a somewhat different shape, was known as the *Clavicymbalum* – the English Clavicymbal – the Italian Clavicembalo or keyed Psaltery, the name appearing as early as 1404.

There is, however, the trace of a yet earlier keyboard instrument called the Echiquier, Exaquir or Eschaqueil. In a letter from King John of Aragon to his brother-in-law, Philip Duke of Burgundy, written at Saragossa in the year 1388, it is described as "like an organ which sounds with strings". The King not only asks that an instrument should be sent to him, but also a player who could perform both on it and on the little organs. In Machault's poem of fourteenth-century date, *Li temps pastour*, it is called "L'eschaqueil d'Angleterre", and, therefore, as the late Mr A. J. Hipkins suggested in his *History of the Pianoforte*, it may be that England was the original home of this instrument. With his unrivalled knowledge of the history and technique of the ancient keyboard instruments – a knowledge which was so freely and courteously placed at the disposal of all musicians – such an opinion is of value, and our own researches into the past seem to confirm it and to show that there is every probability that as our country was, in its school of Virginal music, far in advance of the rest of Europe, so the invention of the first instrument of this type was due to the genius of Englishmen. It is commonly supposed that the name Echiquier or Exaquir, which also means a chessboard, refers either to the shape or to the decoration of the case. It is more likely, however, that it refers to the *jacks*, which, appearing in a row across the sound-board, suggested the idea of chessmen, which was enhanced by the action of "checking" or repulsing the strings as they rose to pluck them. We know that the old English word *chaw* has given us *jaw*, and the Spanish *xaqueta* is the English *jacket*; so the *check* of the Echiquier has become the *jack* of the English Virginal. Dr Farmer would connect it with the Arabic *Al-shaquira*.

Although no illustrations of the instrument of the fourteenth century are now extant, we have nevertheless one which shows us the form it had assumed in England a hundred years later. It is held by one of the winged minstrels carved in wood and placed in the roof of the nave of Manchester Cathedral, which dates between the years 1465 and 1468. As will be seen from the illustration given in Fig. 21, it there appears in the familiar wing-shaped form of the later Harpsichord. Another example of a similar instrument and of the same period is to be found in the manuscript of the *Thoison d'or* in the Bibliothèque Nationale at Paris. In the Certosa at Pavia, built about the year 1474, there is a representation of King David playing upon a trapeze-shaped Psaltery with eight keys; with one hand he presses the keys, while with the other he damps the strings. This is probably the early form of the Italian pentagonal Spinet, which in the sixteenth century became so popular, and of which the so-called Queen Elizabeth's Virginal, now in the Victoria and Albert Museum, is a fine and perfect specimen.

At one time this name Virginal was evidently restricted to the smaller forms of the instrument, which assumed either the pentagonal shape already mentioned or the rectangular outline which has generally been considered typical of the true English Virginal. Before the death of Henry VIII, however, it had received a wider application, and Virginals included Clavicymbals as well as Spinets. A rectangular Virginal by Andreas Ruckers[1] of Antwerp, dated 1610, is illustrated in Plate 24. It is the oldest known

Fig. 20 Clavichord – early 15th cent. (Shrewsbury)

Fig. 21 Clavicymbal – 15th cent. (Manchester)

work of this famous Flemish maker, one of whose instruments was among Handel's cherished possessions.

Concerning the origin of the name Virginal, there can be little doubt but that it arose from the fact, mentioned by sixteenth-century writers, that this

[1] Lists of extant instruments by the various members of the Ruckers family will be found in Grove's *Dictionary* (Fifth Edition); the earliest surviving instrument by Andries (Andreas) is dated 1608.

keyboard instrument was especially favoured by the ladies of the period, whilst the men preferred the Lute.[1] At any rate, Henry VIII and his family, to whose personal skill and enthusiastic example the English music of that century owed so much, were all excellent performers on the "Virgynalls"; and long before the Virgin Queen ascended the throne, the Privy Purse expenses of her sister, the Princess Mary, abound with interesting items of the expenditure on the repair and "setting" (tuning) of "My Lady's Grace Virgynalls", and Mr Paston, her music master, received the sum of £1 2s. 6d. per quarter for "techyng my Lady". Queen Elizabeth's skill on the instrument is well known, and also the clever way in which she managed to show off her talents before her courtiers and the ambassadors of foreign sovereigns. An instrument which is supposed to have belonged to her – as has been also said of many other things, including bedsteads – is not without interest, and has been already mentioned. It is highly decorated, and bears the Royal Arms, though the work was either renewed or restored in 1660. Its shape is similar to that shown on Plate 23, which is dated 1552, and it probably had originally a rectangular and decorated case, as this specimen has, into which it could be placed when not laid on the table for use. The compass is from G' to c''' or $4\frac{1}{2}$ octaves including the "short octave" in the bass. This latter device, which now appears so primitive and incomplete, was in general use on all keyboard instruments during the sixteenth and seventeenth centuries. It arose from a desire to extend the compass downwards on the existing keyboard, which in the earlier instruments ended at E or B', according to the ancient Greek scale. As the sharps and flats of the lower bass notes were seldom required in the simple music of the day, if the keyboard compass descended to E, the $G\sharp$ and $F\sharp$ immediately above were changed to E and D, and the original E became C; if, on the other hand, it descended to B', the $D\sharp$ and $C\sharp$ were used for B' and A', and the B' became G'. In this way the octave was reached without increasing the number of keys. When at the close of the seventeenth century a complete chromatic compass was required, the $G\sharp$ and $F\sharp$ keys were sometimes cut across, the back half giving the sharp and the front half the natural note of the short octave.

As regards the style of music played by the Queen an excellent idea may be obtained from the settings which are found in the handsome volume now at the Fitzwilliam Museum, Cambridge, and popularly known as *Queen*

---

[1] The true etymology of the word "virginals" remains obscure, but it is at least as likely that its name derives from its tone-quality. Early theorists sometimes liken this to a girl's voice (*vox virginalis*). This may well mean that its jacks used plectra of leather or quill, by contrast with earlier instruments in which the strings were plucked by sprigs of metal.

PLATE 21

1. Symphony, early fourteenth century

2. Rotte, Rebecs and Psalteries, eleventh century

PLATE 22

1. Clavichord by Onesto Tosi, Genoa, 1568

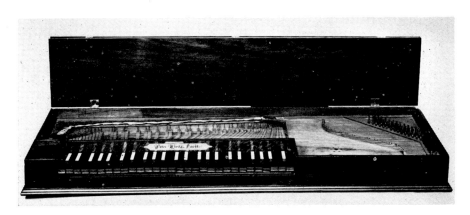

2. Clavichord ascribed to Peter Hicks, *c.* 1700

PLATE 23

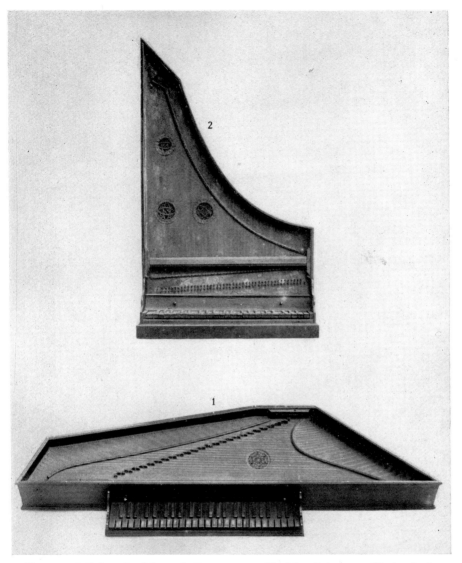

1. Pentagonal Spinet by Marco Jadra, 1552. 2. Upright Spinet or Clavicytherium, seventeenth century

PLATE 24

1. Maker's device in sound
hole

2. Virginal by Andreas Ruckers, 1610

Elizabeth's Virginal Book. It has been conclusively shown by Mr W. Barclay Squire in *Grove's Dictionary of Music* (Art. "Virginal Music") that the compilation is of early Jacobean rather than of Tudor times, but of the 291 compositions contained in the book the greater number are by the eminent musicians of the Elizabethan age, such as Byrd, Bull, Tallis, Farnaby, and others. They chiefly consist of airs with divisions or variations, and as they are written on six-lined staves, require some study in reading and a considerable amount of technique. An excellent reproduction and description of this valuable collection of old English Virginal music has been issued through the joint labours of Mr A. J. Fuller Maitland and Mr Barclay Squire. A photograph of part of a page in the original manuscript is shown in Fig. 22. In reading it the player must remember that the *c'* line is drawn at the bottom of the Treble Stave and also at the top of the Bass Stave. Another interesting collection entitled *Parthenia, or the Maydenhead of the first Musicke that ever was printed for the Virginalls*, was published in 1612. It was republished by Dr Rimbault for the Musical Antiquarian Society (1847), and this edition has recently been re-issued by Mr William Reeves (London, 1907).[1]

It is not until we arrive at the middle of the seventeenth century that we have reliable information with regard to the Virginal-makers and their work. We are inclined, however, to believe, that as the Virginal and similar instruments had for two or three centuries been held in high esteem in our country, English makers of these popular instruments were many and capable. In the early part of the sixteenth century "one Cowtes, of London" must have been able to make as well as to mend Princess Mary's instruments; and William Lewes, who supplied her royal father with several Virginals at an average price of thirty shillings each (£18–£20 in the present value), was certainly something more than a dealer. In connection with these

---

[1] The study of virginals music has been advanced very considerably since Galpin wrote this section. For further information on the sources, see the article "Virginal Music, Collections of" in Grove's *Dictionary* (Fifth Edition). The Fitzwilliam Virginal Book is now known to have been copied by the recusant musician, Francis Tregian the younger, during his imprisonment in the Fleet Prison, 1609–19. *Parthenia* (first published late in 1612 or early in 1613) was issued in facsimile in 1941, and a critical edition of it, edited by Thurston Dart, has been published by Stainer & Bell (1960). A companion volume, *Parthenia In-Violata*, has been issued in facsimile and also in a modern critical edition by the New York Public Library and Peters Edition (1961). The complete keyboard works of John Bull, Orlando Gibbons, Thomas Tomkins, Thomas Morley and others have been published in critical editions by *Musica Britannica* and Stainer & Bell. The article in Grove listed above should be studied in conjunction with the prefaces to all these editions. For more about virginal-makers see the books by Boalch and Russell listed in the footnote on p. 84.

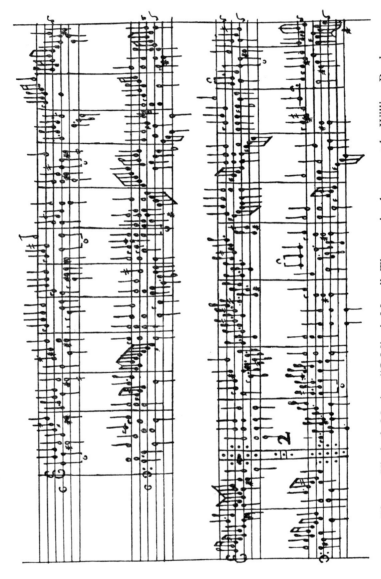

Fig. 22 Virginals Music – "O Mistris Myne". The opening bars as set by William Byrd

instruments the following entry in the King's *Privy Purse Expenses* has puzzled and misled recent writers:

> 1530. Paied to William Lewes for ii payre of Virginalles in one coffer with iiii stoppes brought to Grenewiche, iii[11.]

The late Mr Hipkins, in his *History of the Pianoforte*, considered this to have been an instrument with two keyboards and stops like the double Harpsichords of later times. But there is no trace of such an instrument either in the writings and illustrations of the sixteenth century or in any existing specimen until, towards its close, it was produced by Hans Ruckers, the celebrated Flemish maker. Either the Virginals used in England, therefore, were in advance of the time and forestalled this invention by forty or fifty years, or (more probably) they were identical with the instruments, described as Virginals in the King's Inventory given in our Appendix, where we find a Regal-organ with one or more stops attached to the stringed keyboard instrument. The "one coffer" mentioned in the entry above quoted was apparently only the packing or travelling case; for, on the same date, a payment of £3 was made to William Lewes for "ii payer of Virginalles in one coffer brought to the More", the King's residence in Hertfordshire, and at his death the Inventory gives "Two paires of olde Virginalles" as still at the More, but no mention is made of the "one coffer". On the difficult terms "single" and "double", as applied to the keyboard instruments, a note will be found in the Appendix, and the phrase "a pair of Virginals" is explained in the chapter on Organs.

Of English Virginal-makers the seventeenth century, however, leaves us no longer in doubt; for John Loosemore, Adam Leversidge, Stephen Keene, James White and Thomas White stand forth pre-eminent, and their handiwork has survived to our own time. [In the earlier editions of Galpin's book, Plate 25 showed a virginals made by Thomas White in 1651, and the text was appropriate to this instrument. For the present edition it has seemed preferable to include White's earliest known instrument, dated 1642 and now in the Victoria and Albert Museum. It measures five feet six inches in length, one foot eight inches in width, and the depth, if closed, is but a foot. The dome-shaped cover is painted with an artificial scene. The forty-nine keys give, with the short octave, a compass from A' to c'''. – T. D.] A fine example of the work of Adam Leversidge (London, 1666), said to have belonged at one time to Nell Gwynne, was once the property of Mr Arthur Hill. It is now in America. The painted lid gives a view of St James's Park, and an illustration of it appears in Messrs Novello's *Catalogue of the Musicians' Company's Exhibition* (1904). Its compass is from G'

(short octave) to f'''. These large rectangular Virginals, when constructed by the Flemish makers, whose handiwork became so famous under the skill and genius of the Ruckers family, had sometimes a small instrument of octave pitch inserted in the side. This was removable and could be placed on or near the larger instrument for a second performer.[1] But at the close of the sixteenth century this octave effect had already been included in the mechanism of the larger instrument by the insertion of an octave string in addition to the two unison strings, which had been found in the Clavicymbal at least eighty years previously. Stops, too, for producing loud and soft effects, by bringing into use additional strings, were invented; and thus by improved combinations on both keyboards the Clavecin or Harpsichord, as it was called in England, was rendered capable of great variety and charm.

The usual form or model of the English instrument, as it was constructed in the eighteenth century by the eminent firms of Tschudi or Shudi (now Broadwood) and Kirkman, was that of the older Clavicymbal or the Grand Pianoforte of our own day. A fine example of Joseph Kirkman's workmanship, dated 1798, is figured on Plate 26. The two keyboards of this Double Harpsichord are controlled by six stops. Two, placed on the right hand of the player, called the *Cymbal* and the *Unison*, bring two rows of jacks into touch with two unison strings; whilst of the three stops on the left, one called the *Octave* sets a row of jacks against an octave string, another, called the *Lute* stop, moves a row of jacks which pluck one of the two unison strings close to the bridge, over which they pass, thereby producing a reedy tone much fancied by the old lutenists; and the third stop, the *Buff*, places a set of felt dampers against one or other of the unison strings, giving thereby a less resonant and harp-like effect. In addition to these variations of power and tone, a foot-pedal opens part of the cover of the instrument or moves a Venetian swell of louvred shutters, a device invented by Shudi and afterwards used for the organ. In this way the sound can be increased or diminished at pleasure, whilst a sixth stop, called the *Machine*, places the stop-mechanism under the control of another foot-pedal which enables the player to alter the registering or arrangement of stops without lifting his hands off the keys. Of the keyboards the upper is

[1] These so-called "mother-and-child" instruments seem to have been quite common during the early seventeenth century, the centre for their construction being Antwerp. The underside of the octave instrument had a slot in it; by removing the jackrail of the "mother" and placing the "child" above it, a two-manual instrument was made, in which the lower manual sounded 8′ and 4′ strings and the upper manual (4′ only) could serve for echo effects. A few two-manual instruments were also made by the Ruckers family, the second manual serving as a transposing manual. See Russell's book, cited earlier.

controlled by the Cymbal, the Lute and, in Kirkman's Harpsichords, the Buff stops; the lower keyboard is affected by the Cymbal, Unison, Octave, and Buff stops. In Single Harpsichords (i.e. with one keyboard) the same six stops are found. Continental instruments exhibit further peculiarities; some specimens of the German Kielflügel, as it is called, have a set of strings an octave lower in pitch than the unison,[1] whilst instruments with three keyboards have been made, as Mersenne in his *Harmonie Universelle* (1636) and Jacob Adlung in his *Musica Mechanica* (1768) tell us, and as an existing specimen in the New York Metropolitan Museum of Art clearly shows.

It seems that the attachment of pedal mechanism for varying the power and tone of the Harpsichord was due to our English maker, John Haward, according to the testimony of Thomas Mace in his *Musick's Monument*. The improved instrument was called The Pedal, and, from four little "Pummels of wood" for the player's feet, at least six varieties of tone could be obtained. This important invention must have been made before the year 1664, as in that year, according to the *Lord Chamberlain's Records*, John Hingeston, Keeper of His Majesty's Instruments, was paid for "repairing the organs, harpsichords and pedalls". In 1678 he received for "strings for the harpsichords and pedall for three years and a quarter" £1 10s. 6d., and in 1683 for four-and-a-half years £3 10s. After this the "pedall" is no more mentioned.

The Spinet, so popular in England in the eighteenth century – though, as it had but one string to each key, any gradation or change of tone was impossible – was made in the wing-shape of the Italian Transverse Spinet, the tuning-pins being immediately behind the keyboard as in the Harpsichord and not at the side as in the rectangular Virginal and pentagonal Spinet. It appeared in this country soon after the Restoration; and Mr Pepys, in his *Diary*, under the year 1668, informs us that he bought an *espinette* of Haward for £5, and afterwards obtained a "tryangel" or three-legged stand on which to set it. Not only Charles Haward, but Keene, Thomas and John Hitchcock, Barton, Slade, Mahon, Harris, and Haxby were amongst the favourite makers. The illustration on Plate 27 shows a small instrument by Baker Harris which is furnished with leather plectra and could be taken to the evening party by the performer himself, as we can testify. Its compass is from *C* to *g'''*.

Similar in purpose to our upright pianos, for economizing space, are the

[1] It has now been conclusively shown that sub-octave stops (16′ strings) were unknown during the whole of the seventeenth and eighteenth centuries, with the exception of one or two freak instruments constructed almost by way of experiment. See Friedrich Ernst, *Der Flügel Johann Sebastian Bachs* (Peters, 1955); see also Russell's book, cited earlier.

upright Spinets and Harpsichords, which were made from the beginning of the sixteenth century to the very close of the existence of these "plucked" instruments in the first part of the nineteenth century. We have no evidence, however, that they were much used in this country, though on the Continent they were in general request. That ardent collector of musical instruments King Henry VIII died possessed of "two fair pair of new long Virginalls, made harp fashion, of cipres with keys of ivory, having the King's Arms crowned and supported by his Grace's beastes with a garter gilt standing over the keys"; and in the Long Gallery at Hampton Court there was also "a paire of Virginalles facioned like a harp". It is generally said that these were upright instruments, examples of the *Clavicytherium* (keyed harp), of

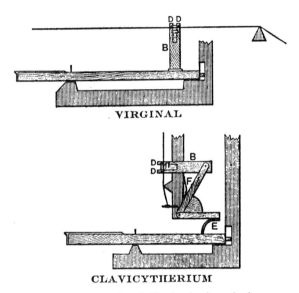

Fig. 23 Virginal and Clavicytherium Actions
B Jack, D Damper, E Lifter, F Spring

which a unique specimen, dating from the early sixteenth century, exists in the Donaldson Collection at the Royal College of Music. It is illustrated by Messrs Hipkins and Gibb in their work on *Musical Instruments*, and an example of a century later is shown on Plate 23. Its "action" will be seen in Fig. 23.

From the list of King Henry's possessions given in the Appendix to the present work it will be observed that he had six Double Virginals, eight Single Virginals, twelve Virginals of which it is not stated whether they were single or double, three Virginals made harp-fashion, four Virginals and Regals combined (of which more will be said in a later chapter), one Virginal "that goethe with a whele without playing uppon" (an automatic instrument on the same principle as the modern Barrel Piano) and two "Claricordes" – in all, thirty-six examples of the Clavichord and Virginal class.

It surely makes us sad when we remember that all these instruments on which the skilled mechanic spent his labour, the decorator lavished his art, and the musician exercised his genius, if they have survived the ravages of Time, are now condemned to the silent confinement of the museum show-case or handed over to the unscrupulous denizens of the country hay-loft. An awakened and, we trust, ever-awakening interest in the music of the past is at last bringing back to our ears their old-world tones, and revealing to us – as they alone can – the true meaning and hidden charm of the musical compositions of their day.

Two points, however, militated against the continuance of their popularity. In the case of the Clavichord, it was the inability to produce a sound loud enough to be appreciated by the many; and with the Virginal and its *confrères* it was the impossibility of giving expression to the music played except by purely mechanical devices. When therefore, in 1709 or there-abouts, the Florentine Harpsichord-maker, Cristofori, invented the *Gravicembalo col Piano e Forte* or the Harpsichord with little hammers, the fate of the Clavichords and Virginals was sealed; for here was an instrument of full tone combined with a delicacy of expression only obtainable by the touch of the player's fingers.[1]

There are, fortunately, two examples of these first pianos in existence, both of them are well known to us; one, dated 1720, is in the New York Metropolitan Museum of Art; the other (1726) was, when we played on it, in the Kraus Collection at Florence, but is now in the Grassi Museum at Leipzig University.

The dominating principle of the invention was the *falling* hammer. The Clavichord had for centuries employed a kind of hammer in the metal or wooden tangent which struck the string and caused it to vibrate; but unless the tangent was kept pressed firmly against the string the sound, such as it was, ceased, for it was bridge and hammer combined. The falling hammer, however, is the direct outcome of the Dulcimer hammer, by which a sharp blow is given and the string, which is tuned to its proper note, left

---

[1] The fullest account of the development of the piano is to be found in Rosamond Harding, *The Piano-Forte* (Cambridge, 1933), and her article in the Fifth Edition of Grove's *Dictionary* (sub "Pianoforte"). Cristofori's invention is almost contemporary with the hammer actions of Marius and Schröter.

free to vibrate. But for this purpose the string must be set at a high tension with a corresponding strain upon the framing of the instrument, and until this latter point could be dealt with and the framing strengthened, the Piano was out of the question. For the Piano e Forte which the Duke of Modena possessed in 1598 was evidently a Harpsichord, with some such contrivance for varying the power and sound of the instrument as has already been described.

The clever device by which Cristofori imitated the action of the Dulcimer hammer consists of a movable tongue of wood called the *hopper* and a notch into and out of which it works. When the finger depresses the balanced key the hopper strikes up the pivoted hammer (or, in the earlier instruments, an under-hammer), and, slipping into the notch, allows it to fall back a little way until it meets the *check* or padded rest, which, being fixed to the end of the key, rises to receive it. The damper meanwhile is lifted off

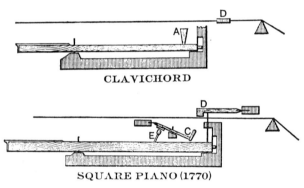

CLAVICHORD

SQUARE PIANO (1770)

Fig. 24 Clavichord and Piano Actions
A Tangent, C Hammer, D Damper, E Lifter

the string. This "falling" distance, called the *escapement*, is carefully regulated to help the repetition of the blow. For when the finger allows the key to rise, even but a little way, a small spring returns the hopper to its original position, and the blow can be repeated. When the finger is lifted entirely off the key the hammer leaves the check for its first position, and the damper drops on the string. Whatever may be the form of the action, and however much it may have been elaborated to give rapidity of repetition and delicacy of touch, these points are essential, though the actual shape may be varied. The very simple action of an early square Piano is shown in Fig. 24.

As the history of the Pianoforte takes us far beyond our present subject and requires more adequate treatment than we can give it in so general a

PLATE 25

Virginals by Thomas White, 1642

PLATE 26

1. & 2. Double Harpsichord by Joseph Kirkman, English, 1798

survey, we must refer those who are interested to Mr Hipkins' excellent History already mentioned, and it must suffice us to say that the now familiar instrument first became popular in this country about the year 1760, when the German maker Zumpe settled in London and constructed small rectangular instruments, resembling the Clavichord in shape, furnished with three stops – two for Forte effects in the treble and bass respectively (produced by lifting the dampers off the strings), and a third for muting the strings with a strip of soft felt. One of Zumpe's instruments, dated 1770, is shown in Plate 27. The compass is barely five octaves from A' to f''', and the tone is thin and wiry; but these little instruments were much admired, and, as the square piano, proved the favourite shape till the close of the century. It is believed that Charles Dibdin was the first person to bring it prominently before the public, for in an old playbill of the Theatre Royal, Covent Garden, for May 16, 1767, it is stated that at the end of the first act of the *Beggar's Opera* Miss Brickler would sing a favourite song from *Judith*, "accompanied by Mr Dibdin on a new instrument called Pianoforte".

Chapter VIII

Recorder and Flute

> The Recorder of his kynde the meane dothe desyre;
> Manyfolde fyngerynge & stoppes bryngithe hym from his tunes clere:
> Who so lyst to handill an instrumente so goode
> Must se in his many fyngerynge that he kepe tyme, stop and moode.
>
> LEKINGFELDE PROVERB (*temp.* Henry VIII)

THERE ARE FEW WHO can refuse a smile and furtive glance at the merry conceits and familiar drolleries of Mr Punch when age forbids a more open surrender, but there are fewer still who remember that the one-man orchestra standing by the show-side is presenting to our ears music of the most remote antiquity. For as the Drum is the recognized sound-producer of savages, so the PANPIPES embody in their row of hollow reeds one of the earliest efforts of that Art which we have been taught to believe can "soothe the savage breast". As the Roman poet Lucretius wrote two thousand years ago, Nature herself may have been the first to suggest the pleasing sound:

> Et Zephyri cava per calamorum sibila primum
> Agresteis docuere cavas inflare cicutas.

But whether it was the whistling of the breeze across the empty reeds which first taught rude man to pass his breath over the hollow stalks, or whether it was Pan, Silenus, or some other equally mythical person to whom the little scale of pipes owes its origin, at any rate the diffusion of the instrument is world-wide. It greets us in the classic sculptures of Greece, in the mosaic pavements and the mural paintings of ancient Rome; it rests in the graves of the prehistoric Incas and forms the basis of China's mysterious music; and as in bygone ages it led the Lydian dance, so does it still enliven the festive gatherings of the dusky islanders of the Pacific: while Jubal's organ and Nebuchadnezzar's flute have both been claimed as Panpipes (Plate 30). Among the Sumerians and earlier Egyptians, however, it seems to have been missing.[1]

---

[1] The instrument is still very much alive in the Balkan countries; the most brilliant performers are perhaps to be found in Rumania. See Tiberiu Alexandru, *Instrumentele Muzicale ale Poporului Romîn* (State Publishing House, Bucharest: 1956).

From the frequency with which the instrument appears in the medieval illustrations and carvings, it is evident that it was considered worthy of the musician's notice. In the Anglo-Saxon Psalter of the early eleventh century, now in the University Library, Cambridge, and shown on Plate 38, it will be seen in Idithun's right hand. At first sight the instrument looks as if it were a form of drum, but trustworthy examples of Panpipes constructed in this semicircular shape are forthcoming from other manuscripts. In the left hand the player holds the *crotala* or clappers, frequently associated with the instrument when used for the dance. In the twelfth-century manuscripts preserved in the University Library, Glasgow, and reproduced on Plate 20, it is associated with the Rebec, Viol, and Recorder; whilst in the Psalter now at St John's College, Cambridge, of the same century, it is seen taking its part in Sacred Music, as opposed to the Profane Music exhibited in the lower half of the page (Plate 43). Among the Norman carvings on the south doorway of Barfreston Church in Kent it appears in the paws of a bear or other beast, as will be seen in Plate 15, and in the thirteenth-century manuscript (Brit. Mus., Lans. 420) it is allotted to a hog; both of these are suggestive of its lowly associations, nor did it regain its high estate in this country until the Italian artist who redecorated the Great Screen in York Minster, after the fire in 1829, placed it to the lips of an angel.

But before primitive man conceived the idea of uniting a set of hollow reeds and blowing across their open ends, the use of a single pipe must have been known to him, on which he could sound simple calls or signals. And these *vertical flutes*, as they are called, have attained as wide a distribution as the Panpipes themselves: though in the form in which we find them, in later prehistoric times, they show a distinct advance in technical skill and musical knowledge, for one or more holes for the fingers are provided, whereby the pitch of the sounds can be altered.

In the ancient Egyptian wall-paintings the long vertical flute called *Sebi* is constantly portrayed, and as the *Nay* (Plate 30) it is still in use among the Arabs. In the Chinese orchestras of the Confucian temples it has a special place, and its mellow tones are heard in the dances of the North American Indians and African incantations. Five thousand years ago it charmed Sumerian ears.

In Europe, however, except for the *Aulos* of modern Greece and the *Kaval* of Bulgaria, the use of the single vertical tube has practically disappeared, although in Italy an attempt was made by Signor Giorgi a few years ago to revive it in an improved form. Its use, however, seems to have lingered among the peasant folk of our country districts for many centuries, for in the illustrations which adorn a manuscript of the early fourteenth century, known as Queen Mary's Psalter (Brit. Mus., 2 B. vii), which was written and illuminated in England, we see a goatherd playing on such a rustic instrument, and with the left hand opening or closing the end of the tube to produce a variety of sound. On the other side of the listening animals is another musician, as Phyllis to his Corydon, playing upon the shawm. This unique example is shown on Plate 28.

Fig. 25 Recorder – 12th cent.   Fig. 26 Recorder – 13th cent.
(Glasgow)   (Oxford)

As the production of a good tone on the simple tube with open ends is difficult, attempts were made at a very early period in the history of the human race to facilitate the process by improving the mouthpiece. A notch was cut in the pipe and the upper part filled with a resinous substance or a wooden plug, save where a small opening allowed a thin stream of air to play on the *fipple* or lower lip of the notch: and hence was evolved the principle which gave to Greeks and Romans the organ pipe, and to medieval Europe the whistle-headed flute, called THE RECORDER or FIPPLE FLUTE, which has played so interesting a part in the music of our own country. The earliest English illustration of the Recorder is given in the twelfth-century

Psalter now in the University Library, Glasgow. As will be seen from Fig. 25, the performer is grappling with the fingering of the instrument. Other reliable examples appear in the Ormesby Psalter in the Bodleian Library (Fig. 26), and among the choir-stall carvings in Chichester Cathedral, both being of the thirteenth century. In the former case the position in which the instrument is held is very characteristic. An early Continental instance is found in a Latin Psalter of the eleventh century in the Bibliothèque Nationale at Paris (No. 1118).

As a more primitive instrument, however, it was known from prehistoric days, when it was probably used for trapping birds by imitating their song as it has since been used for teaching them to sing (Plate 30). It is supposed that for this reason it received the name of Recorder, the phrase "to record" being especially applied to the notes of birds; but as the idea underlying the word is that of repeating or recalling, it may refer to the facility with which this pipe repeats in an upper octave the notes of the lower.[1] The name occurs in the English literature of the late fourteenth and early fifteenth centuries, as in the passage from *The Squyr of Lowe Degre*, quoted in full on page 48, and also in the old Cornish drama *Ordinale de Origine Mundi*; another will be found in Lydgate's *Bochas* (*c.* 1440): "Pan of recorders fond fyrst the melodies." The *Promptuarium Parvulorum* of the same date describes it as a "lytyll pipe, *Canula*"; but the sixteenth and seventeenth centuries saw the days of its greatest popularity: indeed, it was so practised and esteemed in this country that it was generally known as the *Fistula Anglica*, or English Flute, in contradistinction to the *Fistula Germanica* or *Helvetica*, the transverse flute commonly in use at the present day. Shakespeare's allusions to this instrument in his plays *Hamlet* and *Midsummer Night's Dream* are too well known to require quotation. It may be necessary, however, to remark that in the first of the two passages (*Hamlet*, act iii, sc. 2) the "ventages" are the holes pierced in the Recorder for the fingers and thumb, and the "stops" are the required positions of the fingers for the several notes, which Hamlet shows to the spying Guildenstern, who, however, cannot understand them so easily as he thinks he can understand the Prince. The fingering is again alluded to in the second passage (*Midsummer Night's Dream*, act v, sc. 1), with a play on the words "stop" and "not in government", i.e. not under proper control, as an older and more experienced player would have it.

[1] A new document bearing on the history and etymology of the recorder has been discussed by Brian Trowell in his note on "King Henry IV, Recorder-Player", *GSJ*, X, pp. 83–4. The document, dated 1388, uses the spelling "Ricordo", which is the Italian word for a keepsake or memento.

The reference to the Recorder in the Lekingfelde Proverbs of a century earlier will be found at the head of this chapter. It reminds us that the instrument was made, like others of its own day, in various sizes, usually divided into Treble, Mean, and Bass, the first and last being an octave apart in pitch, and the Mean, which did duty for Counter Tenor (alto), and Tenor either a fourth or fifth above the Bass. The compass of each was two octaves, the lowest note of the deepest instruments being at first f; but during the sixteenth century they were made of greater length, so that the Bass was able to descend to c, and the Great Bass Recorder to F or even to D, the length of the latter being over eight feet, a giant in stature but a baby in voice. Owing to the size of the deeper instruments a crooked tube of brass was required through which the wind was conducted from the player's mouth to the orifice of the whistle. This is shown in Plate 29, where two sets of Recorders representing two distinct periods are depicted. Though at first sight this tube resembles that of the Bassoon, it must be borne in mind that it in no way increased the sounding length, which was confined to the wooden portion of the instrument. Smaller Recorders were also made, pitched as much as an octave above the usual treble instrument mentioned above; and at the opening of the seventeenth century there were, according to Praetorius, eight instruments of graded sizes in a perfect set: and these could be purchased complete at Venice for about eighty thaler, or £100 present value.[1]

The *Privy Purse Expenses* of Henry VII show that, notwithstanding his frugal mind, he patronized players on the "records"; but his son and successor appears to have made a speciality of the instrument, for at his decease he left seventy-five recorders made of box, walnut, and ivory: they are set out in the transcript of the Inventory given in the Appendix on pages 218–20, and one particularly fine set is thus described:

> Item. a case couvred with crimson vellat havinge locke and all other garnishments to the same of Silver gilte with viii Recorders of Ivorie in the same case, the two bases garnished with silver and guilte.

There was also "one Greate Base Recorder of woode".

Amongst the King's officers who received a New Year's present from the Princess Mary in 1543 are "The Recorders . . . 10s." The players appear to have been Venetians, and they were quite distinct from "the Flutes". At the funeral of Queen Elizabeth seven Recorder-players were allowed

---

[1] It is not easy to give a present-day (1964) equivalent of eighty thalers in the Venice of Praetorius' day: perhaps £200–£250 is nearer the mark. This price would almost certainly have included the cost of a chest for preserving the instruments safely when not in use.

mourning, five of them Venetians, one a Frenchman, and the other an Englishman. In 1628 there were six belonging to the King's Music;[1] but at a masque presented at Windsor in 1674 this number was reduced to four, for the larger forms of the instrument had disappeared. In the more portable sizes, however, the Recorder was still much admired. Pepys, under the year 1668, writes of his visit to the pipemaker in the following words: "To Dumbleby's, and there did talk a great deal about pipes; and did buy a recorder, which I do intend to learn to play on, the sound of it being of all sounds most pleasing to me"; and a further entry tells us how, when at home, he applied himself "to the fingering of my Recorder and getting of the Scale of Musique without Book", a process which he considered troublesome but necessary. Humphrey Salter, fifteen years after this, published exact directions for the instrument under the title *The Genteel Companion*; probably Mr Pepys' efforts were directed towards learning by heart the intricate fingering of the higher notes, technically known as cross-fingering. In 1679 Evelyn informs us that "the Flute Douce[2] is now much in request for accompanying the voice"; here he uses the French name, derived, as the Italian also was, from the soft sweet tone, a characteristic which was noticed by Chaucer, who, in his *House of Fame* (c. 1384), says that the great array of musicians played "both in doucet and in rede" or, as we should say, "on Recorders and Shawms". Lydgate also associates the two classes of wind instruments, so different in their tone and effect, when he writes "Lowde shalmys and doucettes".

In the first half of the eighteenth century sets of the smaller Recorders continued to be made; there is a complete set of four instruments by Bressan preserved in the Grosvenor Museum at Chester; and in the later of the two sets in Plate 29 the Alto and Tenor instruments bear the name of Stanesby, as father and son the most famous of English pipemakers.[3] Although, as the "Common Flute", its popularity was fast waning before the increasing attention given to the German Flute, yet it survived for some time under

---

[1] For a note on the court wind-players and their music, see Thurston Dart, "The Repertory of the Royal Wind Music", *GSJ*, XI, pp. 70–7. Selections from this repertory have been published by Oxford University Press.

[2] This name seems to have been given to the new and improved kind of recorder perfected at the court of Louis XIV by the Hotteterres and their colleagues. See Joseph Marx, "The Tone of the Baroque Oboe", *GSJ*, IV, pp. 3–19.

[3] See Eric Halfpenny's two articles, "Biographical Notices of the Early English Wood-wind-making School", *GSJ*, XII, pp. 44–52, and "Further Light on the Stanesby Family", *GSJ*, XIII, pp. 59–69. For more recent studies on the recorder in England, see the *Proceedings of the Royal Musical Association* (83rd Session, pp. 49–63) and Walter Bergmann, "Henry Purcell's Use of the Recorder", in *Music, Libraries and Instruments* (Hinrichsen, 1961), pp. 227–32.

Fig. 27 Flageolet Music by Thomas Greeting (*Pleasant Companion*, 1672)

(*Transcription by Thurston Dart*)

another name. For though the whistle-headed Flutes of the early nineteenth century are generally called Flageolets, they were, nevertheless, small Recorders with the typical thumb-hole but a modified scale and fingering (Plate 30). In fact, they were called "English Flutes" by the makers. On the other hand the present Penny Whistle cannot be considered a Recorder or English Flute, as the thumb-hole is absent.

An exhaustive description of the Recorder and the literature relating to it was given by Mr Welch in a paper read before the members of the Musical Association in 1898 and published in his *Six Lectures on the Recorder*.[1]

The true construction of the FLAGEOLET – or the French Flageolet, as it was called, from its extensive use in that country – is frequently overlooked.

[1] Reprinted in part (O.U.P., 1961), with an introduction by Edgar Hunt.

Its peculiar characteristic consists in this, that there are but four holes or ventages in the front of the instrument while there are *two* holes – one for each thumb – at the back. The name is a diminutive form of the old medieval word Flageol, which was applied to Flutes in general; thus we find that in the year 1274 Philip the Hardy's Master of the Flute-players was called by the grandiloquent title of *Rex flaioletus* and the fifteenth-century writer of the *Promptuarium Parvulorum*, when he explains the "Flowte Pipe", adds, as an illustrative quotation, "the schepherd under the folde syngythe well with his gugawe the pype", which shows us that it was a small trivial instrument, probably as readily cast aside as easily made (cf. p. 116 n.). It was constructed of reed, elder, bone, even rush, and Virdung, in 1511, calls it the Ruspfeife, which is said to mean "black pipe", but is more probably a corruption of Ruschpfeife – the Rush-pipe, a simple translation of *calamaula*, the shepherd's pipe. Of its use in England we hear but little till the middle of the seventeenth century, when French fashions abounded, and the "Flageolet", which, according to the French writer Mersenne, was considered of all instruments the most *gentil*, came in with the four-and-twenty fiddlers and the rest. It had already been introduced into the ballroom, but was now studied by amateurs under competent masters. In *Samuel Pepys, Lover of Musique*, the author reminds us that the enthusiastic Secretary of the Admiralty not only lived with his beloved "flageolette" in his pocket that he might pipe on it whilst waiting for his dinner or riding on the coach, but, how, with the help of Master Thomas Greeting, one of the King's musicians, he managed to make his wife play upon it "very prittily – quite beyond my expectations". Sir Frederick Bridge very properly and fortunately possessed Mr Pepys' own copy of Greeting's Instruction Book entitled *The Pleasant Companion, or New Lessons and Instructions for the Flageolet* and published in 1661. From it, by his kind permission, the example of Flageolet music in Fig. 27 was taken and a transcription of the tablature, which has been already explained in Chapter III, is subjoined.[1]

Though remarkable players such as John Banister in England, and Le Vacher in France, were to be found, yet it was reckoned by Thomas Mace, whose heart was set on Lute and Viol, as but a "slight business", and in the closing years of the eighteenth century it was superseded in this country by the modified Recorders already mentioned which were then called Flageolets and were constructed with double or even triple pipes, so that duets and trios, within certain limits, could be played upon them. These

---

[1] For more about the flageolet see Thurston Dart, "Bach's 'Fiauti d'Echo'," *Music & Letters* (October 1960), pp. 331–41. The earliest known edition of Greeting is dated 1672.

interesting instruments, which with the true Flageolet are figured on Plate 30, are always worth preserving when found; and the work of Simpson and Bainbridge, the chief English makers, is remarkably good and ingenious.

Such double flutes were, of course, no new invention; but whether the double Whistle-Flute was known in classical times is doubtful; for most, if not all, of the twin pipes portrayed or discovered are evidently reed-pipes of the Shawm or Clarinet type described in the next chapter. But in the manuscripts and carvings of the Middle Ages the double Whistle-Flute is distinctly shown and can always be recognized by the "notch" which forms the whistle and by the cylindrical shape of the tubes with or without a small expansion

Fig. 28 Double Recorder – early
16th cent. (Cirencester)

at the lower end. In the illustration on Plate 28, taken from an early fourteenth century manuscript of English workmanship (Brit. Mus., 10 E. iv), the two pipes are separate and distinct, but in a sixteenth-century carving on Cirencester Church (Fig. 28) the tubes are united; a difference in arrangement which appears to have been optional, as was also the equality or inequality of the two pipes in length. It is indeed remarkable that in the musical works of medieval writers no description or mention is made of these double Flutes; we are not, however, left in doubt as to their character, for in the library of All Souls College, Oxford, is preserved a double Recorder of late fifteenth or early sixteenth century make, which, by the kind permission of the Warden and Fellows, we have been permitted to inspect and photograph (Plate 35). It is formed of a single block of wood twelve inches in length, through which two parallel tubes have been bored slightly apering towards the lower end. The right-hand or longer pipe is terminated by a small bell, ornamented with a turned bead, and similar to the Recorders of the period. On both pipes there are four finger-holes in front and one behind, and owing to their difference in length their fundamental sounds are at the interval of a fifth apart, the lowest note of the longer pipe being c'' and that of the shorter g''.

It is impossible to make the instrument sound, because it has been badly damaged and the whistle-plugs are lost, which is a matter of no surprise, seeing that it had lain for centuries beneath the soil of the college court. On reproducing the pipes, however, in facsimile the pitch was easily obtained, and it was found that although the larger pipe could only with difficulty be made to ascend above a'', on the smaller pipe the diatonic scale with one or two chromatic notes could be obtained with ease by cross-fingering from g'' to c'''', the extreme limit being two octaves above the lowest note of the longer pipe. It is evident, therefore, that the melody was played on the short pipe, whilst the longer provided a limited second part or a simple ground. In the seventeenth century Double Flutes similarly constructed from one block of wood were in use, but they produced a succession of thirds; and in the same century, one hundred and fifty years before the appearance of Simpson's Double Flageolets mentioned above, Dumbleby, the pipe-maker, had shown Mr Pepys "a fashion of having two pipes of the same note fastened together, so as I can play on one and then echo it upon the other, which is mighty pretty". Upon some such double Flute Banister was a noted player in the early years of the next century.

There was yet another form of Whistle-Flute which took a prominent part in the lighter music of our country. It was technically known as the Three-holed Flute, but is more familiar to us under the English name of Tabor-pipe, for it was usually associated with the rhythmic beat of a small drum. It seems to have been introduced into England from France, where it was in general use during the twelfth century, and soon took its place with the bagpipe and rebec for country dancing. Owing to its purely cylindrical bore this little Whistle-Flute, though possessing but two finger-holes in front and one for the thumb behind, was capable of producing, by the aid of harmonic sounds, a diatonic scale of one and a half octaves from g'' to c'''' with many chromatic intervals, while there were four lower notes from g' to c'', which were usually put outside the practical scale (Plates 28, 30).

The pipe being held and played by the left hand set the right hand free to beat the Tabor or small drum, which was generally hung on the left arm or fastened to the left shoulder; by this means marked rhythm and cheerful melody were combined. In the early days of its popularity the pipe was made about twenty-four or thirty inches in length, and its pitch was an octave or more deeper than that given above, for the English instrument, when it disappeared in the middle of the last century, was but little over a foot long. The size of the drum also has varied. The instrument used by the piper who in 1599 accompanied William Kempe's "Nine daies Wonder of a Morris Dance from London to Norwich", was, as shown in the published account of his performance, of the long and deep model usually employed on the

Continent and still surviving in the modern Tenor Drum; but the typical English Tabor was shallow and provided with a string or snare across one of the parchment heads. It is depicted on Plate 28, as represented in an early fourteenth-century manuscript (Brit. Mus., 10 E. iv), and in its later form in Plate 30. Measurements taken of old English Tabors give the following sizes: $2\frac{3}{4}$ in. in depth by $8\frac{1}{2}$ in. in diameter, and $5\frac{1}{2}$ in. in depth by 14 in. in diameter. The allusions in English literature to these instruments, which we have associated in our description because they were combined in practice, are as frequent as their representations are in illumination and carving. Their light music is contrasted by Shakespeare in *Much Ado About Nothing* (act ii, sc. 3) with the martial strains of Drum and Fife, as being far more after Claudio's inclination when he was in love; and in *A Quest of Inquirie* (1595) the author draws from them a solemn lesson: "Good people, beware of wooer's promises; they are like the musique of a tabor and pipe; the pipe says, 'golde, gifts and many gay things', but performance is moralized by the tabor, which bears the burden of 'I doubt it, I doubt it'."

Though usually played by one and the same person, instances are to be found in which the labour is divided; as, for example, in the late fourteenth-century Psalter of Humphrey de Bohun preserved at Exeter College, Oxford, where one plays the pipe and his companion the drum.

A famous performer of the countryside was old Hall of Herefordshire, who, born soon after Henry VIII came to the throne, was still at his play in 1609 though ninety-seven years of age – "giving the men light hearts by thy pipe and the women light heels by thy tabor. O wonderful piper! O admirable tabor man!" exclaims the enthusiastic chronicler. In the middle of the seventeenth century John Price was known on the Continent as England's greatest performer, and so the merry music went on till the middle of the last century, Oxfordshire (where it was called the Whittle and Dub) and the adjacent counties being its last home. In an old Oxfordshire cottage there lately hung from an ancient beam the Tabor of bygone days, no longer to set the feet a-going, but to act as a weather prophet by the stretching of its time-worn skin.

A yet shorter form of the Three-holed Pipe – only four inches long – formerly in use is shown on Plate 29, and it was brought into special prominence by the wonderful performance of a blind peasant named Picco, who first played in London in 1856; by the use of the palm or the second finger of the right hand, which was placed on the lower end of the tube, he was able, it is said, to obtain a compass of three octaves. Still constructed as a toy, like the Pipes of Bartholomew Fair ridiculed by Mace, it is the last, as well as the least, of the Recorder family.

Of the Flute blown crosswise or THE TRANSVERSE FLUTE, which was commonly known in England in the eighteenth and nineteenth centuries as the German Flute, the early history, so far as our country is concerned, is far more simple than that of the Recorder, because it is so meagre. It is, however, a mistake to suppose, as some writers have done, that our use of the instrument dates from the days of Purcell and Handel. It was certainly admired and practised in the year 1500 or shortly afterwards, as will presently be shown.

The European origin of the Cross Flute (as we shall call it for distinction's sake) is traceable to Eastern influence, for both in India and China it has been a favourite instrument from remote antiquity. It probably came into Europe first of all through Byzantine influence, and is portrayed in ivory carvings and manuscripts of the tenth and eleventh centuries, as, for instance, on caskets in the National Museum at Florence (tenth century) and in the Victoria and Albert Museum, London (eleventh century); also in Greek manuscripts preserved in the Bibliothèque Nationale at Paris (tenth century) and in the British Museum (Add. MS. 19352, eleventh century). Through the same influence it appears in the eleventh-century paintings of the cathedral at Kiev in Russia. Gradually its use was extended into Germany, Spain, and Southern France, where in the thirteenth century we find it as the popular instrument of the Minnesingers; it is illustrated in the *Hortus Deliciarum* written by Herrade de Langsberg, an Alsatian abbess of the twelfth century.

The French poets Machault and Deschamps of the fourteenth century call it the *fleuste* or *fleuthe traversaine*, and, in the celebrated manuscript of the Romance of Alexander, treasured in the Bodleian Library at Oxford, which was illuminated in Flanders by Jehan de Grise in 1344, it is frequently portrayed among the other instruments of the period. In indisputable English work it does not appear till the sixteenth century; on the crozier of William of Wykeham it is seen in the plaques which decorate the crook, but they are of French origin, and it is entirely absent from old English ecclesiastical carvings. Yet shortly before the commencement of the sixteenth century it is mentioned – for the first time, so far as we know – in the *Privy Purse Expenses* of Henry VII, for we find that in 1492 when the King was at his palace of Shene £3 10s. was paid to Guillim for "flotes with a case". A careful distinction seems to have been made in these and similar English writings at that time between "recorders" and "flutes", and we have little doubt but that the instruments for which the King gave so large a sum (about £35) were highly ornamented Cross-Flutes from France or Flanders. His son, Henry VIII, had, indeed, a remarkable collection of them, some tipped with gold and enamelled black, others of ivory and of glass, Flutes called "pilgrim staves" and probably made like the Walking-stick Flutes of later days, as well as "vi phiphes [fifes] of blacke Ibonie tipped withe Silver" – seventy-eight in all. In 1543 we find the Princess Mary making a New Year's gift of ten shillings to the "Flutes" in the King's band, as she did also to the "Recorders". For at King Henry's death there were five Flutes and one Fyfer amongst his musicians, and at the funeral of his daughter Elizabeth there were present seven Flutes as well as seven Recorders. An eye-witness of the decorations erected in 1575 to welcome this much-visiting Queen to Kenilworth observed amongst them a trophy of musical instruments which included "luts, violls, shallms, cornets, flutes, recorders and harpes". And in 1602 Sir Thomas Kytson of Hengrave Hall died possessed of "two flewtes without cases" as well as one case of seven Recorders. Lord Bacon, in his *Sylva Sylvarum* of 1627, draws a sharp distinction between the "recorders which go with a gentle breath" and the flutes and fifes which will not give a sound by a blast at the end as recorders do, but are blown at a small hole in the side. As illustrations from English sources of the sixteenth century we have reproduced in Plate 54 part of a painting in the National Portrait Gallery representing a masque which took place at the marriage of Sir Henry Unton: while in Fig. 47 is shown an engraving from Spenser's *Shephearde's Calendar* (1579), where the month of April is prefaced by a scene depicting four ladies playing on the Lute, Viol, Harp, and Cross-Flute whilst the shepherd sounds the Cornett.

All through the seventeenth century we trace the existence of the Flute in England: Nicholas Lanier, Musician for the Flute under Queen Elizabeth, was succeeded in 1618 by Andrew his son; it was his duty to keep two boys for the purpose of instructing them in the art of "Lez Flutes et Cornetts". In 1667, Flutes and Recorders are again mentioned, and in 1683 Henry Purcell was appointed "keeper, maker, repairer, mender and tuner of all and every His Majesty's Musical Wind Instruments, that is to say, virginalls, organs, flutes, recorders and all other kind of wind instruments whatsoever". His wages were £60 with allowance for the cost of materials required. At his death in 1695 Dr John Blow and Bernard Smith, generally known as "Father Smith", succeeded to the office – Flutes as well as Recorders being again mentioned. This will suffice to show that the German Flute, though probably brought into greater vogue by the Hanoverian succession, was no new-comer to this country in the eighteenth century. In what way and by what steps it was altered from the one-keyed instrument of that time to the "Concert Flute" of the present day is beyond the scope of this work. Such details will be found in such a book as R. S. Rockstro's *History of the Flute*, and in an interesting lecture delivered by Mr John Finn at the exhibition held by the Musicians' Company in 1904 which has since been published in a volume of the Music Story Series entitled *English Music*. It is, however, to be observed that the bore of the earliest Cross-Flutes was cylindrical; but towards the close of the seventeenth century, though the head joint remained the same, the rest of the tube was made conical and smaller at the open end than where it fitted into the head joint, an alteration which was probably due to the French maker Hotteterre. So it remained till 1847, when Boehm reverted to the old cylindrical bore for the lower part of the instrument and contracted the head joint at its closed end, and this is the form now usually adopted. The Octave Flute or Fife, which had retained its old cylindrical bore till the early part of the last century, has been altered to the conical shape which was discarded in the larger instrument by Boehm. Tenor and Bass Flutes have also been constructed, and sixteenth-century speci-mens preserved in the Museo Civico at Verona must have required giants to play them, the Bass, whose lowest note is *c*, being three feet seven inches long with a bore an inch in diameter. Attempts have been made from time to time to revive these deeper-toned instruments; one of the most successful was McGregor's Bass Flute, an octave below the ordinary Flute, which was brought out in London in 1810, the head being recurved after the French fashion of the late eighteenth century. Illustrations of this and a Tenor instrument, with flutes of various periods, will be seen on Plate 31. Of the smaller instruments of this class the most interesting is the FIFE, which, from its use by the Swiss in conjunction with the Drum for military purposes was generally known in the sixteenth century as the "Swiss Pipe". For a like purpose it was introduced into this country (Fig. 44), and amongst the musicians of Henry VIII at his death was "Olyver Fyfer" who played the Fife; to the instruments in the Royal Collection we have already alluded. The Fife seems to have been brought into use shortly before 1530, when the drummers and the fifers were procured from the Continent for the King's Band. In 1539 we find the citizens of London mustering with Drums and Fifes; and George Ferrers, who, as Lord of Misrule at the Christmas festivi-ties of Edward VI, had to give directions for the necessary preparations, writes: "I have provided one to plaie upon a Kettell Drom with his boye, and a nother Drome with a fyffe which must be apparelled like turkes garments." Again, in 1557, when an army was dispatched to St Quentin, in France, a "drumme and phife" at 1s. each per diem were attached to the train of artillery. The shrill notes of the instrument, however, were not appreciated by all, and doubts were raised as to whether the soldier's attention might not be distracted "by the aire of a whistle" from the signals given by the Drum; so in the reign of James II it was banished from the army, for in many regiments the hautboy had already taken its place. In 1748 it was restored, and has been recognized ever since as one of the best instruments for the march.

Fifes and Drums also took part in dramatic representations, for in *Gorboduc*, the first tragedy of the English stage, set forth before the Queen in 1561, the directions are that, as a prelude to act v, which is of a military character, the "Drommes and Flutes" are to play. So also they enlivened the Lord Mayor's Shows of the sixteenth century, and in time became so popular a form of "noyse" for attracting a crowd, that in 1671 a warrant was issued by Charles II for the apprehension of all persons beating Drums, sounding Trumpets, or playing Fifes at dumb shows or models without the licence of His Majesty's Sergeant Trumpeter. From which it is evident that Shakespeare was not the only Englishman who had suffered from the "vile squeaking of the wry-necked fife".

Note for p. 109, added by Canon Galpin to the Third Edition (1932): "Two little whistle-flutes (13th or 14th century) were discovered at Old Sarum and are now in the Museum at Salisbury. One has four holes, the other three. They are made from the tibia of a swan."

PLATE 27

1. Spinet by Baker Harris, *c.* 1750

2. Square Piano by J. Zumpe and Bundebart, London, 1770

PLATE 28

1. Shawm and Vertical Flute, early fourteenth century

2. A Gymnastic Display, accompanied by the Pipe and Tabor and
the Double Recorder, early fourteenth century

Chapter IX

Shawm and Pipe

A Shawme makithe a swete sounde, for he tunythe basse;
It mountithe not to hy, but kepithe rule and space.
Yet yf it be blowne withe to a vehement wynde,
It makithe it to mysgoverne oute of his kinde.

Lekingfelde proverb (*temp.* Henry VIII)

IT HAS OFTEN BEEN ASSUMED that instruments played with the double reed, of which the Oboe and its predecessor the Shawm are typical examples, were introduced into Western Europe at the time of the Crusades; and though we must admit that the closer contact of Europeans with Eastern customs and usages, which the Holy Wars of the twelfth and thirteenth centuries afforded, was probably responsible for the altered form and prominent position which musical instruments of this class assumed at the close of the Middle Ages – for such instruments, as shown in Plate 34, are greatly favoured by Oriental musicians – yet it is very evident, from the illustrations and word-names which exist in the Western languages, that the use of the double reed was generally known, not only in France, Spain, and Germany, but in our own country also many centuries before the crusading spirit called our warriors to distant travel.

For instance, in the supplement to Aelfric's Saxon Vocabulary of the tenth or early eleventh century, the Latin *auloedus* is translated "reodpipere". Nor is it difficult to trace the origin of such usage, for wherever Roman civilization extended (and we do not find any mention of reed-pipes, as we do of the Crot and the Horn, in purely Celtic times) there the *tibiae*, pipes sounded with a double reed, were always found. We see them in our own island figured on a legionary stone discovered near the eastern end of Hadrian's Wall at Bridgeness on the Forth, a relic of the past which is now in the National Museum of Antiquities at Edinburgh; and, though they have recently been claimed by an enthusiastic Scotch writer as bagpipes, this is not so, for their character is unmistakable. Two manuscripts of the Latin author Prudentius, now preserved in the British Museum (Add. MS. 24199 and Cleop. C. viii) and dating from the tenth and eleventh centuries, show

K117

the double pipes as an accompaniment to the dance; though in estimating the value of these works by English artists as portraying instruments of their own time and country, it must be remembered that they were dealing with a Latin author, and also appear to have seen yet earlier drawings by a Rhenish draughtsman. The same may be said of the single and double pipes which are depicted in the illustrations of the Harleian manuscript (Harl. 603) which are of the same period, but evidently inspired by those in the so-called Utrecht Psalter, which are supposed to have been designed at Rheims during the ninth century after Byzantine or Graeco-Egyptian drawings of an earlier date.

Better authorities are the sculptured crosses of Ireland which frequently display the use of the reed-pipe, as at Monasterboice (ninth to tenth centuries) where single pipes appear, and at Clonmacnoise (early tenth century), where double pipes are shown. From the shape of these pipes and the absence of a marked bell at the lower end of the instrument, we may infer that they were lineal descendants of the ancient Roman *tibiae*, as found in the chanter or melody pipe of the Irish bagpipe at the present time.

It is in Norman carving that we first observe reed-pipes of the typical SHAWM class with an expanding bell and a conical tube: in this form the single pipe appears on the Prior's Door at Ely, erected about the year 1200, and at Barfreston in work of the twelfth century, whilst it is grotesquely but clearly portrayed in the mouth of a goat on one of the capitals in the crypt of Canterbury Cathedral carved in the same century. An illustration of this interesting example is given in Fig. 29. In English manuscripts it appears in the Ormesby Psalter (*c.* 1290), now in the Bodleian Library, Oxford, and in that of about the same date formerly in the possession of Bishop Grandisson of Exeter (Brit. Mus. Add. 21926). In the fourteenth century illustrations are much more frequent, for it had then begun to take a definite place in the wind-bands of the period. This is shown on the Braunche Brass[1] at Lynne, where a Shawm and two long Trumpets are represented as being played at the "Peacock" feast, perhaps that given in honour of King John of France. It also adorns the Minstrels' Gallery[2] at Exeter Cathedral, and we are told by the author of the fourteenth-century romance *Lybeaus Desconus* that both "trumpes and schalmuses" were used "for hyegh days in the halle". It is well displayed in a fourteenth-century Psalter of East Anglian work preserved at Lambeth Palace (MS. 233), of which, by the kind permission of

[1] See John Page-Phillips and Thurston Dart, "The Peacock Feast", *GSJ*, VI, pp. 95–8. The brass is reproduced at Pl. X of this issue, from the original at King's Lynn.
[2] Which was in fact the gallery for the organ; no minstrel ever set foot in it.

His Grace the Archbishop of Canterbury, we are able to give a reproduction in Fig. 30; and it is to be seen in combination with other instruments in Plate 53, taken from an early fifteenth-century manuscript (Brit. Mus., I E. ix). The representation of a lady shawmist from the Luttrell Psalter on Plate 33 shows the "tuning" holes bored in the bell, which are characteristic of the earlier shawms and oboes and are still to be found in the Oriental instruments of the present day.

In the early thirteenth century the Shawm does not seem to have been one

Fig. 29 Shawm – 12th cent. (Canterbury)

of the instruments which an accomplished jongleur was expected to play, but by the later minstrels it was readily adopted; and, as by the order of King Henry III, watchmen (waytes) were established in London and other cities, who also made midnight merry with their minstrelsies, the popular instrument assumed the title of the watchman's craft and was called the *Wayghte* or *Wayte Pipe*. The third Edward had three Wayghtes in his Royal Music, and the fourth retained among his thirteen minstrels some with "shalms and small pipes" and, in addition, a "waite" who was required to

119

pipe watch nightly from Michaelmas to Shrove Tuesday four times, and on the summer nights three times and to make "bon gayte" (a good noise) at every chamber door and office as well for fear of "pickers and pillers". Such a minstrel "waite" is shown among the five quaint little figures carved on the well-known Minstrel's Pillar in St Mary's Church, Beverley; his companions are playing on the Pipe and Tabor (though only the top of the Pipe in his mouth is left), the Viol, of which only a small portion remains on the left shoulder, the Harp, of which nothing survives except part of the soundbox, and the Lute, which is unusually perfect.

Fig. 30 Shawm – 14th cent. (Lambeth)

In a *Nominale* of the fifteenth century we find the medieval Latin word *colomaula* (i.e. *calamaula*, a reed-pipe, whence *chalemelle* and *shawm*) is translated "wayte pipe", and in a seventeenth-century manuscript in the British Museum (Harl. 2027) there is a sketch of a "Howboye or a Wayte or a Shawm" – all three names being applied to the one illustration. From the *Edinburgh Town Council Register* for the year 1694 we gather that one Robert Imrie was appointed "one of the good towne's waits or hoyeboyes". Records of payments to these minstrels or waits, both from the royal purse as well as by town corporations and private persons, are so plentiful that it is unnecessary to particularize them. Here are two widely removed in date:

    1438. Livery to the town minstrels voc. waytes. (Shrewsbury Bailiff's
    Accounts.)
    1619. Payde to the Waightes of the citie for ther servyce on all the five
    dayes the somme of £2 13s. 4d. (Lord Mayor of London's Pageant.)

With the Christmas Waits the name, as we know, has only recently become
extinct, and the office is now merged into those of our police bands and
municipal orchestras.

The principle of the Shawm is familiar to most of us because it is still to
be seen in the modern Oboe. The sound is produced by the vibration of two
flat pieces of thin cane whose edges are set in motion by the breath of the
player. In its simplest form this double reed is easily made, and country
children often construct it from the stalks of the dandelion or the hollow
tubes of green rushes. A very interesting survival of a rustic pipe of this
kind is to be seen – if not now extinct – in the Oxfordshire Whithorn or May
Horn, carefully described by Mr Henry Balfour in a paper printed in the
Reliquary (1896) and illustrated on Plate 34. In this case the reed is made of
the green bark of the young willow, the body of the instrument is made of
stouter bark twisted into a conical shape and fixed together with hawthorn
prickles. The writer tells us that this crude Shawm was annually made for the
Whit-Monday Hunt which took place in the forest. In the late fourteenth or
early fifteenth centuries the Shawms were made, like the Recorders, in
various sizes, the larger being called Bumbardes. Hence in the *Confessio
Amantis* (1393) Gower speaks of "the sounde of bumbarde and of clarionne
with cornemuse and shalmele": and in the *Squyr of Lowe Degre* we are told
"ther was myrth and melody . . . with pypes, organ and bumbarde". A
bumbarde depicted in the early fifteenth-century carvings of the nave at
Beverley Minster is shown in Fig. 31. Virdung, in the early sixteenth
century, and Praetorius a hundred years later give us illustrations of these
various forms which, at the later date, numbered seven different sizes from
the Great Bass Shawm or Gross Doppel Quint-pommer which descended
to F', to the Treble Shawm or Klein Discant Schalmey which ascended
to b'''.

This will explain the allusions which we find in English literature to the
"shrillest shawm", as Drayton calls it in his *Polyolbion*; and also to the Shawm
that "tunethe the Bass" mentioned in the Lekingfelde inscriptions quoted
at the head of this chapter. The actual compass of each instrument, however,
was not great, only about one and a half octaves, though the sounds of the

Bass Shawms were extended downwards by additional keys. A set of these instruments will be seen on Plate 32; the perforated box which appears upon the tube just above the bell is intended to protect and cover the mechanism of the key or keys concealed beneath it; the key is visible in the Tenor Shawm there shown, owing to the removal of the box.

King Henry VIII had many "Schalms" in his great collection, as will be observed in the list given in the Appendix, page 219. Shawms called "Pilgrims' Staves" were more like the older Reed-pipes, being of considerable

length with a narrow bore: they were so called, says Mersenne, because they were used by the pilgrims to the shrine of St James at Compostella to while away the tedium of the journey, as bagpipes also were used. Similar instruments, when turned up like a crook at the lower end, were known as Crumhorns or Cromornes: these also the King possessed, having several sets of from four to seven instruments in each. They are probably the "still pipes" mentioned as forming part of the orchestra in Gascoigne's tragedy of *Jocasta*, acted at Gray's Inn in 1566; and Sir William Leighton, in his *Teares and Lamentacions of a Sorrowfull Soule* (1613), calls them Crouncorns. Mersenne, the French writer mentioned above, tells us that when he wrote his great work on Musical Instruments in 1636, they were still made in England; but a diligent search has failed to find any specimens or even English illustrations of their use. Even continental examples are extremely rare. Cremona, the name of a reed-stop on the modern Organ, is taken from this instru-

Fig. 31 Bumbarde –
15th cent. (Beverley)

ment, and, if well voiced, closely resembles its soft veiled tone. A specimen of the Cromorne is exhibited on Plate 32.

From the *Privy Purse Expenses* we find that in 1530 the King paid 26s. 8d. for a "shalme", and "for 2 sagbuttes, 2 tenor shalmes and two trebull shalmuse", £10 10s.

The name "Howeboie", in place of the word Shalm, first appears in the reign of Queen Elizabeth. In 1561 the tragedy *Gorboduc, or Porrex and Ferrex*, was set forth before the Queen, and as a prelude to the fourth act, which represented Furies and Murder, there was the "Musicke of Howeboies". In 1562 we are informed by the *Scottish Treasurer's Account* that the "Trumpeters and Howbois" received a New Year's gift of ten crowns by order of Queen Mary, and in 1575 the music of the Lord Mayor of London's Pageant was varied by "a sett of hautboits playinge".

The word, which is variously spelt as above, and also as Hoboy, Hoeboy (as in Shakespeare), Howboy, Hautboy, and now Oboe, is probably derived from the pitch – the *Haut-bois*, i.e. the "high wood" – and appears to have been first applied in France to a form of treble Shawm, perhaps with an improved bore or reed, which enabled the performer to ascend three or four notes higher than the ordinary instrument. It is shown in an early form in Plate 34. In the seventeenth century writers on musical instruments treat it as identical with the Shawm, but in English and Scottish literature the two are constantly mentioned as if distinct. For instance, at the Kenilworth Festivities in 1575 the harmony of "hautbois and shalms" is recorded, and in 1607 we find the magistrates of Edinburgh engaging John Oley to provide five musicians with "chalmes and howboyis" to play through and in the town every day at morning, noon, and night. Probably the word Shawm was retained for the deeper-toned instruments for some time, but in 1665 we read in the records of the King's Music that Isaac Staggins was admitted to it "for the tenner Hoboy". This instrument is mentioned by name and employed by Purcell in the score of his Opera *Dioclesian* (performed 1690, published 1691);[1] its use was long continued in this country, where towards the close of the seventeenth century bands of Hautboys, after the French manner, supplanted the Drums and Fifes for military service. It is probably for this reason that the tenor Oboe was called the *Cor anglais* or English Horn, a title which appears to have been given to it in the early part of the eighteenth century, when on the Continent the Horn, or *Cor de chasse*, an instrument of the same pitch, had already superseded the tenor Oboe in the wind-bands. This suggestion seems to receive some corroboration in an extract taken from a newspaper, which describes a performance given in Paris in 1782, on the *Cor de chasse anglais*. This the writer says, would be more correctly termed a *Cor anglais* or *Hautbois de forêt* – a tenor Oboe with a soft sound. In our country it appears to have been always constructed in a straight form, as shown in Plate 34, with a spreading bell; but when made on the Continent it was curved in the arc of a circle, and the bell was contracted to give a veiled tone (same Plate). The eighteenth-century Oboes,

[1] See Margaret Laurie's revised edition of the full score, published for the Purcell Society in 1961. See also Eric Halfpenny, "The 'Tenner Hoboy'," *GSJ*, V. pp. 17–27, and his important technical surveys of the French Hautboy in nos. VI and VIII of the same periodical.

and Flutes also, were often fitted with an additional and longer upper joint, by the use of which the pitch could be lowered a quarter tone.

Before the close of the sixteenth century another instrument appears in this country called the Curtall. In the Household Accounts of Sir Thomas Kytson, of Hengrave, who died in 1602, is the following entry:

December, 1574. For an instrument called a Curtall . xxx[s].

And in the inventory of his effects there is this item:

Three hoeboys with a curtall and a lysarden.

It is a corruption of the French word *Courtaut*, the name given to a bass instrument with a cylindrical bore made in a "short" form by recurving the tube (Plate 32). A yet shorter instrument of bass pitch with a cylindrical-shaped tube, recurved eight times, was called the *Racket*, or from its quaint appearance, the Sausage Bassoon. In France it was known as the *Cervelat*. Mersenne, in his work on musical instruments, gives an illustration and description of the Courtaut and says it was rare in his day; but Praetorius, in 1618, informs his readers that the English "Corthol" was identical with the Bassoon or Fagotto, and this it certainly was in the later years of the seventeenth century. It is not known to whom we are indebted for the simple device of recurving the long straight tube of the deeper-toned Shawms; the idea is embodied in the *Phagotum* of Canon Afranio, constructed about the year 1539, but his instrument was an elaborated form of Bagpipe and furnished with single beating reeds of metal.[1] The "short instruments called Dulceuses", which were in Henry VIII's possession at his death, were a form of Curtall, for the name Dolcian or Dulcino was also given to it, as it was to the Bassoon of later days. It seems therefore, that this form of instrument was invented, probably in Italy, about the year 1540, and that it was at first used for instruments with a cylindrical bore throughout, as in the *Phagotum*. The convenience and portability of the shape becoming at once recognized, it was applied to instruments with a conical bore like the Shawms. Praetorius enumerates five different sizes, and tells us that in his country a little form of the instrument was the "single" Corthol and a larger size the "double" Corthol. A single Curtall is depicted on Plate 32. In a manuscript in the British Museum (Harl. 2027), dated 1688, a sketch is given of a Curtall, which closely resembles a small Bassoon in shape, and the author tells us that the double Curtall is "8 notes deeper than other

[1] See William A. Cocks, "The Phagotum: An Attempt at Reconstruction", *GSJ*, XII, pp. 57-9.

PLATE 29

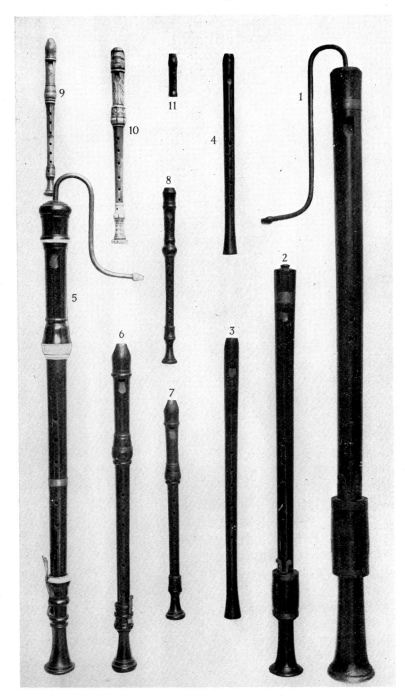

1–4. A set of Recorders as used *c.* 1600. 5–8. A set of Recorders, eighteenth century. 9–10. Recorders of Ivory, eighteenth century. 11. Picco Pipe

PLATE 30

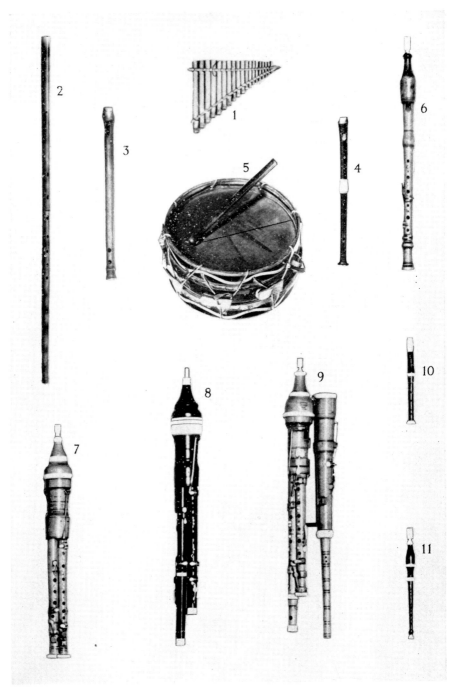

1. Panpipes. 2. Nay or Vertical Flute. 3. Tabor Pipe. 4. Tabor Pipe by Potter, eighteenth century. 5. Tabor by Potter. 6. Flageolet, early nineteenth century. 7. & 8. Double Flageolets by Simpson, early nineteenth century. 9. Triple Flageolet by Bainbridge, early nineteenth century. 10. Flageolet by Thibouville, eighteenth century. 11. Bird Pipe, c. 1800

PLATE 31

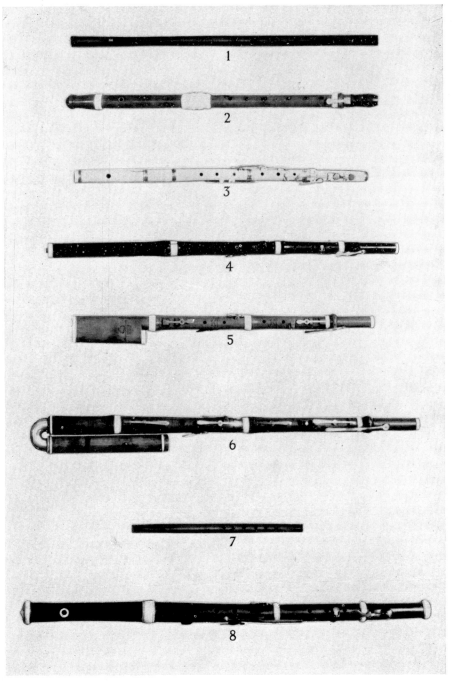

1. Flute as used *c.* 1600. 2. Flute by Chevalier, *c.* 1670. 3. Flute of Ivory by Potter.
4. Alto Flute by Potter, eighteenth century. 5. Tenor Flute by McGregor, 1810.
6. Bass Flute by McGregor, 1810. 7. Fife, eighteenth century. 8. Bass Flute by
Bainbridge, early nineteenth century

PLATE 32

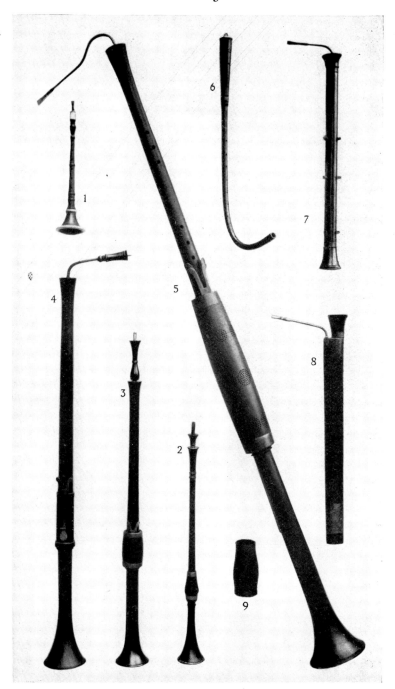

1. Bombarde, Breton. 2–5. A set of Shawms as used in the early seventeenth century. 6. Crumhorn as used *c.* 1600. 7. Courtaut, after Mersenne, seventeenth century. 8. Single Curtall as used *c.* 1600. 9. Key Cover of Tenor Shawm no. 4

and double the bignesse". This deeper instrument corresponds with Praetorius' description, which informs us that the "doppel Corthol" had the compass of the ordinary Bassoon, without additional keys, viz. from C to g. The use of the words "single" and "double" in this connection is probably due to the old English method of denoting the pitch of the notes in the scale. The note called Tenor C and now usually expressed after the continental fashion with a small c was, in our country, marked by a large or capital C, and called single C, whilst the C an octave below was denoted by CC or double C, the intervening notes below G being also represented by double letters. Therefore a "single" Curtall was one which descended to single C and a "double" Curtall, like a "double" Sackbut, touched CC, or some deep note represented by double letters. In later times the analogy was lost sight of, and a "double" means today any instrument or series of sounds whose pitch is an octave below a recognized standard. A further note on this subject will be found in the Appendix (p. 212).

Dr Cummings, in his interesting *Life of Henry Purcell*, mentions that at a festival service of the Knights of the Garter held at Windsor about the year 1660 a hymn was sung with the additional accompaniment of "two double sackbuts and two double curtalls placed at convenient distances among the classes of the Gentlemen of both Choirs, to the end that all might distinctly hear and consequently keep together both in tune and time"; and in 1662 the double Curtall was used on Sundays and holy days in His Majesty's Chapel Royal; in the following year "three good Curtalls" were purchased for His Majesty's service at £50, and six years later two double Curtalls were bought for £52 for the service of the Queen's Majesty. In 1731 the "Grenadier music" of the Honourable Artillery Company, according to the history of the band, written by Henry Farmer (1904), consisted of "one curtal, three hautbois and no more", but in 1762 the regimental music was altered to "2 trumpets, 2 French horns, 2 bassoons, and 4 hautbois or clarinetts" played by Germans. An English Bassoon will be seen on Plate 34, and the tenor instrument, sometimes called the Tenoroon, is also shown.

The still larger instrument known as the Double Bassoon, four or five notes deeper than Praetorius' largest instrument and an octave below the ordinary Bassoon, appears in the orchestra of the eighteenth century. In the *London Daily Post* of August 6, 1739, we read that "to the usual Evening Concert at Marylebone Gardens will be added two Grand or Double Bassoons made by Mr Stanesby, Senior, the greatness of whose sound surpasses that of any other Bass instrument whatsoever; never performed with before". One of these instruments, which had been made with Handel's approbation, was used the next year by him in his *L'Allegro*, and an amusing advertisement, which appeared in the *General Advertiser* of October 20 – as a skit on the large orchestras of the period, together with the opening of Handel's season at the Haymarket – announced "a concerto of twenty-four bassoons accompanied on the violoncello, intermixed with duets by four double bassoons accompanied by a German flute, the whole blended with numbers of violins, hautboys, fifes, trombones, French horns, trumpets,

Fig. 32 Double Shawm—early 14th cent.
(Luttrell Psalter)

drums and kettledrums, etc." According to Dr Burney, one of Stanesby's double Bassoons was to have been played by Lampe at the Coronation of King George II, but either the player or the reed failed; it was, however, used at the Handel Commemoration in 1784 in Westminster Abbey. The instrument is now in the National Museum at Dublin, where its gigantic proportions are a source of wonder and amusement to visitors. It is eight feet four inches in height and descends to the low $B\flat''$. Modern instruments are generally made with four parallel tubes instead of two, and are therefore shorter but thicker.

Double Shawms, like double Recorders, were used in medieval times, as they had been in those of Greece and Rome; but no details are given as to their construction. Double pipes with separate tubes are depicted in Abbot Litlington's Missal at Westminster Abbey of the late fourteenth century and in the reproduction in Fig. 32, taken from the Luttrell Psalter, written and illuminated in the earlier part of the same century. On the nave of St John's Church, Cirencester (early sixteenth century), and also at Hull the double Shawm appears with the upper parts united in one block.

There is yet another class of reed wind instrument beside that with which we have already dealt. The single or beating reed, which we find in the Clarinet, is an invention of hoary antiquity: it appears in the Egyptian pipes and finds a place in many forms of the modern Bagpipe, both Oriental and European. In our own country, however, it is first seen in connection with a very interesting Celtic instrument called the HORNPIPE, whose festive strains are said to have given the name to the well-known dance. In the six-teenth century there was a dance tune called "a Wales Hornpipe", and the instrument, which Bulstrode Whitelocke in his *Memorials* classes with "northern music", was still to be found in Wales until the middle of the last century, as the Pibcorn, Pibgorn or Cornicyll, and as the Stockhorn or Cornepipe in the Scottish Lowlands. In 1779 the Hon Daines Barrington described the instrument in a paper read before the London Society of Antiquaries, and the Hornpipe which he presented to them on that occasion is still preserved in their rooms at Burlington House. By their kind per-mission we have been allowed to examine and photograph it for this work. The form will be seen in Plate 35. Barrington's paper, published by the Society in the *Archaeologia* for 1779, fortunately gives us an illustration of the reed which was used, and we find that it was of the single-beating type, which renders the instrument distinct from the old English Hautboy, with which it has sometimes been confused. In a portfolio of eighteenth-century drawings and prints of musical subjects in the British Museum is an illustra-tion of a Pibcorn by Moses Griffith. The end of the single reed is shown within a wooden cap.

"The hornepypes of Cornewayle", of which Chaucer speaks in his *Romaunt of the Rose*, are probably identical with this instrument; as the poem, however, is only a translation of a French original, "Cornewayle" may be the well-known district of Brittany. In a fifteenth-century *Nominale* we find "Hornpipe" given as a translation of the Latin *Cornubium* and also of *Salpo*, and, in the *Promptuarium Parvulorum* of the same century, "a Hornpiper" Latinized as *Palpista*, which should probably be *Salpista*. But still more interesting is the word which occurs in a Saxon vocabulary of the eighth century where *Sambucus* – the ordinary name for a pipe – is translated "swegelhorn" – Swegel is connected with the old German *schwägel* formerly used to denote the long bone of the leg below the knee usually called the *tibia*. From this straight bone not only were the Roman pipes originally constructed, but, as we were informed by an aged Welsh peasant many years ago, the *tibia* of the deer – if it could be procured – was con-sidered the best material for the tube of the Pibcorn. We find the same meaning in the old High German *Swegel-bein*, which is explained in medieval

Latin as *"cornus-tibia"* or Hornpipe; the word *bein* occurs in the early English *beme* or *byme* and the Celtic *buinne* as the name of a horn. Swegel-horn then, as Pibcorn, simply means Pipe-horn, a designation which its construction amply warrants. For the ends of the tube, whether it is made of bone, elder, or other convenient substance, are tipped with the horns of cattle, the smaller horn covering the reed (so that, like the Cromorne, it is not touched by the lips) and the larger forming a rudimentary bell, which is generally ornamented with serrations. A Stockhorn in the Museum of Scottish Antiquities at Edinburgh shows the interesting and uncommon form of a double tube like the Egyptian Zummarah; and in the National Museum at Dublin there is a small bone of a deer ornamented and pierced with nine holes, which once probably formed the tube of a Hornpipe, as there are pinholes at the larger end for the horn attachment. The details of the eighteenth-century specimen preserved at the Society of Antiquaries are as follows: length of the wooden tube, $6\frac{1}{2}$ in.; of the upper horn, $4\frac{1}{2}$ in.; of the lower, $7\frac{1}{4}$ in. The bore is $\frac{1}{4}$ in., and the scale produced is $f'\ g'\ a'\ b\flat'$ $c''\ d''\ e''\ f''$. There are six finger-holes in the front and a hole, for the thumb, at the back. The diameter of the holes is $\frac{1}{8}$ in.

Mr Henry Balfour, in an important paper read in 1890 before the members of the Anthropological Institute, draws a comparison between the Hornpipe and similar instruments found in the islands of the Greek Archipelago, in Persia, and in India; and he comes to the conclusion that the Hornpipe probably came in with the Celtic migration and has, within historical times, still held its own in Wales, Cornwall, Lancashire, South Scotland, Ireland and Brittany. It is possible that this is the instrument which is represented on the sculptured Irish cross at Durrow, erected about the year A.D. 1000.[1]

In the seventeenth century a rustic pipe called the Chalumeau, derived like the word shawm from *calamus* (a reed), was raised to the level of a recognized musical instrument and, in the next century, found a place in the scores of Gluck's operas and the pages of Diderot's famous Encyclopaedia. It is believed that, from this instrument, Denner, of Nuremberg, about the year 1700, evolved the Clarinet, which now plays so charming and im-portant a part in our military bands and orchestras. As it superseded the use of the high-pitched and difficult Trumpet called the Clarion, the older form of word, *Clarionet*, is more correct from an English standpoint. The

---

[1] For new light on the history of instruments of this class, see an important review (of Stuart Piggott's "The *Carnyx* in Early Iron Age Britain") by Anthony Baines, in *GSJ*, XIII, pp. 108–11.

eighteenth-century Chalumeau is figured in Plate 34.

As with the Hornpipe so with the BAGPIPE,[1] its introduction is attributed by Mr Henry Balfour to the Celtic migration from the East. It may be so, for on the high Syrian plain which formed the cradle of the race, the bag-pipe has existed from time far remote and spread eastward to Persia and India and westward to the civilizations of Greece and Rome, and possibly by the northern route to Britain and Gaul. Or it may be that we owe this precious possession to Roman soldiers and Roman settlers, for the *tibia utricularis* was used in the Imperial army. Beneath the crumbling walls of the old Roman castle at Richborough, in Kent, was unearthed in the eighteenth century the bronze figure of a piper which evidently formed part of a horse-trapping. It was depicted in the second volume of the *Munimenta Antiqua*, and from this our illustration in Fig. 33 is taken.[2] The instrument appears, as we should naturally expect, with a bag and chanter (or melody pipe) only; and in this same primitive con-dition it remained till the fourteenth century, as shown in Fig. 34. By the Saxons it is said to have been called *Sweghleothre* or "sound-ing skin", while in Germany in the twelfth century it was known as the *Swegel-balch* (pipe and bag). In Ireland its name was *Piobmala*, but the word does not seem to be of great antiquity. In Scotland there

Fig. 33 Bagpipe – 16th cent. (Richborough)

appears to be no early name for it; in Wales it is generally supposed to be represented in the *Ancient Laws* by "Pibau", but as this merely means "pipes" (*fistulae* or *tibiae*), it might, with equal propriety, be referred to the double pipes, or perhaps some form of Hornpipe like the Scotch double

---

[1] See the outstanding study by Anthony Baines, *Bagpipes* (Oxford, Pitt Rivers Museum, Occasional Paper . . . no. 9: 1960), based on the collection of bagpipes left to the Museum by Henry Balfour. This study, 140 pages long, with 16 plates, 78 line-drawings and a comprehensive bibliography, renders all earlier discussions obsolete, and is a major contribution to the history of musical instruments.

[2] But the Richborough figure has since been shown, by W. A. Cocks, to be a sixteenth-century cutlery handle, of which almost identical specimens have been found at Whitby Abbey and elsewhere. See Grove's *Dictionary* (Fifth Edition), sub "Bagpipe".

Stockhorn previously mentioned. And this is probably what Giraldus intended when, early in the twelfth century, he enumerated as the characteristic instruments of his own people *cithara, tibiae et chorus*, harp, pipes and crwth; for although we now speak of Bagpipes in the plural, the old form of the word was in the singular until additional tubes were added. Since, moreover, the *Chorus* has been shown to be the Crwth or Crowd, it is evident that Giraldus does not mention the existence of the Bagpipe in Scotland in his own day, nor does he allude to any use of it in Ireland; and this is borne

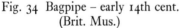

Fig. 34 Bagpipe – early 14th cent.   Fig. 35 Bagpipe – early 14th cent.
(Brit. Mus.)   (Gorleston Psalter)

out by the evidence of carving and of illustration, for Sir John Dalyell, in his *Musical Memoirs of Scotland* (1849), very truly says: "The Bagpipe occupies more frequent notice in English than in Scottish History and is a more frequent object both of delineation and sculpture." We have but to glance at the manuscripts illuminated by English artists in the thirteenth, fourteenth, and fifteenth centuries to realize how important a part it took in the social life of their country. The piper, be he man or beast, gazes at us from church tower and carved pillar, he peers at us from beneath the "miserere" seats and often finds a corner near "Our Lady's altar", for were not shepherds the first to greet the Holy Infant? We hope – without bagpipes.

The instrument was also in royal favour: Edward II and Edward III both had performers in their musical establishments, and the latter gave his bagpiper leave to visit the minstrel schools beyond the sea. In the Account Book of Eleanor, his sister, there is the following entry: "cuidam menestrallo vocato Bagpiper facienti menestralsiam suam coram Domina Eleanora per proprias manus xiiˢ·," which shows how thoroughly the good lady appreciated the piper's minstrelsy. In 1489 "Inglis" pipers came to the castle gate at Edinburgh, and were rewarded by King James. Henry VIII had his "Baggepiper", though no Scottish crown graced his head; he left in his collection four instruments "with pipes of iuorie".

It seems to have been considered a cheering adjunct to a long journey, and so Chaucer's pilgrims were brought out of town to the strains of the Miller's pipe. Early in the fifteenth century we find the following reason given: "I say to thee that it is right well done that Pylgremys have with them both singers and also pipers, that when one of them that goeth barefoote, striketh his too upon a stone, and hurteth hym sore and maketh hym to blede it, is well done that he and his fellow begyn then a Songe, or else take out of his bosome a Baggepipe for to drive away with soche myrthe the hurte of his fellow." For this charitable object, we presume, the clergy were permitted to play the instrument if they would or could, for in Veron's *Hunting of Purgatory to death*, issued in 1561, we read: "I knewe a priest (this is a true tale that I tell you and no lye) whiche when any of his parishioners should be maryed, woulde take his Backe pype, and go fetche theym too the churche, playnge sweetelye afore them, and then would he laye his instrument handsomely upon the aultare, tyll he had maryed them & sayd a masse. Which thyng being done, he woulde gentillye bringe them home agayne with Backe pype. Was not this priest a true ministrell, thynke ye: for he dyd not conterfayt the ministrell, but was one in dede." On the other hand, in the year 1592, at Skilgate, in Somersetshire, Humphrey Sydenham was summoned for interrupting divine service by "causing the bells to be rung, and dyvers baggepipes to be blown, to the grete dishonour of Almighty God".

The author of the *Complaynt of Scotland* (1548) appears to allude to the yet simpler form of the instrument, which was known in Germany as the Platerspiel: it consisted merely of a reed-pipe and a bladder, the latter being sufficiently elastic to continue the sound of the pipe by its own contraction without the pressure of the arm. It may be, however, that he is only describing the droneless Bagpipe which still lingered in use in the sixteenth century.

For soon after the year 1300 we find the first addition to the instrument, namely the Drone, which continues to sound a bourdon or buzzing bass note to the melody of the chanter. The illustration in the Gorleston Psalter (*c.* 1306), reproduced in Fig. 35, is one of the earliest we have noticed; it will also be seen in Plate 48 on a page from the Luttrell Psalter (*c.* 1330). It has been suggested that the French *Muse* – whence came a form of Bagpipe called Musette – was called the *Cornamuse* when the drone was added, the long pipe being often tipped with a curved horn. The word, which appears in the French Romances of the fourteenth century, is used by Drayton in his *Polyolbion*. The second drone was added about the year 1400, for it is seen in the ancient Bagpipe belonging to Messrs Glen, of Edinburgh, probably the oldest in existence – which bears, at the branching of its drones, the date 1409. The instrument with these additions is frequently alluded to in writings of the sixteen century as the "Drone" or "Dronepipe". Henry VIII, in 1532, gave ten shillings to "a Droner that played upon the Drone". In the next century a third drone appears on the smaller instruments.

Bagpipes with double chanters are sometimes depicted, and examples will be found in the fifteenth-century carvings at Beverley and Malvern. This is the usual form of the Greek and Oriental Pipes which are without the drones of the European instruments. There is also another important difference, namely that in the latter the chanter is sounded by a double reed like that of the Shawm and Oboe, but in the Oriental Pipes there is a single-beating reed like that of the Hornpipe and Clarinet. The *drone* reeds of the British Pipes are, however, of the single type. The only English instrument which has maintained its existence until recent years is the Northumbrian Pipe – a small instrument seen in Plate 34 – with three or four drones, which can be silenced at will, inserted into one block or stock. It is sometimes called the Border Pipe and is used for dancing, the wind being generally supplied by bellows blown by the right arm. In bygone days there were Lincolnshire and Lancashire Bagpipes, but how they were constructed is now unknown. The compass of the chanter of the great Highland Pipes, which are used in military service, is from g' to a'': the two small drones are tuned to a and the long drone to A, but sometimes they are tuned in fifths. An old ivory chanter, blown directly from the mouth, is also shown in Plate 34.

The Irish Pipe since the sixteenth century has been blown by means of bellows beneath the arm, though now there is a reversion to the earlier form for use in the army. In the second half of the eighteenth century keyed "regulators" were added to the Irish Pipes, and before the year 1800 three of these tubes had been fitted enabling the performer to obtain a limited progression of chords as an accompaniment to the melody of the chanter,

PLATE 33

2. The Nakers (Luttrell Psalter)

1. The Shawm (Luttrell Psalter)

PLATE 34

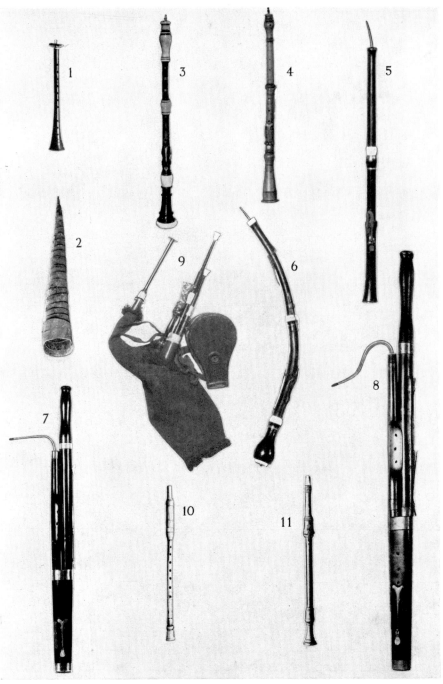

1. Zamr, Arabic Reed Pipe. 2. Whithorn, nineteenth century. 3. Hautboy, seventeenth century. 4. Hautboy by Milhouse, eighteenth century. 5. Tenor Hautboy by Milhouse. 6. Cor Anglais, Italian, eighteenth century. 7. Tenoroon, eighteenth century. 8. Bassoon, *c.* 1800. 9. Northumbrian Pipes. 10. Pipe Chanter, eighteenth century. 11. 2-keyed Clarinet, as used *c.* 1720

after the manner of the Neapolitan Surdelina of the seventeenth century. These were called Union Pipes, either as immortalizing the legislative Union of Great Britain and Ireland in 1801, or more probably from a mistaken rendering of the native name *Uilleann* or "elbow" pipes.

Chapter X

Horn and Cornett

Of bras thay broughten Beemes and of boxe,
Of horne, of boon, in whiche thay blewe and powpede
And therwithal thay schrykede and thay howpede;
It semede as that hevene schulde falle.

GEOFFREY CHAUCER (*c.* 1390)

THE MUSICAL DEVELOPMENT of the human race has been divided by some writers into three stages. In the first our forefathers delighted themselves with the rhythmic beat of the Drum, in the second they made merry with the cheerful strains of the Pipe, and in the third they began to appreciate the subtle refinement of the Stringed Instrument. Although this theory is largely supported by conditions present in the various grades of civilization of the world today, yet the fact that in Africa, for instance, we find stringed instruments in constant use among the most degraded savages appears to discountenance the rigid necessity of any such order.

Leaving, then, this interesting but open question for further ethnological research, and assuming that the Drum – probably in the form of a hollow tree – was the first to serve man's purpose as a musical instrument, the next development – representative, we may so say, of the Pipe stage – is found in the gentle and dignified art of horn-blowing. For the office of the horn-blower has from early times been considered honourable. Were not the ram's-horn-blowing priests, as they encircled the walls of Jericho, men of mark? And are not His Majesty's State Trumpeters in their gorgeous array much the same? Certainly, whether it be the blast of the skilful witch-doctor in Central Africa or the "coo" of the yet more skilful Corno Primo of a London orchestra, we are sure that the Horn is in the hands of the "gentle-man" – the man of caste and distinction.

Now, as Mr J. F. Rowbotham remarks, our musical progenitors applied themselves to the blowing of Horns for two chief reasons – to bring them victory in war and rain in peace.[1] The original idea underlying both these

[1] This discussion of Horn and Trumpet somewhat obscures the clear organological

134

purposes was to frighten someone: in battle to frighten their enemies into running away, especially if the horns were made, as they often were, from the bones of their deceased relatives, and in their rain-making to terrify the evil spirits who held back the needed showers, a result usually achieved only after the fees had been fully paid. That this is not theory, but fact, the customs of the savage tribes of Africa amply testify, and what they do today our forefathers did in the far-off prehistoric times. For Greek and Roman writers alike allude to the use of these horns, and the instruments themselves have frequently been found in the Irish peat-bogs, lost probably in tribal raids and kept for 2000 years or more to adorn the magnificent collection of Celtic antiquities in the National Museum at Dublin. Even the Roman legionaries quailed before their sound, as Polybius relates in the second book of his History. "The parade and tumult of the army of the Celts," he writes, "terrified the Romans, for there was amongst them an infinite number of horns and trumpets which, with the shouts of the whole army in concert, made a clamour so terrible and loud that every surrounding echo was awakened, and all the adjacent country seemed to join in the horrible din." So also Diodorus and Livy in their historical works. Regarding the rain-making propensities of our forefathers, it is sufficient to allude to the idea long prevalent in our country districts that the advent of a German band is a prelude to a coming shower.

The ancient horns which have been discovered in our islands and more especially in Ireland are made either of wood or of bronze; of the latter the earlier examples are cast and the later formed of thin pieces of hammered bronze riveted together. The wooden instruments, like the pastoral horns of Norway, Switzerland and Austria still in use, were made of willow or sallow wood, split in half, hollowed out and then bound together again with strips of bark or, as in the Irish specimens, by metal bands. A most interesting feature of some of the cast bronze horns (which are believed to date from the fifth century before Christ) is the mouthpiece, which is placed in the side of the instrument and not at the end, as in the usual form. In this respect the instruments are the exact counterpart of the African Ivory Horns which are used for signalling as well as for war. It is possible that this similarity is due to the common home of our race, for among the early

---

distinction between the two families: Trumpets, with cylindrical bores, and Horns, with conical bores. The two families appear in general to have had different functions, the trumpet having to do with warfare and the horn with the hunt, but the early history of the families is very obscure. The most up-to-date discussions will be found in *Musical Instruments through the Ages* (Penguin Books, 1961). For a note on the Scandinavian *Lur* – a bronze horn – see Galpin's article in the Fifth Edition of Grove.

remains of prehistoric man in this country bones have been found with a side orifice which may have served the same purpose.

To pass, however, to historical times. The recognized distinction between the Horn and the Trumpet is found in the shape of the tube. Instruments of the Trumpet type have for the greater part of their length a tube of cylindrical bore opening out towards the end into a broader bell, and this form, which we find in the Buzine, Clarion, and Sackbut of later medieval times, will be described in the next chapter. The Horn type includes those instruments in which the tube tapers gradually from the mouthpiece to the bell, and it is represented by the Bugle, Hunting-horns (great and small), and by the two classes of Cornetts or Cornets, ancient and modern.

Fig. 36 Circular Horn – late 14th cent.
(Worcester)

The BUGLE carries us back to the earliest form, for it takes its name from the bugle or wild ox, an animal form-erly common in this country and whose horns were used for the chase and the banqueting-hall. Foresters still blow the ox-horn, and an instrument, said to have been the Watchman's Horn used of old time at Saffron Walden, is illustrated on Plate 37. It is made of a fine twisted horn thirty-six inches in length and terminated at the larger end by a copper bell. These Bugles appear in the earliest illustrations of our English manuscripts, as, for in-stance, in the so-called Psalter of St Augustine of the eighth century, now in the British Museum (Vesp. A. 1) and shown in Plate 2. Similar horns appear in manuscripts of the tenth and eleventh centuries also in the British Museum. When suitable and obtainable, the horns of other animals were used; the famous Horn of Ulphus, for instance, now in the Treasury of York Cathedral, is made from an elephant's tusk curiously carved and originally decorated with gold. It is said that Ulph, the son-in-law of King Canute, in order to prevent his sons quarrelling over their inheritance, vowed he would make them equal, so he went to the altar of the cathedral, filled his horn with wine, drank it off and dedicated all his lands to God and

St Peter. The valuable relic was lost during the Civil War, but restored by Lord Fairfax after the Restoration and in 1675 redecorated by order of the Dean and Chapter, for whom it forms the title to several of their estates.

The tradition attached to this horn illustrates the use to which they were often put as drinking-cups; on festive occasions, with the finger placed over the mouthpiece, the "metheglin strong" was quaffed off in one draught and the horn blown to show it was emptied. It also affords an example of the Oliphant or Elephant Horn, whose sound was supposed, in the Middle Ages, to be of magic power, for Roland's or Rollo's Horn, as described in the Anglo-Norman romances, could be heard at a distance of thirty miles. Unfortunately the hero died after one of those terrible blasts. A Forester's Horn appears on Plate 37, and with it an Oliphant of the seventeenth century carved with scenes in the life of St Hubert. The short Bugle, as depicted in the illustration of an English hunting scene in an early fourteenth-century manuscript (Brit. Mus., 10 E. iv), is reproduced on Plate 36, and in *The Squyr of Lowe Degre* the poet describes how the sound of the chase echoed from the glen as you could

> here the bugles ther y-blowe.

In 1525 "the Inglisman that brocht blawin hornis, leschis and dog collars fra the King of Ingland" was rewarded by the Scottish Soverign with "lx unicornis", and a long list of Henry VIII's hunting-horns, white and black, large and small, garnished with silver and gay with bright baudricks for hanging across the shoulder, will be seen in the list of his musical instruments given in the Appendix (p. 221). In the sixteenth century they were often made of wood, covered with leather or satin, and of brass or other more precious metal; and, as the length was increased, they were turned in a semicircle. On the Continent one or more turns were added for this same reason, until, in the later part of the seventeenth century, the large *Cor de chasse* – an altered form of the *Trompe de chasse* – appeared with several turns and encircling the body of the performer. This latter feature, however, adopted for ease of carriage, was not new, for horns so turned are seen in illustrations of much earlier date, as, for instance, on the choir-stalls of Worcester Cathedral erected at the end of the fourteenth century, from which the example in Fig. 36 is taken.

In England the shorter horn (Plate 37) seems to have been more generally preferred; on it rhythmic signals only were played, and it was not until the very close of the seventeenth century that the French Hunting-horn (but in a more compact form) was made in this country, as shown on the same

Plate by the fine work of William Bull, of London, dated 1699. This shape is frequently depicted in Caldecott's charming illustrations of old country life. The Hunting-horn with its musical calls was introduced by Lully and other composers into the ballets and divertissements of the French Court, and thence it seems to have won a permanent place in the orchestra, though strong objections were urged at first against it. Probably the tone was much forced after the manner of the strenuous calls of the chase; in fact, the instrument was held with the bell upwards on a level with or even above the player's head. This custom continued in England for a long period; the horns were so held in the Handel Celebrations in 1784; and in an old coloured print showing the band playing in Vauxhall Gardens the expanded bells of the horns are still pointed upward. Owing probably to its extensive use as the *Trompe de chasse* by the French, the Horn as employed in the orchestra was known by their neighbours in England as the *French* Horn; but the Bohemian players were probably the first to cultivate the softer tone and to hold the bell downward; and about the year 1760 Hampl, of Dresden, introduced the practice of placing the hand within the bell to flatten the natural notes and so to obtain a more complete scale. In 1773 the Hand Horn was played by a foreign *artiste* named Spandau at the Opera House in London with remarkable effect. Other devices to render the instrument more serviceable were suggested and tried, such as additional lengths of tubing, called *crooks*, to alter the pitch, keys covering holes in the side of the instrument, and even a slide like the Trombone, but they have all disappeared owing to the invention of the valves or pistons, which were applied to the Horn in Germany in 1813. A Hand Horn is depicted on Plate 37.[1]

Beside the instruments of horn or metal used for directing the movements of men in battle or in the chase, and to which the name *byme* or *beme* is given in the Anglo-Saxon Vocabularies and early English literature, as shown by the quotation at the head of this chapter, there were also two kinds of a much larger size, sometimes equalling or even exceeding the height of the player.

The first kind is always represented in drawings and illuminations as made of metal and tapering from the small mouthpiece to a large open end without an expanding bell, and frequently ornamented with bands of gold and silver. In a tenth- or eleventh-century manuscript in the British Museum (Add. 24199) two soldiers or uniformed officials are depicted, each holding a large horn of this form, and the same appear in the very similar manuscript known

[1] For a more detailed history of the Horn, see Morley Pegge, *The French Horn* (London, 1960), and also his article in the Penguin Book mentioned above.

as Cleopatra C. viii. Possibly in both cases the artists intended to represent instruments of a yet earlier date.

It is in the illuminated scenes of the Apocalypse that these large horns most frequently appear (held by attendant angels), and they seem to increase in length and size with the loftiness of the theme. In an early eleventh-century manuscript of the Apocalypse in the Bodleian Library at Oxford (Bodl. 352) they are magnificently displayed, and their open ends are resting on the ground. An example from an early fourteenth-century Apocalypse (B. 10. 2, Trin. Coll., Cam.) is shown in Plate 36. This type of Horn appears to have been especially used for the calling of assemblies, and it is represented in practical form by the Burgmote Horns, which many of our ancient corporations still possess. For instance, in 1234, Henry III gave to the citizens of Canterbury the right to hold a burghmote once in fifteen days, the court to be assembled "by the sound of the horn". The bronze horn used for that purpose is still in existence, and, including the mouthpiece, which is cast in one piece with the rest, the length of its gentle curve is thirty-seven inches and the open end six inches in diameter. There are two projections with ring-holes for suspension, but otherwise it is quite plain. Its fundamental note ($e\flat$) is fine and resonant. The Folkestone Horn, thirty-six inches long, is made of beaten brass ornamented with bandwork. It is more semicircular and engraved on the bell is the word FOVLSTAN in Lombardic letters. Its note is g.

The Canterbury Horn, and that of Dover (which is probably of German workmanship), are well illustrated and described in Hipkins and Gibb's *Musical Instruments, Historic and Rare*. The minutes of these Burghmotes are often headed, "At a comyne Horne Blowyng." New Romney, Hythe, and Faversham still possess their horns. The *Corporation Book* of the last-named place has under the year 1542 the entry: "For mendyng of the Brasen Horne, the Cokyngstole, etc., xvi[d.]"

The "Great Court Trump" of Ipswich, which is said to have been presented by King John, is of cast metal, thirty-five inches long and straight for the greater part of its length, with a sharp upward curve at the open end. Its shape is very similar to the Roman Lituus. The Ripon Horn more closely resembles the continental Foresters' Horns of the seventeenth century. It is still blown by the city *Wakeman*. An interesting and well illustrated account of this and other old English Horns with the curious customs attached to them, written by Dr J. C. Bridge, will be found in the *Chester Archaeological Society's Journal*, vol. xi.

The other type of medieval Horn is quite straight. It was apparently made originally of wood hollowed out as in the ancient Celtic horns and bound together with metal bands. It is seen in the hands of two of David's attendants standing on the right in the illustration given in Plate 2 from the eighth-century manuscript (Vesp. A. 1) already mentioned, and in one of the eleventh century (Brit. Mus., Tib. C. vi) it appears resting on a forked stand or prop, as if needing support owing to its length or weight. The straight Lurs and Alp-horns of the present day are often so supported, and it is probable that this type of Horn was the Trumba or Trumpe of medieval writers and was used in its largest form by herdsmen and in its more portable size by men-at-arms, until it was superseded by the lighter "Trumpette", which we shall presently describe.

Before dealing with the Cornett it may be useful to explain why the Horns and Trumpets have not been allowed to remain in their natural and primitive form, but have been the subject of constant experiment and alteration.

A plain open tube, when the air within is set in vibration by the player's lips, can only yield certain fixed sounds known as the harmonics of the fundamental note, and commonly represented as: C c g c' e' g' $b\flat'$ c'' d'' e'' f'' g'' a'' $b\flat''$ $b\natural''$ c''' d''' $e\flat'''$ $e\natural'''$, etc., a possible range of over four octaves, but practically much limited, being dependent upon the length of the tube and other conditions. In the short horns and trumpets of early times only the first two or three notes could be obtained; on the Roman Buccina, however, which somewhat resembled the large encircling horns already mentioned, nine harmonic notes are easily sounded, though the fundamental note is impracticable with the usual mouthpiece. But even on this instrument the upper notes do not seem to have been employed, or the Roman musicians would have learnt to appreciate the interval of the major third, which occurs twice at least. In fact they are not obtainable if the cheeks of the player are puffed out according to the practice of those times.

When, however, the scale was developed and melodic progressions were admired, human ingenuity set out to discover a way whereby the gaps in the lower part of this harmonic series of notes could be filled up, partly with a view to obtain the desired freedom for melody and also to obviate the use of the upper notes, which become increasingly difficult the higher they are, and can only be reached on tubes of great length.

Now the simplest and earliest way by which our forefathers attained this result was by boring holes in the side of the short, curved horn, six or seven in number, and covering them with the fingers, as on a reed-pipe. The melodic instrument thus formed was known in the later Middle Ages as THE CORNETT, and we adopt this spelling in order to distinguish it from

the modern brass instrument of the same name. It is interesting to remember that the invention, such as it was, was probably due to our own
countrymen, for the earliest illustrations are all of English workmanship. It
appears, in a British Museum manuscript (Harl. 603) of the late tenth or
early eleventh century, in the Anglo-Saxon Psalter written shortly after the
year A.D. 1000 now in the University Library, Cambridge (Plate 38), and
in a manuscript in the British Museum (Tib. C. vi) of the same century. It is
also seen in a Psalter, due to an English artist, in the Bibliothèque Nationale
at Paris (MS. Lat. 11550). In the twelfth cen-
tury it is represented in the St John's College Psalter at Cambridge, amongst the
instruments used for sacred music, as will
be seen on Plate 43 and again in the carvings
on the twelfth-century capitals in the crypt
of Canterbury Cathedral shown in Fig. 37.
In this century it also appears on the Continent in a French manuscript preserved at
Trier.

The original form was doubtless decided
by the natural shape of the horn from
which it was made: in Norway a goat's
horn pierced with four or five holes at
the side is still used as a rustic instrument
and called the Bukkehorn or Prillarhorn;
but by the twelfth century the Cornett
had been constructed of wood or ivory
and had taken its characteristic six-sided
outline.

Fig. 37 Cornett – 12th cent.
(Canterbury)

The success of this application of
holes to the short curved horn naturally suggested their use with other
instruments of the same class, and accordingly we find in the eleventh
century the straight "Trompe" pierced with side holes, but employed
at first only in Germany, and especially in the Rhine Provinces, from
which it apparently emanated. The German name was Zinke. It does
not seem to have been used in England till the thirteenth century, for it
appears in a manuscript of that date (Brit. Mus. 14 B. v), the curved form
being preferred by our forefathers. The earliest mention of the Cornett
which we have observed in English literature is in *Octavian Imperator*,
a poem of the fourteenth century.

> Ther myghte men here menstralsye
> Trumpys, taborns and cornettys crye.

Aimeric de Peyrac, of the same century, thus speaks of the closing of the holes with the fingers:

> Quidam triplices cornu tonabant
> Quædam foramina inclaudentes.

In the sixteenth century the instrument had taken a definite place in the wind-bands of the period.

In 1503 Bonatus, who was attached by the English King to the train of his daughter Margaret, Queen of Scotland, played the Cornett in the Royal Chamber. Henry VIII, who died possessed of many "Cornettes", some of ivory and others of wood covered in the usual way with black leather, made special provision for their use in the statutes which he granted to various ecclesiastical bodies at the Reformation. In the list of officers appointed for the Cathedral Church of Canterbury in 1532, there were two *Cornetters* and two *Sackbutters*. The "Musicke of Cornettes" sounds in England's earliest tragedy, *Gorboduc* (1561), heralding the King and Nobilities who appear in the second act, and similar instruments are present at the performance of *Jocasta* four years later. The translators of the Bible, too, considered it a fitting instrument to find a place in Nebuchadnezzar's band. A small treble Cornett of wood, covered with leather and garnished with silver, is shown on Plate 39. It is dated 1518: on the same page is an ordinary treble Cornett.

In the sixteenth century the fame of English musicians as well as of English music was great on the Continent; and in 1604 Charles III, Duke of Lorraine, sent his cornett player, Jean Presse, to our country "to look for different sorts of instruments to accompany his music". He secured two sackbut players, John Robinson and Robert Parker, and two cornett players, John Adson and William Burt. In 1628 we find Robert Parker again in England as one of the King's musicians on the double sackbut, and in 1633 John Adson appears as a musician for the flute and cornett; both of them died in 1640. At Westminster Abbey, at York, at Durham, and probably in most of the cathedrals, the cornett was used with the organ and sackbut to support the voices of the singers. At the funeral of James I two "shagbutts" and two "cornitors" appear among the singing men of Westminster, and in the Abbey Accounts for the year 1664 a payment of £4 is made to John Hill "for playing on the cornett in the Church this yere". There is in the British Museum (Add. 17801) a composition by Matthew Locke "for His Majesty's

Sagbutts and Cornets", supposed to have been written for the triumphal progress of Charles II through London on April 22, 1661.[1]

But at that date its days were already numbered, and Evelyn in his *Diary*, under the year 1662, writes after attending the Chapel Royal "now no more heard the cornet which gave life to the organ. That instrument quite left off on which the English were so skilful." Roger North too appreciated a good player on the Cornett, for he says in his family *Memoirs*: "Nothing comes so near or rather imitates so much an excellent voice as a cornett pipe; but the labour of the lips is too great and it is seldom well sounded." About the same time Randle Holme, from his *Academy of Armory* (Brit. Mus., Harl. 2304), tells us, "It is a delicate, pleasant wind musick if well played and humered."

In 1660 William Child was appointed for the Cornett in the King's Musick, and, as Dr William Child, he still held the post in 1684, though, having been born in 1606, it is doubtful whether at the later date he did much more than draw his salary of 20*d.* per diem and £16 2*s.* 6*d.* a year for livery. Michael Wise, a much younger man, was his companion and probably played the Cornett at the Coronation of James II, where it appeared for the last time. For the Hautboy had proved its successful rival, as we gather, for instance, from the entry in the *Edinburgh Town Council Register*, which informs us that in 1696 the Cornetts of the Town Waits were superseded by the "French hautboye and double curtle, instruments far more proper than the instruments they now have to play upon". The brilliancy of the old Cornett to which Evelyn alludes was nevertheless copied and maintained in the Cornett stop of the Organ, which took its place, and Cornett Voluntaries were at one time in great request. In order to give piquancy to the tone, the pipes, of which four or five sounded for each note, were placed on a special sound-board, and the stop was then called a Mounted Cornett.

On the Continent, however, the instrument itself still continued to be used and found a place in the chorales of Bach and the operas of Gluck, but England, its birthplace and home for six centuries, knew it no more; the original parts written for it by Handel in his opera *Tamerlano* were transferred for the English performance of the work to Clarinets.[2]

The Cornett, like the other instruments, was made in various sizes,

---

[1] See the article footnoted on p. 107 for a fuller discussion of the Royal Wind Music. Editions of Locke's music for Sackbuts & Cornetts, as well as other English wind consort music of the seventeenth century, have been published by Oxford University Press.

[2] For a discussion of these somewhat doubtful parts for Cornett in *Tamerlano*, see R. B. Chatwin, "Handel and the Clarinet", *GSJ*, III, pp. 3–8.

generally three. The High Treble Cornett, with a compass of two octaves from d', the Ordinary Cornett a fifth lower, and the Great Cornett an octave lower in pitch. These details are gathered from existing instruments, and the set, which is shown in Plate 39, was technically known as a "Nest of Cornetts". The instrument most commonly used was the second of the nest, and, at the lips of an experienced player, it had a compass of nearly three octaves. The Great Cornett, which was generally used as a Mean or Tenor with a sackbut for the bass, was bent somewhat like the letter S. All the Cornetts are sounded by means of a small cup-shaped mouthpiece having a very thin edge: they are not reed instruments, as has been sometimes stated. There are six finger-holes in front and one at the back for the thumb, as in the Recorder; a key or an extra hole at the lower end was sometimes added on the larger instruments. Beside the Curved Cornetts, of which we have been speaking, there were also Straight Cornetts, some made with detachable mouthpieces and others with the mouthpiece one with the instrument: the latter were called Mute Cornetts and were softer in tone.

Simply constructed as the instrument is, specimens are now exceedingly rare and valuable. Of the prices given for them at the time of their greatest popularity we may gather some particulars from old records. In 1595, according to the *Bursar's Accounts* of Trinity College, Cambridge, "a Cornett bought for the Chappell" cost £1, and in the following century the *Lord Chamberlain's Records* of the King's Musick supply us with many details. The average price of a Treble Cornett was £2 10s. and Tenor Cornetts £3 each, though in 1633 a Tenor Cornett was bought for His Majesty's use which cost £13, probably a very richly mounted instrument. In 1631 three Mute Cornetts were purchased for £9. The Mute Cornett is shown in Plate 39; with it appears a curious form made of horn with six holes only, which was found in a Norfolk village, where for many years it had been known as the Harvest Horn. In the Hengrave Hall Inventory of 1603 one item consists of "iiii Cornutes, one being a Mute Cornute", and in Sir Thomas Kytson's Household Accounts there is an entry in January 1573-4 of the purchase of "vii cornetts bought for the musicians iiii^{li}". Annual payments were regularly made during the next hundred years to one of the King's musicians for instructing boys in the art of "Les Flutes et Cornetts".

At the close of the sixteenth century a true bass instrument of the Cornett type was invented by a Canon of Auxerre, Guillaume by name. Though it does not seem to have been recognized in Germany for some time, if at all, yet in France it was at once adopted for supporting the plain-chant and is well described by Mersenne in his *Harmonicorum Libri XII* (1635). It was called THE SERPENT from its peculiar shape, necessitated by the length of tubing required, which was drawn together something after the fashion of a snake. In the year 1603 it probably appears under the name Lysarden in the Inventory of the musical instruments at Hengrave Hall in Suffolk. In the *Lord Chamberlain's Records* of the seventeenth century we do not find any mention of it, unless the £13 Tenor Cornett already mentioned was a Serpent in disguise. In the eighteenth century it figures in the parts of Handel's *Water Music* of the year 1717, and also in the *Firework Music* of 1749. We also hear of a famous player in the reign of George III, one Hurworth, of Richmond, in Yorkshire.

In a group of the Sharp family painted by Zoffany before the year 1785 and showing a musical party on a yacht on the Thames at Fulham, there is a fine representation of the Serpent in the hands of Mr James Sharp, whilst other members of the family are shown with the Harpsichord, Violin, Violoncello, Theorboe Lute, Hautboy, two Horns, and two Whistle Flutes for use as a Double-Flute with the Serpent (Plate 56).

The admission of the Serpent into the army bands at the close of the eighteenth century was probably due to King George's fatherly interest in this unwieldy instrument: it is said that he suggested the method of holding it sideways so as to avoid the movement of the player's knees when marching, and he also proposed the turning outwards of its open end in order to increase the tone. For supporting the voices in the church bands of the early nineteenth century it was in reality returning to its original purpose, though some of the English clergy considered that its use in Divine worship was unscriptural. In the seventeenth century the compass of the Serpent was from *E* to *g'*, but at the zenith of its glory in the early nineteenth century it had a compass of three octaves from *C* or even a note lower.

The English form as improved by His Majesty is shown on Plate 39. The instrument is of wood, covered with parchment and black leather: we have heard of one that was covered with green baize, and military Serpents were sometimes constructed of metal. If not overblown it yields a peculiarly soft *woody* tone which no longer has its counterpart in the orchestra, though it is found in certain organ stops. The objection to it was the inequality of its notes, but this had already been overcome by the addition of many keys before it gave way to younger members of its family, the Bass Horn and Ophicleide (also shown), which in their turn have disappeared before the onward march of the valved Tubas, introduced about 1830 and improved by Adolphe Sax, of Paris, ten years later. Both the Ophicleide and the Serpent are still to be met with in curiosity shops and old country houses;

for old time's sake they are worth preserving, and as we have frequently been asked to supply a few instructions for the Serpent we hope that there is more than one player still left. As is well known, there are fine parts for the instrument in Mendelssohn's oratorio *St Paul*, in his overture *A calm Sea and prosperous Voyage*; in Wagner's *Rienzi* and Bennett's *May Queen*, and in the works of Auber, Rossini and Verdi. So it has moved in respectable company. "There's worse things than serpents," as the village shoemaker rightly says in Thomas Hardy's *Under the Greenwood Tree*. "Old things pass away, 'tis true, but a serpent was a good old note; a deep rich note was the serpent."

One other effective attempt was made to perpetuate the instruments of the old Cornett type. In 1810 Halliday, Bandmaster of the Cavan Militia, placed five side holes covered with keys on the Bugle.[1] Owing to the length of the tube, this number was sufficient to give a complete compass of two octaves from c'. This was undoubtedly the first attempt to obtain the *chromatic* scale on the Bugle; but, judging from a French instrument with only two keys in our possession, made by Courtois Neveu, who was working in Paris at the date of Halliday's invention, it is possible that the Bugle had already received sufficient keys to enable it to produce the open notes of the ordinary Trumpet. Other keys, including one for the low $b\natural$ and for the better production of certain notes, were afterwards added, and as the Keyed or Royal Kent Bugle – so called in honour of the Duke of Kent – the instrument, seen on Plate 39, was welcomed into the military music, village bands, and theatre orchestras for the first half of the nineteenth century; in fact, it was not until the year 1835 that its rival, the Cornopean or Valve Cornet, began to dethrone it from its leading position as a solo instrument. The charm of its melody is not yet forgotten by our old folk, who tell us of the stage-coach rattling along the high road and hill and dale echoing some familiar strain as the guard played on his Keyed Bugle "in the days when we went gipsying a long time ago".

[1] See further Morley Pegge, "The Regent's Bugle", *GSJ*, IX, pp. 91–6.

Chapter XI

Trumpet and Sackbut

Immoderate wyndes in a Clarion causithe it for to rage;
Soft wynde and moderate makithe the sounde to assuage.
Therfore he whiche in that instrument wolde have sweete modulacion,
Bustius wyndes must leve and use moderacion.

LEKINGFELDE PROVERB (*temp.* Henry VIII)

THE STORY OF THE TRUMPET is the story of panoply and pomp. It is the "nobleman" amongst the instruments of music, standing at the king's right hand. The watchmen might blow their horns through the gloomy streets, the huntsmen might "poup their bemes" across the woodland glade, the town pipers might make merry holiday for all good citizens, but the trumpeters, with their attendant drummers, stood apart, awaiting their lord's commands. Early in the history of the Middle Ages we find the Trumpeters with the "Taberettes" formed into a special corps, which afterwards became an exclusive guild. They journeyed with the sovereign or nobleman to whose retinue they were attached: as he passed through the towns they played brilliant tuckets and fanfares; acting as heralds, they announced the dinner hour, and during the meal stood behind their master's chair. At the siege of Rochester in 1087 William Rufus would not allow the besieged to evacuate the city, unless at the sound of his trumpets; and while they quitted the place in shame, the royal trumpets sounded for joy. In the days of Good Queen Bess we were told by a foreign visitor to England that, whilst her guard were bringing in the dinner, twelve trumpets and two kettledrums made the hall ring for half an hour together; and at a pageant called *The Royal Oak*, exhibited in London in the year 1660, twenty-eight trumpeters beside the sergeant trumpeter were employed.

The instrument, which had thus been annexed exclusively for noble purposes, appears in the English manuscripts of the thirteenth century as a straight cylindrical tube of metal terminated by a spreading bell. An illustration taken from the early fourteenth-century Psalter in the Library of All Souls College, Oxford, is reproduced in Plate 36.

We find the word itself used in the *Squyr of Lowe Degre* (*c.* 1400), and

147

Edward III had five Trumpetters in his suite. Machault, the Provençal poet of the early fourteenth century, mentions both the *Trompe* and the *Trompe petite*; but, notwithstanding the similarity of name, the true Trumpet, with its cylindrical tube, was not evolved from the older Trumba or Trompe, described in the previous chapter and having a conical bore. The idea was doubtless derived originally from contact with the East through the Saracenic settlers in Sicily and Northern Africa, though popularized more widely at a later date by the Crusades. It appeared in Europe in two forms, the shorter, with a clear, ringing sound, being called the *Claro*, whence our word Clarion, while the longer was known as the Buzine or Bocine, a corruption of the Latin *Buccina*, though in no way resembling that instrument. The earliest illustration of it occurs in a wall painting of the eleventh century at Formis in Southern Italy, where its perfectly straight tube is distinctly seen. Early in the following century William of Malmesbury speaks of the "loud melody of the *Clarasii*", and in the thirteenth century we are told by an old charter that an assembly was to be summoned by the common herald "with the tuba or claro, as the custom is". The word Buzine is also found in general use, as, for instance, in Machault's *La Prise d'Alexandre*, where the poet groups together "Trompes, buzines et trompettes". A Buzine is depicted on Plate 36 from an early fourteenth-century manuscript (Brit. Mus., 2 B. vii), and an existing specimen dated 1460, made by Sebastian Hainlein, is shown on Plate 41.

It was rather in the manner of its construction than in its actual shape that the instrument, whether short or long, was new to Western Europe; for one type of the Roman *Lituus* used by the cavalry was a true trumpet, its cylindrical tube being made by placing a long strip of thin bronze on a metal rod, over which it was turned and its edges neatly flanged and riveted together, after being coated with wax to render the seam quite air-tight. This is clearly shown in an ancient specimen discovered in Etruria. In the Buzine, however, and the straight Trumpet, various lengths of prepared tubing were fitted together and the joints covered by a ferrule or ornamented band. In this way tubes of any length could be made, and, if we may safely draw an inference from the illuminations of the medieval artist, the Buzines must have been at least six feet long and the straight Clarones about half that length.

The advantage which these longer tubes gave for the elaboration of fanfares was not lost sight of by the trumpeters. The objection which might naturally be urged against their use was that they were extremely awkward to carry. So about the year 1300 we hear of "crooked" horns (*cors crocus*),

PLATE 35

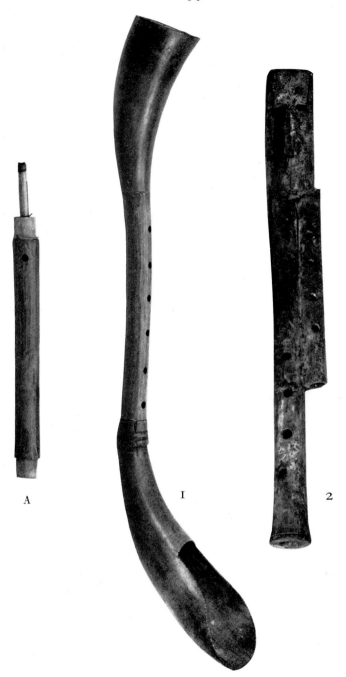

1. Pibcorn or Hornpipe, eighteenth century. A. The pipe dismantled. 2. Double Recorder, sixteenth century

PLATE 36

1. Buzine   2. Trumpet

3. Horn   4. Bugle

Horns and Trumpets of the early fourteenth century

and from that period we date the step which was destined to give the Trumpet its high place in the realm of music as well as of pageantry. This step was the folding of the tube by means of a U-shaped elbow or *potence*, requiring, it is true, careful workmanship, but at once securing unlimited length without loss of portability. It is interesting to find that, as with the making of a cylindrical tube, so with its folding into a more compact form, the Romans had been in advance of medieval Europe; for on the walls of the House of the Gladiators at Pompeii there is a fresco of the first century A.D. which shows that a trumpet, very similar in shape to our modern military instrument, was in use in classical times. An illustration of this fresco will be found in a paper on the *Evolution of the Sackbut*, read by the writer before the Musical Association in 1906 and published in their *Proceedings*. But, like so many of the arts of classical days, it had been put aside and forgotten with the decline and fall of the great Roman Empire, until, at the close of the thirteenth century, it appeared again in Northern Italy, where a great revival in technical skill and industry had taken place. It may be that the old idea of bending the tube was reconceived in these later minds by contact with a distant Oriental source, for a folded Trumpet has for many centuries existed in India, and Venice had become the principal port of Eastern trade and commerce since the insecurity of Constantinople. At first the tube was bent in a zigzag form and in the same plane: so it is figured in the masterpieces of Fra Angelico and Luca della Robbia. An early instance of this form occurs in a tournament scene carved beneath one of the choir-seats of Worcester Cathedral, erected in 1397. The trumpeter is on the right hand, and his attendant kettle-drummer, who is in great difficulties, on the left. The carving is reproduced on Plate 49. Another is to be seen in an early fifteenth-century manuscript (Brit. Mus., 1. E. ix) and is shown in Plate 53; and yet a third in an almost contemporary description of a joust held by King Richard II at Smithfield (Lambeth Palace Library, MS. 6). This is reproduced in Plate 40. In the same manuscript, which is known as the St Alban's Chronicle, there are represented, in an illustration of Henry V at the battle of Agincourt, two mounted trumpeters, one with the long straight Buzine and the other with the more compact instrument. But the zigzag form, though more portable than the long Buzine, was weak in construction. The next step, therefore, was to turn the third length of the tube over the first, which gives us the shape of the instrument as we know it today; though, for some time, the two tubes were not actually fixed together but kept apart by a piece of wood inserted between them, over which canvas strapping and coloured cords were wound to secure rigidity. It seems probable that this improvement also took place in Italy, although at a later date the circular form of Trumpet was known in Germany certainly as the Italian Trumpet. The name usually given to it, however, was derived from that which it bore in its earlier straight form: it was called the Claron, Claronceau, or Clarion. In 1529 Horman tells us that "a Trompette is straight, but a Clarion is wounde in and out with a hope". Trumpets and Clarions in this sense appeared in the English army at Crécy in 1346, and two Clarions, as well as five Trompetters, were on the musical establishment of the King. In a ballad, of which the subject is the defeat of the Scots at Halidon Hill in 1333, we read:

> This was don with merrie sowne
> With pipis, trompes and tabers thereto,
> And loude clarionis thei blew also.

Attached to the fleet under Richard Earl of Arundel, in 1377, were "one claryoner", two trumpeters and four pipers.[1]

Chaucer in his *Knighte's Tale* (line 1653), speaks of

> Pypes, trompes, nakers, clariounes,
> That in the bataille blowen blody sounes,

and in the *Squyr of Lowe Degre* the "claryon clere" is mentioned with "the trumpette". The Proverb (taken from those at Lekingfelde), which has been placed at the head of this chapter, will show us the good advice given to the Clarion player shortly after the year 1500.

The earliest English illustration which we have noticed of the folded form as distinct from the earlier zigzag shape is that given in Plate 40, taken from the Harley Roll (No. 7353) in the British Museum. It dates from the first part of the fifteenth century. Another early illustration will be found in the metrical *Life of St Edmund*, written about the year 1433 for Henry VI, and now in the British Museum (Harl. 2278). His father had ten "clarionners" in his military music.

Virdung, in his *Musica getutscht* (1511), gives illustrations of three kinds of bent and folded Trumpets; the earlier shape, already described, is called by him the Thurner Horn, and was used by the Tower watchmen; the Clarion he calls the Clareta, and a more robust form with larger tubing the Field

---

[1] It appears that the word "clarion" was an exact synonym for the medieval "trompette des ménéstrels" or slide-trumpet – an instrument therefore capable of playing a fully chromatic scale, with quite low lip-pressure, within the range from c' to a'' or so. The instrument's defects were its lack of agility and its rather dull tone; both were remedied in the cornett and, later, in the clarinet ("little clarion"). See also Jan LaRue and Jeanette B. Holland, "Stimmer's Women Musicians: A Unique Set of Woodcuts", in *Music, Libraries and Instruments* (Hinrichsen, 1961), pp. 261–8, and (in particular) plate 177.

Trumpet. When, however, the long straight instrument was entirely discarded, the word Trumpet, was used indiscriminately for the Clarion and the Field Trumpet though in the actual performance of music they were distinct, the former, with its smaller bore, taking the higher notes in the fanfares and the latter sounding the lower.

So they appear when, liberated from the exclusiveness which had guarded them for so many centuries, they took their places in the orchestras of the seventeenth century. The clarion player had, by assiduous practice, acquired perfect mastery over his instrument, combined with a marvellous command of compass and execution, its small tubing enabling him to reach the extreme harmonic notes. It is for this reason that composers like Bach and Handel were able to find players who could reach the high f'''. That this is quite possible was clearly shown by the well-known player Mr Walter Morrow at one of the Gresham Lectures in 1909. The instrument on which he performed was made at Nuremberg in the seventeenth century, and the tone produced was flute-like, forming a pleasing accompaniment to the voice. It is illustrated on Plate 41; and at the bottom of the same Plate is shown a rare specimen of an English long Trumpet made by Augustine Dudley, of London, and dated 1651. It is said to have been used at the battle of Worcester, and its former owner was Mr A. H. Littleton, to whom we are much indebted for permission to illustrate it. It is now, with Bull's, in the London Museum.

But the invention and rapid popularity of the Clarionet, which, as its name implies, was considered an effective substitute for the high clarion notes, soon caused the older instrument to disappear: so totally indeed was it abandoned, that Mozart was obliged to rewrite the trumpet parts found in the works of his predecessors. The long instrument now used in the orchestra and called the Bach Trumpet is certainly not the Clarion of that great composer's time, but a return, with very modern additions, to the straight Buzine of the Middle Ages.

In the records of the King's Music we find frequent allusions to the provision of Trumpets for His Majesty's use. In 1639-40, for instance, £60 was paid to "Cuthbert Collins for twenty Trumpets made by him for His Majesty's service in the northern expedition"; and, at the death of H.R.H. the Duchess of Saxony in 1666, mourning liveries were provided for "the Sergeant, 18 Trumpetters and a Kettledrummer", and also for "the Drumme Major, fowre drummers and a Phiphe".

The following instrument-maker's acknowledgment will explain why old examples of Trumpets and other instruments of metal are so rare:

"Received Simon Pierson's trumpett, broke to pieces, weight 27 oz. Received Thomas Barwell's trumpet, all broke to pieces, weight 16 oz. These two above-mentioned trumpetts delivered to Mr Bull, Feb. 20, to be new made.

"Received by me. Wm. Bull."

This was in 1685, or 1686 according to the new reckoning, and the old metal was melted down and used again with any addition necessary to make the new instruments of standard weight. William Bull was famous for his work, and a fine instrument of copper with silver mountings made by him which belonged to Mr T. A. Harper, is illustrated in Messrs Hipkins and Gibb's *Musical Instruments*. A horn by him is shown on Plate 37 and is dated 1699. Two Bull Trumpets are in the London Museum.

A very interesting and useful improvement on the ordinary Trumpet was introduced in England at the close of the eighteenth century: a slide was added to the instrument, whereby the false harmonic notes could be tempered and the pitch lowered a half or whole tone at will.

The slide, unlike that of the Trombone of which we shall presently speak, was automatically returned after being drawn out, by means of catgut strings wound on springs.

This Slide Trumpet was brought before the public by the celebrated player John Hyde, who wrote an instruction book for it. He seems to have been but partly the inventor of it, for on the instrument, depicted in Plate 42, the inscription of the spring-box is "Woodham, Inventor and Maker, Exeter Court, Strand".[1] It was never adopted on the Continent, but in this country became the solo instrument for use in the oratorios; and under its greatest exponents – the Harpers, father and son – was popular for nearly a century, until superseded by the valved Trumpets.

The shorter straight Trumpet, as we have seen, became the Clarion and the Field Trumpet: in the same way the longer Buzine has given us THE SACKBUT or TROMBONE, for the earlier form of the folded Trumpet had only to receive the addition of a slide and an attachment of metal stays (for greater rigidity) to appear as the first form of the Sackbut. But what a step!

Unnoticed by the Fraternity of Trumpeters, who fortunately did not appropriate it, as they had done the Clarion, to their own exclusive use, probably little accounted of by the actual inventor, whoever he was, and his immediate contemporaries and successors, it was fraught, nevertheless, with

[1] This trumpet is in fact by G. H. Rodenbostal, and only the slide-mechanism was made by Woodham.

untold value to the musical resources of after centuries, and by its perfect simplicity, yet perfect tonality, rose to meet every requirement of Music's Art as it progressed from cacophony to harmony. For, be it Sackbut or Trombone, it is the only wind instrument which, like its stringed associates in the orchestra, can within its compass produce the smallest interval which the human ear can appreciate.

It is impossible to say how or when the Slide principle first arose. The ancient Roman Trombone said to have been given to King George III cannot be traced, but as others still extant were found in Italy at the same time it was evidently only one of those large Horns or *Buccinae* such as form part of the treasures of the National Museum at Naples. The eleventh-century "Sackbut" of the famous Boulogne Psalter (MS. No. 20) is undoubtedly a lyre or harp. We know, however, that the slide was in use in the fourteenth century; for not only does the occurrence of the words Sacabuche and Saquebute imply it, but it is clearly shown in a representation of the instrument, together with shawms, on an ivory chessboard of Burgundian workmanship in the National Museum at Florence. An illustration of this instrument, which still retains more of the Trumpet shape than the later form, is given by the writer in his paper on *The Evolution of the Sackbut*. As it is also mentioned as forming part of an orchestra which played during a great feast held in Lombardy at the close of the fourteenth century, it seems that either in Northern Italy or in the south of France the new instrument took its rise. In Germany it retained the name of its progenitor, and was called the Buzaun, a word which has now become Posaune; and this is probably the reason of the German tradition which places the Posaune or Trombone in the hands of the Archangel of the Judgment Day. It should, of course, be the long Buzine, as shown so repeatedly in medieval manuscripts of the Apocalypse. In Italy it was simply called the Trombone or Large Trompe; but in Spain it received the nickname from which we have the old English name Sackbut. The Spanish name *Sacabuche* also denotes a kind of pump, and is derived from *sacar* (to draw) and *bucha* (a tube); for it was only natural that the action of the hand on the slide of the instrument should have suggested the similarity; and it is surely rather far-fetched to suppose that the word is a contraction of the phrase *sacar del buche* (to exhaust the chest), no special effort being necessary to produce the sound. In the fifteenth century the name and the instrument appear in England, for in the *Privy Purse Expenses* of Henry VII there is the following entry:

1495, May 3. To foure shakbusshes for ther wag[s] vii[li].

Whatever the instrument may have been, the name was a trying one for English ears, and it took a long time to settle into shape; we find it as sayke-bud, sakbud, sacbut, shackebutte, sagbut, shagbushe, and shagbolt; but sackbut was the English form which survived in the end.

King Henry VII's players were of foreign extraction; but the instrument took at once a recognized place in English music, for we find in 1501 that Hans Naille and John Browne, both of them members of the King's Band, paid a visit to the Court of Charles of Austria, who was then in the Low Countries, and received £37 10s. for their performances.

Henry VIII maintained ten Sackbut players, of whom the three principal received £4 per quarter. In his private collection, however, he left no specimen of the instrument.[1]

An example of the instrument, dated 1557, and the work of the famous maker, Jorg Neuschel, of Nuremberg, is shown on Plate 42. It is the oldest known Sackbut in existence. Neuschel has left some interesting business letters to customers, in one of which, dated 1545, he says that he will make five large Trombones and a "Mittel Busone" (a smaller instrument) for £60; whereas for such a set the King of England, the King of Poland, and other great personages always gave him £120 (1910 values).

Sackbuts ever since their introduction in the fifteenth century have been retained in the household music of our sovereigns, and have played their part at coronations and funerals, in the olden days with the Shawms and Cornetts and in later times with the Trumpets and Drums. As they were not "royal" instruments, they were also in popular use by the watchmen or waits, and appeared as integral parts of ecclesiastical foundations. The Canterbury Cathedral *Account Books* inform us that they were there used *pro melodia* – that is, to support the plain-song; while for stage plays and pageants they were in constant requisition. John Howes, Gatherer of Lega-cies for Christ's Hospital, in *A familiar and friendly Discourse* (1587), says: "I also think it convenient that the children should leearne to singe and play uppon all sorts of instruments, as to sounde the trumpett, the cornett, the recorder or flute, to play upon shagbolts, shalmes and all other instru-ments that are to be played uppon either with winde or finger." In Campion's Maske, performed at Whitehall on Twelfth Night, 1607, on the occasion of

---

[1] Henry's private collection of instruments seems to have consisted only of those used by himself, by his immediate entourage, and by the musicians of the Privy Chamber. Instruments played exclusively by professionals – e.g. such instruments as trumpets, drums, church organs, harps, etc. – would have been in the care of their players. The Neuschel Sackbut mentioned in the next paragraph is now the emblem of The Galpin Society.

the marriage of Sir James Hay, there was a "doble sackbote" in one of the two orchestras. This instrument was the Bass of the set of Sackbuts which, until the end of the seventeenth century, consisted only of the High Sackbut (which did duty as the Descant or treble and is now the Alto Trombone), the Ordinary Sackbut a fifth lower (which we now call the Tenor Trombone), and the Bass or Double Sackbut, an octave below the highest instrument and reaching as its lowest note C or, according to the old English designation, double C. The Treble Sackbut, illustrated in Plate 42, was an octave above the Tenor, and is wrongly called the Slide Trumpet (*Tromba da tirarsi*) of Bach's scores. It was apparently first used in England in Purcell's time, as a part for it appears in the *Canzona* written by him for the funeral of Queen Mary II in 1695. The title "Flat Trumpets" given to the instruments required for the performance of this piece is certainly unusual, but it evidently refers, first of all, to the minor key in which the composition is set, and also to the use of instruments which could be played in that "flat" key.[1] So far as we know, the Sackbut, which was also called the Trumpet Harmonious and the Double Trumpet, was the only brass instrument which, at that period, was recognized as adapted to the minor or flat key, or could truly render the music written by Purcell. An interesting allusion to Trumpets played in a flat key is to be found in a note given in the *St Cecilia Day Celebrations* by Husk, where, under the year 1691, we read that during the feast "while the company is at table, the hautboys and trumpets play successively. Mr Showers hath taught the latter of late years to play with all the softness imaginable: they plaid us some flat tunes with a general applause, it being a thing formerly thought impossible upon an instrument designed for a sharp key".

It is somewhat peculiar that during the latter part of the eighteenth century the Sackbut disappeared from popular use in England; it may have been owing to the disuse of the Cornett, its old partner in the wind-band, or to the peculiar charms of the Serpent and the Horn. An inventory of the contents of Canterbury Cathedral, taken in the year 1752, has the following entry:

In the Vestry.

Two large chests (N.B. in one of these chests are contained only two brass Sackbuts not us'd for a grete number of years past, the body of an old Bass Viol without strings and such like trumpery).

This entry is again repeated in 1761.

[1] Fuller descriptions of "flat" and other trumpets are to be found in James Talbot's manuscript (Christ Church, Oxford, MS 1187: *c.* 1695–8): see Anthony Baines, *GSJ*, I, pp. 9–26. Purcell's March and Canzona for the Funeral of Queen Mary will be found in volume XXXI of the Purcell Society Edition (London, 1959).

Sackbuts were then heard only in the King's private orchestra, and they certainly were not included in the military bands which were at that time beginning to be organized. According to Dr Burney, the King's players were the only performers available for the Handel Celebrations of 1784, and they were Germans. With the revival of Italian Opera, however, the instrument reappeared in full force, but under the Italian name Trombone instead of the old English title. A writer in the *Encyclopaedia Londinensis* (1819) evidently found their presence (as then played) anything but welcome, for he writes: "Trombones and Double Drums are now so frequently used in the Opera, Oratorios, etc., that they are become a nuisance to lovers of pure harmony and refined tones; for, in fact, the vibrations of these instruments produce noise not musical sounds, though in certain peculiar situations they have a noble and grand effect." How different would it have been had these players remembered Mersenne's advice to performers on the Sackbut in the early part of the seventeenth century: "It should be blown," he says, "by a skilful musician, so that it may not imitate the sounds of the Trumpet but rather assimilate itself to the sweetness of the human voice, lest it should emit a warlike, rather than a peaceful, sound."

As has been already said, the mechanism of the Sackbut or Trombone is extremely simple, though the knowledge of it was carefully guarded by the players of the fifteenth and sixteenth centuries. As a tube of fixed length can only produce a certain series of harmonic notes, by lengthening the said tube another series of lower pitch is sounded; and by fitting together the several series thus obtained a chromatic scale can be produced, if sufficient lengths of tube be taken. It requires seven lengths (called *positions*) on the Trombone to effect this, the performer extending or shortening the tube by means of the slide.

The same result is produced by the valves, which are placed on the brass instruments of the present day: for whether they revolve as taps (called *rotary valves*) or pass up and down as *pistons*, they simply add to the original length of the tube such extra lengths as are necessary, either by themselves or in combination, to give the required harmonics. A Cornet with revolving *discs*, the invention of an Englishman, John Shaw, about the year 1835 is represented on Plate 42.

It is not, however, within our present scope to explain the various forms of valve which have been suggested or adopted; one of the first forms of Cornet with two piston-valves only, and called at that time (*c.* 1820) the Cornopean, is shown on Plate 42. But we think it is only fair to the genius of one of our countrymen to draw attention to a method of valve-action which was given

PLATE 37

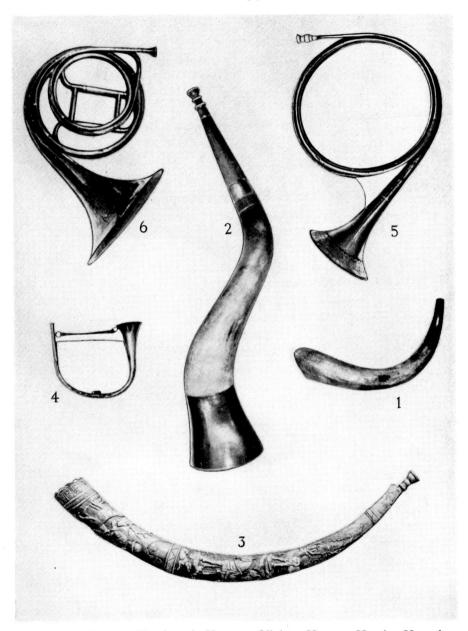

1. Forester's Horn. 2. Watchman's Horn. 3. Oliphant Horn. 4. Hunting Horn, late eighteenth century. 5. Hunting Horn, seventeenth century. 6. Hand Horn, nineteenth century

PLATE 38

Musical Instruments of the early eleventh century: harp, rote, crowd, cornett, panpipes and clappers

PLATE 39

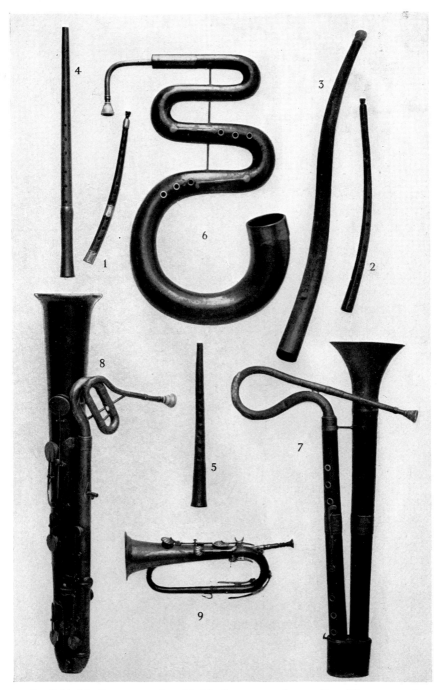

1. Small Treble Cornett, 1518. 2. Treble Cornett, *c.* 1600. 3. Great Cornett, *c.* 1600.
4. Mute Cornett, seventeenth century. 5. Straight Cornett or Harvest Horn.
6. Serpent, late eighteenth century. 7. Bass Horn, *c.* 1800. 8. Ophicleide, early
nineteenth century. 9. Keyed Bugle, *c.* 1820

PLATE 40

1. Trumpet and Clarion, *c.* 1400

2. Clarions, early
fifteenth century

to the public and practically employed seventeen years before Blümel and Stolzel patented in Germany their piston mechanism.

Charles Clagget, born at Waterford, but afterward of Greek Street, Soho, who describes himself as a "Harmonizer of Musical Instruments", in the year 1788 produced his "Chromatic Trumpet and French Horn", capable, as he says, of producing just intervals and regular melodies in all keys, minor as well as major, without the assistance of crooks or any change in the instrument. In 1793 he published a description of his invention in a treatise called *Musical Phenomena*, with a drawing of the instrument and scale of fingering. The device consisted of the union of two trumpets with one mouthpiece, but separate tubes and bells, their pitch being a semitone apart. Just below the mouthpiece a rotary valve was fixed, and its action was twofold: by turning it, either to the right or left, one or other of the trumpets was brought into use; and by an extra turn, right or left, the same trumpet was lowered a whole tone: thus a chromatic compass of twenty-seven notes was obtained. The idea of the two instruments conjoined seems cumbersome, but the device of adding an additional length of tubing for the half-tone by means of a valve is the very principle that underlies the present-day Cornet.

Claggett received the praise of Dr Burney and other musicians for his ingenious invention, which, as one of his correspondents says, "will be of the first importance in the cause of music". At a concert in Bath, duets in major and minor keys, accompanied by the orchestra, were played on Chromatic Horns before several hundred auditors – the soloists, who were horn-players, having had only eight hours' practice on their strange instruments; but Claggett was already past the prime of life, and the prejudices of practical musicians were against him, so his invention went for naught, and Germany has the credit of having given to the world the first valved instruments.

Chapter XII

Organs Portative and Positive[1]

The swete Orgayne pipis comfortith a stedfast mynde;
Wronge handlynge of the stoppis may cause them sypher from the kynde.
But he that playethe of pipis, wher so grete nowmber is,
Must handill the keyes all lyke that [by] mysgovernaunce they sounde amysse.

LEKINGFELDE PROVERB (*temp*. Henry VIII)

FROM THE RECORDS OF ANTIQUITY, so far as they are preserved to us, it is unmistakably evident that the first musical instrument which was distinguished by the application of a Keyboard was the Organ. In the second century before our era, Ctesibius, the mathematician and mechanician of Alexandria, had attached to the slides of the Hydraulus or Water Organ a series of lever keys, which, when depressed by the fingers of the performer, pushed in the pierced slides and thus admitted the wind into the pipes placed immediately above them.

The detailed treatise of his pupil Hero, and the minute description which the architect Vitruvius has given of the Water Organ as it was constructed in the first century A.D., had for some time suggested the idea that the keyboard was well known to the Greeks and Romans; but it was not until the year 1885, when a small earthenware representation of an Hydraulus was found in the ruins of Carthage, that the idea became a certainty and the actual form of the Keyboard was revealed to us. From this interesting relic now preserved, with portions of others, in the museum of St Louis at Carthage, we gather that, at the commencement of the second century of our era, the Water Organ possessed nineteen keys, each about eight inches in length and two inches wide, arranged in the same plane and according to the six Greek scales required on the instrument. It had, moreover, three ranks of pipes, probably of unison, octave and super-octave pitch, controlled by three stops on the right-hand side of the organ; but instead of the primitive horn springs and catgut used by Ctesibius for bringing the keys back to the normal position when the fingers were lifted, it had the metal springs des-

[1] For more about the classical and early medieval organ, see Willi Apel, "Early History of the Organ", *Speculum*, vol. XXIII, no. 2 (April 1948), pp. 191–216.

cribed by the later writer Vitruvius. We do not, however, propose to enter here upon a detailed explanation of the working of the ancient Water Organ – a full description with many illustrations and diagrams has been given by the writer in the *Reliquary* (1904) and in Grove's *Dictionary of Music* – nor can we find any trace of its use in our own country, for the illustration in the Eadwin Psalter at Trinity College, Cambridge, though by an English artist, is undoubtedly copied from that in the Utrecht Psalter, which is presumed to have been illustrated from drawings in a much earlier Byzantine or Alexandrian work. In fact, from our own practical experience of a Water Organ, constructed according to the Carthaginian model, it is evident that it was unsuitable for northern climes, as the freezing of the water in winter renders it unplayable. It may, nevertheless, be advisable to say this as a brief description – that the Hydraulus was not a steam organ played with boiling water, according to one suggestion and as William of Malmesbury endeavours to explain, nor was it similar to those pretty devices of the seventeenth century called Water Organs, in which the bellows were worked by a water-wheel. In the ancient instrument air was forced by two or more side pumps into a metal retainer standing in water and similar to a diving-bell. As the water was driven out the air within became subject to heavy pressure, and when the channels to the organ pipes were freed by the inward movement of the slides, the air rushed upwards and the pipes continued to sound until the water had found its level once more within the retainer. In the organs of the present day exactly the same process takes place, but, instead of water-pressure, the necessary force is obtained by heavy weights placed on the upper board of the reservoir. This simple device, however, for continuing the sound of the pipes was not applied to our large organs till the eighteenth century.

It is almost incredible that, once the utility and advantage of the keyboard had been known, it should have entirely disappeared from practical use and required a rediscovery in the twelfth century. Yet so it was, and the fact is probably due to the abhorrence with which the early Christians regarded an instrument used in the gladiatorial contests and licentious orgies of heathendom.

In the Eastern Empire the principle of the Water Organ seems to have been longer continued, for in the year A.D. 826 an hydraulic organ "after the Greek manner" was erected in the palace of Louis the Pious at Aix-la-Chapelle; but in the Western Roman Empire the simple pneumatic principle asserted itself, and by the seventh century the Organ was recognized as a fitting accompaniment to the choral music of the Church. Saint Ealdhelm, whose skill on the harp we have already recognized and who died in A.D.

709, mentions a large organ "with windy bellows", and we are told that in A.D. 814 the organ (*orcin*) in the church of Cloncraff, Co. Roscommon, was destroyed by fire. In the following century not only does the instrument take its place amongst the necessary adjuncts of divine worship, but the description by the monk Wolstan of the large organ erected by Bishop Alphege before the year 951 in Winchester Cathedral enables us to form some idea of its construction and capabilities. It had four hundred pipes, being ten pipes to each of the forty sliders, for keys were unknown. The forty sliders were divided into two sets, and each set of twenty sliders was manipulated by an organist, the two brothers being, fortunately, "of concordant mind", who pulled them out and pushed them in again as required. According to the scale given by Odo of Cluny, who died in the year 942, each of these sets would have a compass from *G* to *c″* with additional sliders for two *b* flats, as Wolstan informs us. On each slider the letter denoting the sound was written, and so the sets were called "the alphabets". In an English manuscript of the thirteenth century (Brit. Mus., Arundel 339) containing a treatise on the measurements of organ pipes it is stated that if the organist, who was in those days organ-maker as well, wished to exceed two "alphabets" (i.e. octaves) and to add another whole "alphabet" or less, the size of the additional pipes must be proportioned to the rest, so that they may all sound in tune.

As there were no stops in this great Winchester organ, but all the ten pipes to each note gave voice simultaneously, it is not to be wondered at that a noise "like thunder" battered the auditory nerves of the listeners, or that they all "stopped their ears with their hands and were unable to draw near or bear the sound".

The wind supply, too, for this instrument was correspondingly magnificent, for there were twenty-six bellows (no kind of air reservoir being provided), and these were arranged in two rows, fourteen below and twelve above. Seventy strong men "labouring with their arms and covered with the effects of their efforts" incited each his fellow to drive up the wind with all his strength.

In the twelfth-century Psalter at St John's College, Cambridge (Plate 43), a smaller instrument, but worked and constructed on similar lines, is portrayed in the upper left-hand corner; the "strong men" are much in evidence, but the organist is absent. The sliders are shown projecting from the sound-board beneath the pipes, and on their round ends the names of the notes were written. An organ with copper pipes, given by Count Elwin to the convent of Ramsey in the tenth century, cost £30; and history does not relate the value of the instrument provided for the Abbey Church of Malmesbury by Dunstan;[1] but organs appeared everywhere; in fact, the great churches both in England and on the Continent became so "over organized" that in the twelfth century Abbot Aelred, of Rievaulx, in Yorkshire, exclaimed with horror against their size, the noise of the bellows and the roar of the pipes. It is true that the blowing apparatus was sometimes placed on the other side of the wall, so that the creaking and wheezing were less evident; but even then the noise must have seemed tremendous to ears accustomed only to the soft strains of Rote and Harp.

An anonymous treatise of the twelfth century (Cod. Bernensis) on the making of organs, edited by Schubiger in *Musikalische Specilegien*, speaks of keys (*lamina*) which, when pressed down, pushed in the sliders (*linguae*) as far as an iron pin; while, on releasing the keys, horn springs drew them out again. As the whole account, however, savours of Hero's description of the keyboard mechanism of the Water Organ, written in the second century B.C., it is very doubtful whether such a device was in actual use at the time when this treatise was compiled; nevertheless, it is probable that either in the twelfth century or early in the next some kind of keyed mechanism was applied to the organs, and first of all to a small instrument which was called THE PORTATIVE, because it could be carried about and played at the same time by one performer. But the mechanism employed in these small instruments was entirely different from that of the Hydraulus keyboard, and in its earliest form consisted of little buttons or pins, each passing through a closely fitting hole and pressing open a hinged valve placed immediately beneath, which allowed the air to enter from the bellows into a channel leading to the organ-pipe. By taking the finger off the button the valve was closed by the pressure of a metal spring.[2] Such a primitive keyboard is shown in the illustration, given in Fig. 38, from an early fourteenth-century Psalter known as the Peterborough Psalter; and the instrument itself agrees well with the description given of these little organs by Jean de Meung a century earlier:

> Orgues bien maniables,
> A une seule main portables,
> Ou il mesne souffle et touche.

[1] What may well have been the organ-loft for this instrument is still to be seen at Malmesbury – a rather unsightly stone box high up at one side of the nave. There can be little doubt that the so-called "Minstrels' Gallery" in the nave of Exeter Cathedral is in fact the loft in which the fourteenth-century organ was placed; the room behind it would have housed the rather noisy bellows mechanism, and the no less noisy bellows-men.

[2] Such button mechanisms are still used on concertinas and accordeons.

The same keyboard action was retained for all the smaller organs at least till the seventeenth century, though the little pins or buttons of the earlier instruments were soon covered with thin strips of wood, hinged at the farther end, and affording a more convenient surface for the fingers, as shown in an English manuscript (B. 10. 2) at Trinity College, Cambridge (Fig. 39). Thus was re-formed the keyboard of classical times, though it was left for the stringed instruments first to receive the balanced keys, which turning on central pins now move the stickers and trackers of our more modern

Fig. 38 Portative – early 14th cent.
(Peterborough Psalter)

Fig. 39 Portative – 14th cent.
(Cambridge)

organs, and communicate by this action with the valves, which are no longer placed immediately beneath the keys, but removed to some distant part of the instrument.

From the little Portative the keyboard passed to THE POSITIVE ORGAN, that is, to those instruments which were of such a size as required them to be "set down" or "placed in position" before being played upon. In the Belvoir Psalter of the thirteenth century (Plate 44) an organist, probably intended for King David, is depicted performing on a Positive Organ and depressing the keys with his fingers, whilst the blower, or bellows-treader, is supplying the wind in an improved manner. In the Peterborough Psalter, which was for some years in the National Library at Paris, but is now at Brussels, a Positive Organ of the fourteenth century is seen, in which one brother is furnishing the wind by working two small bellows, one grasped by either hand, to another brother, who modulates the sweet sounds by touching the keys. The illustration is reproduced in Fig. 40.

In the large organs the blower's duties, as we have already realized, were more onerous; but the performer's task was far from easy, for the valves were not only fitted with stronger springs and, being on a higher level than

Fig. 40 Positive – early 14th cent. (Peterborough Psalter)

the keys, were pulled down by cords attached to the long key-shafts, but the effort required to draw them open against the heavy pressure of wind, which the great number of pipes to each note necessitated, needed the use of the whole hand and even the clenched fist. The oldest large organ of which we have a detailed account is that at Halberstadt erected in 1361 and repaired in 1495. It is described by Praetorius in his *Syntagma Musicum* (1618). There were four so-called keyboards; two for the hands, consisting of twenty-two keys each, with a chromatic compass (except the g' sharp) from B to a', the upper one acting on from thirty-two to fifty-six pipes to each key and the lower one on a single row of pipes (an open diapason) for quieter music. The third keyboard of fourteen chromatic keys from *B* to *c'*, also for soft effects, was played by the hand or at times by the knee, much in the same way, we presume, as a celebrated London organist was wont to do in the days when pedals were few and feeble, by catching down the ends of the long finger-keys with his knee-cap. The fourth keyboard in the Halberstadt Organ was for the feet and had a compass of an octave from *B'* to *B*, each key acting on from sixteen to twenty-four pipes. As Praetorius truly says, the sound produced was a deep, coarse roar and fearsome grumbling, to which the number of little mixture pipes added an overpowering noise and a mighty scream. No doubt it was just as much admired as the Winchester Organ. The three forms of early slider and keyboard actions are illustrated on the next page.

The invention of stops to alter the tone and volume of sound, which the Halberstadt Organ with its four keyboards had already attempted, took place in the fifteenth century, although they had been anticipated in the Roman Hydraulus. At first they assumed the shape of large iron levers, which, at the will of the performer, cut off the wind by means of little spring boxes from any particular row or rank of pipes; but soon afterwards the slider (Ctesibius' slider under another form) was used and this, being pierced with holes, stopped or opened the channels to the several ranks of pipes according as the slider was moved out or in.

The shape and character of the pipes have also changed. In the organs of Greece and Rome they were of metal only and all of the same diameter or *scale*, though varying, of course, in length; some were stopped with plugs, others were open and fitted with sliding caps for tuning purposes. It has been suggested that *reeds* were also used in these instruments, but all extant illustrations of the Water Organ show only the long flute or *flue* pipes. There is, however, no reason why they should not have been employed, for the beating reed now found in the Organ was known in the days of ancient Egypt. It is interesting also to observe that Wolstan, in his description of the tenth-century Winchester Organ, uses the word *musa* for organ pipes; now *muse* or *musette* is the medieval name of a reed-pipe, such as is found in the bagpipe. Perhaps, however, it was only a poetic licence, though *voces* was the usual word where the exigencies of metre forbade *fistulae*.

In the fourteenth-century Halberstadt Organ there were certainly no reed-pipes, and the first definite mention which we have of them is about the year 1460, when, according to Praetorius, Henry Traxdorff, of Nuremberg, constructed an organ of which the sound, we are told, "resembled that of the shawm". This was probably the beginning of the Regal and soon

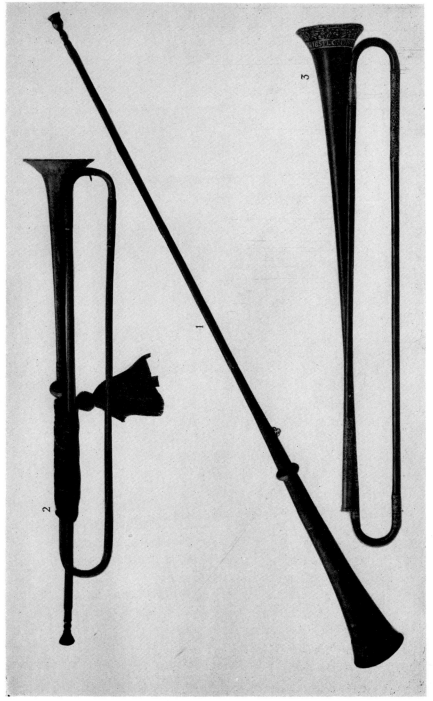

PLATE 41

1. Buzine by Sebastian Hainlein, 1460. 2. Clarion by J. W. Haas, *c.* 1650. 3. Trumpet by Augustine Dudley, 1651

PLATE 42

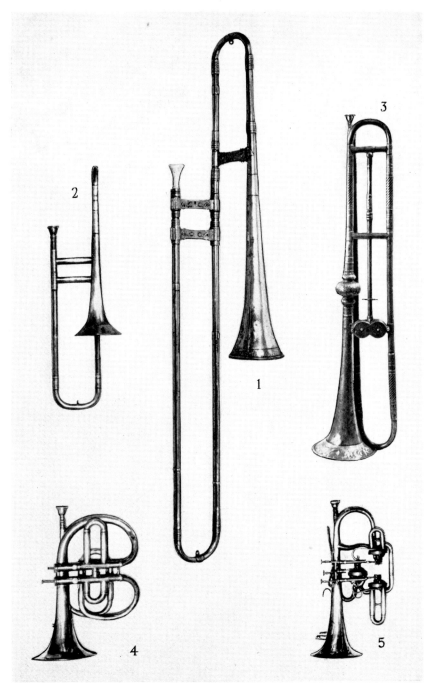

1. Sackbut by Jorg Neuschel, 1557. 2. Treble Sackbut by Schmied, 1781.
3. Slide Trumpet by Rodenbostal, *c*. 1800. 4. Cornopean, *c*. 1830. 5. Cornet,
c. 1840

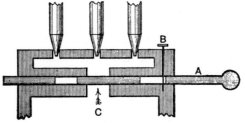

A. SLIDER ACTION (12TH.CENT.)

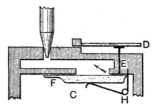

B. PIN ACTION (13TH.CENT.)

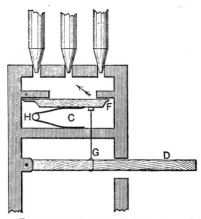

C. TRACKER ACTION (14TH.CENT.)

Fig. 41 Organ Actions
A Slider, B Check Pin, C Wind Chest, D Key, E Push Pin or Sticker,
F Valve or Pallet, G Pull-down or Tracker, H Spring

afterwards it was introduced into the large organ as the first reed-stop of which we have definite information.

In the thirteenth century all organ pipes were made of metal, generally a mixture of tin and copper: they were, like those of classical times, cylindrical and of the same diameter throughout, but in that century Odington tried to equalize the tone by making the length and width of each pipe proportional.

In the instrument (*c.* 1270) pictured in the Belvoir Psalter (Plate 44) the pipes are conical. Wooden pipes appear in the sixteenth century, and various other materials have been tried, such as glass, clay, stone, quill, horn, bark, and paper – the last with a certain amount of success, not only in Henry VIII's Regals, but in organs of the present day. A small Positive Organ of the sixteenth century with paper pipes is in the Victoria and Albert Museum collection.

In many of the representations of medieval organs one or two pipes much larger than the rest will be noticed: oftentimes they are placed on the right-hand side of the instrument. In the Belvoir Psalter (Plate 44) and in that of Peterborough of the next century (Fig. 40) they are very marked. These large pipes were added in the thirteenth century to sound bourdons or deep-toned drones, after the manner of the bagpipe, and a small wooden catch, placed over the drone keys, when turned, held down the required note, leaving the player free to use both hands in descant or extempore melody. This long-sustained note afterwards developed into the so-called pedal-point, which forms so important a feature at the close of many of Bach's grand fugues.

A good idea of an English organ of the early sixteenth century is given by the specification drawn up in 1519 by Anthony Duddington for the instrument at All Hallows, Barking. A full description will be found in Rimbault's *History of the Organ*.[1] From it we learn that all the pipes of this "payer of organs" were to be of pure tin, and it was to have twenty-seven "playne" keys or, as we should say, naturals, beginning from C and reaching to c''' with the necessary sharps and flats, a compass of four octaves with allowance for the usual "short octave" in the bass. Three stops are mentioned, a diapason for the bass of 16 foot pitch and two principals of 8 and 4 feet. The cost was £50 sterling.

The curious and oft-recurring phrase, a pair of organs, calls for notice. This term has no connection with the ranks of pipes, the number of the bellows or the duplication of keyboards. It is simply intended to take the place of the old Latin name *Organa*, the plural number of the word *Organum* which the Greeks and Romans used for any sort of machine whether musical or not. Mr Abdy Williams, in a useful paper on *The Evolution of the Choir Organ* (*Musical Times*, January 1907), states that, owing to the use of the

---

[1] Rimbault's *History of the Organ* is now quite superseded by W. L. Sumner's outstanding *The Organ: Its Evolution, Principles of Construction and Use*, first published in 1952. Chapter V, "The Organ in Britain until the Nineteenth Century" (pp. 97–186) is indispensable. See also Cecil Clutton and Austin Niland, *The British Organ* (Batsford, 1963).

singular number *organum* by medieval musicians to denote a special method of singing, the plural had to be employed for the instrument, and he supports this theory by an apt quotation from *The Customs of the Cathedral Church of Lincoln*, which certainly shows the necessity for this distinction. Under the date 1321, in the celebrations at the tomb of St Robert, it was agreed that the man who conveyed the organ (*trahenti organa*) was to receive 6s. 8d., while each of those who sang the *organum* (*cantantium organum*) was to be paid three pence. This may be so, but, on the other hand, St Augustine, in the early part of the fifth century, tells us that the custom of calling the musical instrument inflated by bellows *organa* was already prevalent in his day and therefore long before the use of the word *organum* for a certain method of singing; he says, moreover, that it was so called to distinguish it from the word *organum* which meant any kind of machine; probably it came from the fact that the organ seemed, from its complexity, to include several machines requiring several men to work them. At any rate, the words "a pair of organs" represent the Latin *organa* and, as a conventional phrase, they were applied to other keyboard instruments, as "a pair of Regals", "a pair of Virginals", etc. On the meaning of single and double organs we reserve a note in the Appendix, page 212.

Owing to their popularity, English literature and records provide many references to the small organs as well as to those of larger size. In 1518 Richard Fitz-James, Bishop of London, mentions in his will his "payre of portatyves" in the chapel of his palace in London, and his organs in the chapels at Fulham, Hadham, and Wykeham. The Inventory of Henry VIII's "Householde Stuffe and other Implementes", taken in 1547, shows us that in the Privy Chamber at Hampton Court there was "one payre of portatives, with the Kynge's and Quene Jane's Armes", and in another room "one paire of portatives covered with crimson satten". In the old Romances also the name of this little instrument appears, as, for instance, in *Clariodus and Meliades*:

> The dulcet playet also with portative
> Sad hevie myndis to make exultative.

For this small organ is frequently depicted in the medieval illustrations with dancers and mummers; probably it was on this instrument that "Janin L'Organistre" played at the Westminster Feast in 1306, and also "Little William, Organist of the Countess of Hereford", who received five shillings for his performance.

It is unfortunate that no specimen of the true Portative is now in existence, the instrument at Blair Castle being a large Regal. Several reproductions are to be found in continental museums, and the example here illustrated is in the writer's possession (Plate 45). It was constructed after the design shown in one of Luca della Robbia's famous plaques of the fifteenth century: the compass, which is chromatic, extends from c' to a'', about the compass of the treble voice. There was usually only one bellows and, as no air reservoir was thought of at that time, the wind had to be drawn in according to the phrases of the plain-song, as the breath is in singing. A Portative, with two bellows lifted alternately, is shown among the fifteenth-century carvings in Manchester Cathedral and is reproduced in Fig. 42. St Cecilia is frequently depicted with this form of instrument in her hands, and for processional purposes it was and would still be eminently serviceable. It disappeared in England in the sixteenth century, being no longer required for church purposes and already superseded in popular use by the portable Virginals and Spinets. Artists would do well to remember that this little organ was not automatically blown, and that if the fingers of the right hand are represented touching the keys the left hand should be placed on the bellows at the back. The instrument was supported either on the knee or by a strap over the shoulder.

Of the Positive Organ we have fewer indications by name, but the Annals of Winchester College inform us that in 1420 a linen cloth was purchased for covering the college organ and carrying it to Clere, and that 8*d*. was paid for two ash staves for carrying the said organ. This was probably a Positive similar to that shown on Plate 45, though in this sixteenth-century specimen a workman of the next century has placed the bellows on the top with a primitive air reservoir instead of the two bellows which originally were attached to the back of the instrument, as in the Regal (Plate 45). Note the blowing strap (left) and the stop handles (right).

A large instrument of this kind is found still in some great churches, especially on the Continent, and being put on wheels can be moved about as required; but its usual position is now fixed, for it has been incorporated into the Great Organ as the Choir Organ, which in Germany is still called the Positive, and is often placed in a separate case in front of the main instrument.

The REGAL, as has already been stated, was invented about the year 1460. It is a form of Positive but provided with one or more *reed*-stops. Of its construction we fortunately have very accurate information. The metal reeds were of the clarinet or beating type, and therefore must not be confounded with the *free reed* of the Harmonium, which was adopted from China and the East at the close of the eighteenth century. The origin of the name Regal has called forth many suggested solutions, the most usual being that it was first made as a present to a king. Others have said that it is a corruption of the name *Rigabello* given to an instrument formerly used in the Italian churches before the introduction of the Organ. But the old English orthography of the sixteenth-century "Rigol" or "Regol" suggests that it is a contraction of the Latin *Regula* and shows that its original purpose was to "rule" or "keep in order" the plain-song of the monastic choirs.[1] In old German the Latin *Regula* appears as *Rigel* or *Regul* and in Italy as *Rigola* or *Regolo*. The utility of the new instrument was speedily and widely recognized and Regals became the rage. Its portability was still further increased by George Voll, of Nuremberg, about the middle of the sixteenth century, for he made it in the shape of a book, the keyboard and pipes being closed after the performance within the covers, which formed the bellows. There are in England at the present time three specimens of this Book or Bible Regal. The writer's example, shown in Plate 46, dates from the later part of the seventeenth century, and was still employed during the last century to accompany a village choir in Germany. The compass is four octaves (chromatic)

Fig. 42 Portative –
15th cent.
(Manchester)

from *C* to *c'''*, and it is capable of sustaining a large number of voices. Owing to the shortness of the pipes the tone in these smaller instruments is not so fine as that of the large and less portable Regal, such as that which formerly belonged to the late Mr Hipkins and is now in the collection of the Royal College of Music.

In the first part of the sixteenth century the name Regal was applied to any small organ which served a similar purpose, even though it did not wholly consist of reed-pipes. This is clearly shown by the description of Henry VIII's Single and Double Regals which is given in full in the Appendix; one of the Single Regals, for instance, had "one stoppe pipe of tinne, one Regale of Tinne and a Cimball". Another had "one stoppe of pipes of wood with a Cimball of tinne and the Regall of papire", the last-named

---

[1] The etymology of the word remains somewhat obscure, but it may well be connected with the current Italian word for "present" or "gift" – *regale*. Canon Galpin's Bible Regal, like his big clavichord, is now in the possession of The Galpin Society; they are housed with the Benton Fletcher Collection of keyboard instruments, at Fenton House, Hampstead.

material being, of course, used for the tube of the pipe and not for the reed, which was of metal. The "Cimballe of Tinne" was a small Mixture or Compound Stop like the German *Zimbel* and could only be drawn in combination with others; and that is the reason why, in the description of one of the Regals with three stops, it is said "the same hath but two stoppes of pipes and thother stoppe is but a Cimball". Lord Bacon, in his Natural History called *Sylva Sylvarum*, writes: "in Regalls (where they have a Pipe, they call the Nightingale-Pipe, which containeth Water) the Sound hath a continuall Trembling"; and a seventeenth-century manuscript in the British Museum (Harl. 4160) gives us "the way of making an artificial nightingale as it is in waterworks with pipes of metal or wood like a flagellat". It is therefore doubtful how far the following entries refer to the Regal proper, consisting *only* of reed-pipes, or to the more comprehensive instrument which we have just described.

Jan., 1537.	Gevene to Heywood's servante for bringing of my Lady Grace's Regalles from London to Grenewiche	xx$^{\text{d.}}$
May, 1538.	Paid for a payre of Regalls . . .	iv$^{\text{li.}}$ x$^{\text{s.}}$
Jan., 1543.	Paied to Betynes servante for mending the Regalles	vii$^{\text{s.}}$ vi$^{\text{d.}}$

These are taken from the *Privy Purse Expenses* of the Princess Mary; Heywood was Virginal player to her father and afterwards to her brother, who also appointed Beton as his organ-maker at a salary of £20, while William Tresorer was retained as Regal-maker at a salary of £10.

From the *Lord Chamberlain's Records* we find that in 1582 payment was made for crimson vellat, or velvet, for covering, lining, and ornamenting divers of Queen Elizabeth's Regals and Virginals. In the Mystery plays the Regals figure largely, and in the accounts of the Coventry performances from 1534 to 1565 the instrument is carefully distinguished from the Organ.

A fine example of a large English Regal is preserved in the castle at Blair Atholl, and by kind permission of his Grace the Duke of Atholl we give an illustration of it in Plate 47. It stands on a frame of wood with four legs, the natural keys are of ivory with black sharps, and the compass is four octaves, including the "short octave". The pipes are all of wood and are turned and mitred in the bass, showing that originally they were concealed beneath an ornamental cover of open-work, now lost. The stops are divided into treble and bass, as in the case of some of Henry VIII's instruments, and the small ivory sliders project from the right and left sides of the case; they are drawn out by loops of cord. The stops are as follows: Fifteenth,

Principal, Stop Diapason, Twelfth and Trumpet, the last representing the old Regal stop. At the back are two bellows, which are raised alternately to supply the necessary wind. On the bellows are painted the initials I.L. and the date 1650; so we conclude that the work, which is evidently English, is that of John Loosemore, of Exeter, who was born in 1613 and in 1665 constructed the great cathedral organ of his native city, with its famous Double Diapasons.

Thomas Mace, in his *Musick's Monument* (1676), describes an instrument which he calls a Table Organ and claims as his own contrivance. It was like an oblong chest, 7 ft. 5 in. in length, 3 ft. 3 in. in height, and 4 ft. 3 in. wide. Eight flaps, acting as desks, in the top allowed the sound to be regulated according to the number of players which it accompanied. The keys were ivory and ebony, and the six stops consisted of an Open Diapason, a Principal, a Twelfth, a Fifteenth, a 22nd, and a Regal; the longest pipes were, of course, turned and mitred as in Loosemore's Organ. There was in addition a Hoboy Stop[1] worked by the foot which, with the Regal, produced the "Voice Humane". The bellows were within the case close to the ground, and could be worked either by the player's foot or by a cord, as in the small Positive Organ shown in Plate 45.

The name Regal for any Reed Organ survived many years after the original instrument had disappeared; in 1684 we find Henry Purcell appointed to the office of keeper, maker, repairer, mender and tuner of the "King's Regalls, Virginalls and Organs", and he was succeeded in 1695 by Dr John Blow and Bernard (Father) Smith. The office is said to have been abolished in 1773 when Bernard Gates, who had held it, died at the age of eighty-eight; but six years later "the tuner of the regalls" was in receipt of £56 per annum.

In the early part of the seventeenth century our English cathedrals and churches had been well supplied with organs, and frequent mention is made, by those who heard them, of their sweet tone and excellent construction – "neat, rich and melodious". The days of the Commonwealth proved, however, for these choice productions of English craftsmen a "common woe", for nearly all of them were wantonly destroyed as superstitious ornaments. Some, however, miraculously escaped, as at St Paul's, York, Durham, Lincoln, and in several of the colleges of Oxford and Cambridge. The Restoration naturally created a demand for their re-erection, and a German, Bernard

---

[1] This appears to have been some kind of tremulant. A single regal stop survived on many English organs well into the twentieth century; usually labelled as "Vox Humana", it was traditionally drawn with a tremulant.

171

Smith, commonly known as Father Smith, to distinguish him from his nephew of the same name, began to make good the loss, whilst Renatus Harris, a rival from France, but of English parentage, challenged his supremacy. Smith was favoured by the King, and Charles II appointed him organ-maker, allotting to him in 1681 the apartments in Whitehall called "The Organ-builder's Workhouse"; but both makers were worthy of their craft, and have left the impress of their skill and genius on the history of organ-building in this country. In the next century the Jordans, an old English family, invented the *swell*, which gives to the instrument so much of its present charm. This was in 1712, and although the method at first employed was clumsy, it was afterwards improved by the substitution of the louvred swell, which had already been applied by Shudi to the Harpsichord. The swell was not adopted on the continent for at least fifty years after its invention in England; on the other hand, the English organists were very slow in using the pedals; in fact, these were rarely found in this country until the end of the eighteenth century, and then they only consisted of small projections from the case, pressed by the player's toes, like those of the fourteenth-century organ at Halberstadt. They had, moreover, no pipes of their own, but simply pulled down the finger or manual keys, which extended a fourth or fifth lower than the usual continental compass. One of the earliest notices of a complete organ in this country is found in the account of an instrument erected in 1824 in St James' Church, Bristol, by Mr Smith, a local organ-builder. It had four manuals and two octaves of pedals from *C*. Dr Hodges, the organist, was, however, mindful of his weaker brethren, for, like the organ in St James' Church, Bermondsey, there was a row of keys which could be used "if the performer was not accustomed to pedals".

The application of pneumatic and electric power to the mechanism of the Organ is a development of more recent times, into the description of which we do not intend to enter, for this has been ably done by such recent writers as Mr Abdy Williams, Dr Hinton, and Mr Audsley in their histories of the king of instruments; but before we close this chapter we must notice some very interesting attempts which have been made in the past to combine the two classes of keyboard instruments, viz. strings and pipes. The combination was generally called the Claviorganum. Thus in 1480 the Chamberlain of Queen Isabella of Spain had in his keeping two "Claviorganos" with painted cases, and Henry VIII was the proud possessor of four such instruments, described in the Inventory of 1547 as instruments "with a Virgynall and a Regall", or as "Virginalles with pipes underneath". It appears to have been known in England in the days of his royal father, for the proverb on the Clavycymbal or the Claricymbal, which is distinct from that on the organ quoted above, can only be explained by supposing that pipes and strings were combined. It is as follows:

> He that covytithe in Clarisymballis to make goode concordaunce
> Ought to fynger the keyes with discrete temporaunce:
> To myche wyndinge of the pipis is not the best
> Which may cause them to sypher wher armoney shulde rest.

In 1552 Rabelais mentions a similar combination under the French title *Espinette organisée*; and in an inventory of furniture at Kenilworth in the days of the great Earl of Leicester (1584) there is this entry: "Item, an instrument of organs, regalls and virginalles covered with crimeson vellatt and garnished with Goulde lace." Here it is evident that the word "organs" stands for the flue pipes, and "regalls" for the reeds. An example of the Claviorganum is to be seen in the Victoria and Albert Museum, South Kensington. On the lid of the wing shaped Clavicymbal, which rests on the top of a large rectangular case, is inscribed "Lodowicus Theewes me fesit 1579". Theewes was a famous Flemish maker, being a member of the Guild of St Luke in Antwerp, and this is the oldest part of the instrument. In the case beneath there are the remains of the organ, which had five stops, probably Stopt Diapason, Principal, Twelfth, Fifteenth and Regal, the latter partly formed of paper, as in Henry VIII's regal. The stops were made in halves, treble and bass, and three stops have been added to obtain variety of tone on the Clavicymbal, which has two unison strings and one octave string. The organ with painted case (*c.* 1600) is well described and figured by Mr Philip James in *Early Keyboard Instruments*.[1]

Kircher, in the second volume of his *Musurgia* (1650), gives a large illustration of a wonderful Clavicymbal in which strings and pipes were combined: he considers it new and unheard of; in fact, each succeeding century produces it as a novelty. A specimen made in 1712 for the Elector of Hanover, afterwards George I of England, is now preserved in the Metropolitan Museum of Art, New York. It has forty-eight stopt diapason pipes below the sound-board of the stringed instrument. A more elaborate example, made by Crang, of London, in 1745, was shown at the International Inventions Exhibition, 1885: it possessed two keyboards with the usual Harpsichord stops, and the Organ attachment had in addition four stops, a Stopt and

---

[1] See also Frank Hubbard's important study of this instrument in *GSJ*, III, pp. 12–15.

Open Diapason, a Principal and a Twelfth, the two latter divided into Treble and Bass.

The combination was even attempted with the Hurdy-gurdy, and the *Vielle organisée* is still sometimes to be met with. In more recent years it has been tried with the Piano and the Harmonium, but though we may admire the ingenuity of the maker the difficulty of maintaining the same pitch in the two instruments and their great dissimilarity of tone must convince us, as the Arched Viall did Mr Pepys, that the Claviorganum at present "will never do".[1]

Of the Barrel Organ, which supplanted the Church Bands in towns and villages during the early part of the last century, many amusing stories have been told, and in some of our more remote parishes the instrument may still be found. The principle, of course, was not new; Henry VIII had a Virginal that went with a wheel "without playing upon". The remarkable manual and mechanical organ made in 1598 by Thomas Dallam for the Sultan of Turkey at the command of Queen Elizabeth had self-acting trumpeters, blackbirds and thrushes, with chimes and solemn music, while Kircher, in his *Musurgia* (1650), devotes a large part of his second volume to these and other automatic instruments.

The Barrel Organ, formerly used in St Michael's Church, St Albans, possessed four stops (Open and Stopt Diapasons, Principal and Fifteenth). The two interchangeable barrels were pricked with ten hymn-tunes each, but as only certain notes were required the scale was incomplete, being – *G A d e f♯ g g♯ a b c' c♯' d' d♯' e' f♯' g' g♯' a' b' c'' c♯'' d'' d♯'' e'' f♯'' g''*. A fine instrument by Willis, which recently stood in an Essex church, met with a sad end. The pipes were sold to a journeyman tinker, the bellows presented to the village blacksmith, the boards of the air reservoir were used as a bed for the clerk's aged father and the case was adapted to the requirements of a pigsty. *Sic transit gloria!*[2]

---

[1] Claviorgans seem to have been made more for convenience than for the artistic effect of pipe and string sounded together; for continuo-playing in such works as Handel's oratorios, or in trio-sonatas around 1700, such instruments were almost essential. For a note on the combination of piano and organ, see Albert G. Hess, "The Transition from Harpsichord to Piano", *GSJ*, VI, pp. 75–94.

[2] Various short notes on barrel-organs may be found in *GSJ* from time to time (vol. I to date), but the most thorough discussion is Canon Noel Boston's article "The Barrel-Organ", *Transactions of Ancient Monuments Society* (London, 1959), pp. 99–124. This includes a full list of all known surviving barrel-organs in England, with lists of their tunes. See also H. B. Sharp, "Church Band, Dumb Organist, and Organ", *GSJ*, XIV, pp. 37–40.

Chapter XIII

Tabors and Nakers[1]

With Shackbuts noate that pierce the skies,
   With Pipe and Taberret,
What tunes by reedes or canes arise,
   Do not His praise forget.

SIR WILLIAM LEIGHTON (1613)

IT IS COMMONLY REPORTED by those who have travelled among the snow-bound Eskimo that the only musical instrument used by them is the drum or tambourine, which is found everywhere, from Greenland to Siberia. Its loud, resonant and somewhat musical note accompanies all their actions. Nothing is done, nothing contemplated without sounding the drum. If a person is ill, the drum is beaten; if he is well, the drum is beaten; if the hunting and fishing are prosperous, the drum proclaims the fact; if death has robbed them of a comrade, the drum sounds his knell.

Does not this show that, in dealing with the Drum, we are speaking of an instrument of sound-production which has probably entered more largely than any other into the destinies of the human race, by its ominous roll and measured beat summoning the bravest hearts a nation can offer to do and dare, or by its alluring thrumming and merry tapping leading in mazy dance the twinkling feet?

Nor is the simplicity of its construction a drawback; after all, the joy of life consists, not in the multitude of our possessions, but in our appreciation of the few. For as with the city urchin, whose old-fashioned, broken-down toy is as great a delight to him as the latest working model is to the spoilt child of fortune (and probably a greater), so with the denizens of these Arctic climes, the drum is the recognized panacea for the many ills of their existence and a source of unbounded delight when the heart is merry and young.

The group of instruments which we generally include under the name of

[1] The best current treatment of this topic is by James Blades in *Musical Instruments through the Ages* (Penguin Books, 1961), pp. 327–49; he has a full-length book in preparation, dealing with all percussion instruments.

175

Drum resolves itself into three distinct types. We have, first of all, the *Timbrel* or *Tambourine*, a shallow circle of wood covered with skin on one side only. Then there is the *Tabor* or Drum proper, with its barrel-shaped frame of wood, varying in depth, but skin-covered on both sides; and lastly we have the *Nakers* or Kettledrums, in which a hemispherical body (generally of metal) is covered with skin over its open top.

To those who associate the Tambourine only with negro minstrelsy or gipsy dances, it may be a surprise to hear that in this Timbrel or Tambourine – for they are the same instrument – we have one of the oldest of the world's music-makers. In the civilizations of the most ancient nations, in Assyria and Egypt, in Greece and Rome, the Tambourine has sustained its part. The hoop Drums of China, the rectangular *Daff* of India and the *Chilchiles* of the Peruvian Incas, like the *Aelyau* of Greenland, are but varying modifications of this one widely distributed instrument.

Fig. 43 Timbrel – early 14th cent.
(British Museum)

Its simple form was doubtless known to the Celtic tribes who in prehistoric days found their home in Britain. Suetonius, in his *Life of Augustus*, describes a Gaul who played upon it, and he tells us that it was circular and struck with the fingers. And even were it not so, the advent of the Romans to our island with their Bacchic rites, to which the Tambourine was a constant accompaniment, would accustom the vanquished to the seductive charm of its rhythm and the pleasing tinkle of its jingles. For in classical times these little plates of metal, called by the Romans *tintinnabula*, had already been added, and throughout the Middle Ages, in the manuscripts illuminated by the English artists, we find that the instrument is almost precisely the same in form as it is today. The old English name was "Tymbyr", which is explained by the author of the *Promptuarium Parvulorum* (1440) to mean "a lytyl Tabore" *Timpanillum*, and it is from the word Tymbrelle, a diminutive of Tymbyr, that we obtain the word Timbrel. This is probably the instrument which, according to our English translation, Miriam and her maidens took in their hands to celebrate their nation's triumph, for the Hebrew *Toph* was a small hand-drum of which the Arabian

Duff is the present-day representative. For this reason, undoubtedly, the Timbrel or Tambourine – the latter name another diminutive of the word Tabor introduced into our language from France or Italy – was frequently represented in medieval ecclesiastical carvings, and is placed by artists and sculptors in the hands of saints and angels.

In the nave of Beverley Minster, beneath the outside parapet of St John's Church, Cirencester, and among the old figures which adorn the front of the Exeter Minstrels' Gallery,[1] the Timbrel with its jingles is well displayed. Gower, in his *Confessio Amantis* (*c.* 1393), says of his heroine:

> When as she passeth by the streate
> Ther was ful many a tymbre beate
> And many a maide carolende.

And in *The Romaunt of the Rose* the dexterity of the Timbrel players and dancers is thus extolled:

> There was many a Tymbestere
> And saylours that I dare wele swere
> Couthe ther crafte ful parfetly
> The Tymbres up ful subtelly
> They caste and hente ful ofte
> Upon a fynger fayre and softe
> That they fayled never mo.

While Drayton two centuries later, in his poem *David and Goliath*, thus describes the victor's return:

> Field, town and city with his fame do ring,
> The tender Virgins on their Timbrels sing
> Ditties of him.

An illustration of the old English Tymbyr in the hands of a Tymbester will be seen in Fig. 43. It is taken from a manuscript of the early fourteenth century in the British Museum (Harl. 6563) and shows that at that time a cord of catgut was stretched across the parchment head in order to give a sharp rattling sound when the instrument was struck, as in the side drum of the present day. On many of the Oriental forms of the Tambourine this detail is still found. The vibrating cord is called in England the *snare*, but in France it is known as the *timbre*, which suggests that the snare was originally derived from the Oriental Timbrel by Western contact with the East during the Crusades, shortly after which we find it so constantly depicted. It is somewhat curious that on the Continent the Tambourine is popularly called

---

[1] For the purpose of this gallery, see footnote on p. 161.

the *Tambour de Basque* or *de Biscaye*; an early allusion to this name is to be found in Aimeric de Peyrac's Latin poem of the fourteenth century:

> Quidam tabreta vasconizabant
> Leves pedibus persaltantes.

"Some were imitating the Basques with their tabret, leaping lightly with their feet." In Spain, however, in the fifteenth century, we find it called the Tamborino.

Late in the eighteenth century we were indebted to Eastern Europe for a strange revival of the instrument in connection with military music; and it was at this time that the old name Timbrel, which had been continually in use during the previous century, was supplanted by the word Tambourine. About the year 1785 Bass Drum, Cymbals or Clashpans, Triangles, Tambourines, and "Jingling Johnnies" – the latter a sort of ornamental standard decorated with little bells which tinkled as the instrument was shaken – were added to our army bands after the fashion of the famous Janissary music of Turkey. Men of colour were generally obtained for the tambourines and the clashpans. Dr Farmer, in his interesting *History of the Royal Artillery Band*, tells us that the blacks who marched in front were expected to perform all sorts of capers whilst striking or *thumbing* their tambourines – such capers as we now see only in negro minstrels, where the instrument is, ethnographically, quite out of place.

As with the Timbrel, so with its close associate the TABOR, its use dates from the most remote ages, though in all probability the form of drum with one skin-covered head preceded that with two. The ancient Egyptians used the double-headed drum, and in 1823 an actual specimen was found at Thebes, which showed that, by a system of cords which we now call *braces*, the skins could be tightened when required. The Romans had a similar instrument and, on the fine tessellated pavement discovered at Brading in the Isle of Wight, in 1881, a dancing girl with her *Tympanum* or Tabor suspended at her side and a man accompanying her on the panpipes are distinctly shown. From this source the Tabor, like the Timbrel, became common in Britain, though we find but little mention of it except in Wales; for the Timpan of Ireland and Scotland, as has been already explained, was not a drum but a stringed instrument of the psaltery kind. In Wales the *Tabrwdd* was recognized as the instrument of one of the inferior orders of musicians and was used by the minstrels on feast days and at the dance. The tabor-player, like the piper, the juggler, and the rebec-player, had to

178

perform standing and only received a penny for his fee. He was usually furnished with a small whistle-pipe upon which the melody of the dance was played, while the rhythm was accentuated by strokes upon the little drum which was fastened to his left arm or shoulder. This primitive orchestra, popularly known as the Pipe and the Tabor, has been described in a previous chapter. An English monk, Bartholomew, writing in the year 1360 says, "the Tympanum maketh the better melody yf there is a pype therewyth". In the Luttrell Psalter of the first part of the fourteenth century a view is shown of the city of Constantinople; armed men are marching out of the gate with long trumpets and preceded by a taborer with his pipe. Illustrations of the instruments will be found on Plates 28 and 30.

The word Tabor, which in Queen Elizabeth's day received a diminutive form Tabourell to denote the smaller sizes of the instrument, is a corruption of the old Spanish name Atambor, which was applied to the largest specimens of its class. The larger Tabor will be seen in front of the comical figure which stands as the central representation of Profane Music in the English illustration reproduced from the twelfth-century manuscript of St John's College, Cambridge, on Plate 43; and a similar instrument is shown in an English manuscript of the same century in the British Museum (Lans. 383). In both instances they are played with the hands and not with sticks. A yet larger form, which, during the later Middle Ages and for two centuries afterwards, took so important a part in military service, came into use in the thirteenth century when the armies of Western Europe adopted so many of the customs of their Oriental foes.

When King Edward III entered Calais, he did so, as we are told by Froissart, "à foison de trompettes, de tabours, de nacaires et de buccines", but earlier still, in 1306, at the great feast made at Westminster, Tabourers and Trompours were present, many of the nobility having also their private musicians, as "the Tabrer of Lady Audham", "Guillot the Tabrer of the Earl of Warwick", a custom very prevalent two centuries later, when bishops as well as titled laymen had their drummers.

This instrument, which was sometimes called the Taberett, was destined to receive a further increase in size in the fifteenth century, when, suspended at the side of the player and beaten on one head only, it became with its accompanying Fife, the first organized form of military band, a step which seems to have been taken during the struggles of Switzerland for freedom, for the Swiss "Fife and Drum" became the envy and admiration of the crowned heads of Europe. The earliest notice of this larger Drum in our country which we have observed is in the *Privy Purse Expenses* of Henry

VII, who in 1492 gave to "2 Sweches grete taborers" the sum of £2. We find the word Swesch or Swische frequently used in Scotland in the next century to denote the large Tabor. At Edinburgh, in 1560, "Cutberth Brown, tabernar, playit on the Suesche quhen our Soverane came furth of Dumbar to this Town"; but in England the name drom or drume was used for the new instrument, which by its booming sound reminded the listeners of thunder and noise. In the list of the King's musicians made in 1547 the "Tabretts" appear no longer, their places being taken by the "Dromslades", the Dutch word for drum-beaters. In 1534 the word was evidently strange to the ordinary Englishman, for a licence was granted in that year to Bartheu Roumbaugh, "Dronslade *player*", to export one hundred tuns of double

Fig. 44 Drum and Fife – *c.* 1540
(British Museum)

beer. In an old sketch (Brit. Mus., Aug. A. iii) showing the English army taking the field about 1540 each squadron is headed by a "Drome and a Phiphe" (Fig. 44), and from an instrument which was used in Queen Elizabeth's reign, we find that the size of the military drum was two feet in depth and two feet in diameter. It was on this rather unwieldy instrument, which hung at the player's side and was struck with two sticks on its upturned head, that those famous drum marches were beaten which so often led the English troops to victory. They were slow and dignified, and when Marshal Brion, a French general, happened to say to Sir Roger Williams, a gallant Welsh soldier of Queen Elizabeth's time, that the English march beaten on the drum was slow, heavy, and sluggish, he was met with the crushing retort, "It may be true, but slow as it is, it has traversed your master's country from one end to the other." In the seventh year of the reign of King Charles I a royal command was issued for the revival of the old English march "so famous in all honourable Atcheivements and glorious Warres of this our Kingedome in foraigne Parts, being by the approbation of strangers themselves confest and acknowledged the best of all Marches", because "through the negligence and carelessness of Drummers and by long discontinuance so altered and changed from the ancient Gravitie and Majestie thereof, as it was in danger utterly to have been lost and forgotten". "A true

PLATE 43

Musical instruments – sacred and profane – of the twelfth century. For sacred music:
chime-bells, monochord, organ, harp, panpipes and cornett. For profane music: rebec,
bugle and drum

PLATE 44

Organ and Symphony, *c.* 1270 (Belvoir Psalter)

Copie of the originall signed by His Majestie" is given in Fig. 45.

In the royal *Privy Purse Expenses* we find frequent mention of payments and gifts to these drummers: the earliest, in 1532, to "Hans Pyper and Bartholomew his Felowe Dromslade for their lyverayes 45 shillings." The Churchwarden's Accounts of St Margaret's, Westminster, informs us that in 1579 there was "paid to the sojers, the ansyant-bearer, and to him that played upon the Drome the sum of £1 7s. 4d." – probably for a muster of the citizen army in Tothill Fields; and Queen Elizabeth paid her three "Drumsleds" £18 5s. each per annum. In the thirteenth century Drums (*taburae*)

Fig. 45 Drum Music – 17th cent.

were employed to warn rowers of approaching danger: but a still more curious use is shown in an old painting on wood of about the year 1620, which represents a football match. The game is in progress, the players in felt hats with feathers, and each side is accompanied by a drummer in uniform who is doing his best to rally his team and to drown the groans of the wounded who are being attended to by a number of doctors in another part of the field.

The use of the "side drum" for military purposes is still well known, but the proportions of the instrument have been much decreased. Its size in the sixteenth century has already been given, but a drum of the eighteenth century, left in 1745 by a straggler of Prince Charles Stuart's army at Arkholme in Lancashire, measures only 1 ft. 5 in. in depth and the same in width. In the British army of today it is represented by an instrument of yet smaller dimensions but of brilliant tone. The Tenor Drum, which more nearly resembled the old English instrument, is now seldom used; for the deep tones of the older form are provided by the Bass or Long Drum, so called because it used to be made of greater length than width. It was formerly known also as the Turkish Drum, having been introduced into the army bands with the Cymbals and other Eastern music at the close of the eighteenth century. Mr Kappey, in his *History of Military Music*, informs us that in the Janissary bands while one side of the Drum was beaten with a heavy felt-headed stick the other was rubbed with a kind of broom or swish held in the left hand, and giving the unaccented beats of the measure. This curious contrivance is represented in an engraving of the Pandean Minstrels at Vauxhall in 1806, contained in a portfolio of prints of musical subjects in the British Museum.

The Bass Drum appears in our English music before the year 1787, for in an old bill of the Royal Artillery Band for that year we find payments of 16s. for three large drumheads for the Bass Drum, as well as 6s. 6d. for two large drumheads for the Tamborins. The dimensions of an existing example of a Bass Drum of that period are 2 ft. 6 in. long by 1 ft. 10 in. across the ends. Owing to its great size, the instrument was often borne on the back of an attendant, leaving the musician free to put all his strength into the performance. This practice was sometimes resorted to with the large medieval Drum, and still more frequently with the Kettledrums described below. In France the very large Drum seems to have been known as early as the fifteenth century, for an example of that period is figured among the stall carvings of Rouen Cathedral. It is supported by one man, whilst another wields the stick, and across the skin is stretched a *snare* to which the little bells are attached, a refinement of torture which is not found in our modern instruments.

We can hardly realize the effect which all this drum-beating and jingle-rattling had in the days of sweet Recorders and soft-toned Viols; but in 1511 the worthy Virdung thus gives vent to his feelings: "These drums are to the taste of those who cause much disquiet to pious old people, to the sickly and weakly, the devout in their cloisters and those who have to read, study and pray. I verily believe that the Devil must have had the devising and making of them, for there is no pleasure nor anything good about them. If the noise of the drumstick be music, then the coopers who make barrels must be musicians." He has our sympathy.

But as there is "music in the bellow of the blast", so there is music, and very sweet music, to be obtained from the skin-covered drum-top. For though on these instruments you may emulate the din of the cooper's shop, yet at the touch of a true musician the drums shall win you to sleep with the lullaby of a cradle song. It is so with the KETTLEDRUMS. Their origin is undoubtedly Arabian or Saracenic. The name by which they were known in medieval times, *nakers*, is but a European corruption of the Arabic word *nacareh* or *naqqaryeh*, which is now represented by the *naqqareh* of Turkey, Syria and Arabia – small hand-drums with bowl-shaped bodies of wood or metal covered with skin. Like the Kettledrums they are usually used in pairs; the smaller forms can be held by one hand while the other grasps the stick with which they are beaten; but in the larger sizes they are either placed on the ground or slung one on either side of a camel (Plate 50).

As we do not find them at an early date in Spain, we may probably infer that their introduction into the West was due, not to the Moorish invaders, but to the Crusades, which brought also the Long Trumpet called the Buzine, with which they were closely associated. They appear in English literature in the old Cornish drama, *Ordinale de Origine Mundi*, written at the end of the fourteenth century, where "Psalmus (shawms), gytrens and nakrys" are mentioned together. "Trompes and nakerys" are associated in the old romance of *Sir Gawayn and the Grene Knight*; whilst in *Belshazzar's Feast*, another old English poem, they take their place amongst the instruments of their class as "the nakeryn noyse, notes of pipes, tymbres and tabours". Chaucer's use of the word has already been quoted in connection with the Clarion.

But the earliest appearance of the Kettledrums in our country is in the list of King Edward I's minstrels, where in 1304 Janino le Nakerer appears; the same man may have been "Le Nakarier" who attended the Westminster

Feast two years later. Edward III had a Nakerer as well as a Tabrete among his musicians, and in 1347 "nacaires" helped to celebrate the entry of the victorious King into Calais.

The representations which we have of these instruments in illumination and sculpture – and they are of frequent occurrence – display them as small, and generally suspended in front of the player by a strap round the waist or from the shoulder, a stick being held in each hand; but in the Luttrell Psalter of the early part of the fourteenth century we find them placed on the ground, as shown in Plate 33. The more usual position is also depicted in that Psalter, as will be seen in Plate 48; and in the carving of a tournament scene on the choir-seats at Worcester Cathedral, erected in 1394 (Plate 49), the Nakerer is represented in dire distress, having been upset by the backing horse of one of the combatants. There are also carvings of the Kettledrums in Beverley Minster and in Duston Church, Northamptonshire, both examples being of the fifteenth century.

The introduction of the larger size, borne on either side of a ridden horse, for cavalry purposes, was due to the Hungarians, who, leaving Scythia about the ninth century, brought with them their military customs as well as their national dances and songs. It is recorded of Henry VIII that he sent to Vienna to procure Kettledrums that could be played on horseback, "after the Hungarian manner", and hence they became the special instruments of the Hussar regiments, a title derived from the Hungarian word for cavalry. The novelty of these instruments had much impressed the Archbishop of Cologne in the previous century, when in 1457 he interviewed the chief of the magnificent embassy sent by Ladislaus, King of Hungary, to treat for the hand of Madelaine, daughter of King Charles VII. Whether the English King procured his Kettledrums and his drummers we have no knowledge, but in the arrangements made by George Ferrers as Lord of Misrule for King Edward VI's entertainment, at Christmastide, 1551, we read that he had provided one "to plaie upon the Kettell Drom with his boye".

This is the earliest instance we have observed of the use of the name, which has ever since been attached to this kind of drum, and probably the "boye" was the unfortunate being who had to bear on his back the noisy burden.

In the reign of Queen Elizabeth the drum-players were called *timpanists*; but this does not necessarily imply that the instruments on which they played were Kettledrums, as it would in our own day. They appeared, however, during the great entertainment made by James I in honour of Christian, King of Denmark; among the sights of the Royal Procession was "the

Kinge of Denmarke's Drume, riding uppon a horse, with two drumes, one on each side of thee horse's necke, whereon hee strooke two litle mallets of woode, a thinge verie admirable to the common sort and much admired". It is not until the year 1660 that the *Lord Chamberlain's Records* give us the actual word, when John Barteeske was appointed kettledrummer. In 1682 we find the following entry: "£12 to be paid to Sergeant Price for a new pair of Kettledrums, provided him for His Majesty's service, a pair of kettledrums having been lately lost at sea." In 1685, when James II ascended the throne, the cavalry or kettledrums became the recognized appanage of every regiment of horse. Sir James Turner, writing the year previously, seems to speak of them as uncommon, for he says: "There is another martial instrument used with the Cavalry which they call the Kettledrum; there be two of them, which hang before the Drummer's saddle, on both which he beats. They are not ordinary. Princes, Dukes and Earls may have them with the troops which ordinarily are called Life Guards." They were also allowed to other regiments, if captured on the battlefield.

By the historian of the Royal Artillery Band we are informed that Kettledrums were purchased for the train of artillery in 1689, and appeared for the first time in the field during the Irish Rebellion of that year. They cost £158 9s., and were mounted on a chariot drawn by six white horses. They also accompanied the Duke of Marlborough to Holland in 1702. They continued in use until the year 1759, when they were deposited in the Tower of London, and probably perished with their ornate carriage in the fire of 1841. But the cavalry drums are still with us, and what more inspiring sight can be witnessed, as the mounted squadrons pace and parade before our eyes, than the kettledrummer leading his regiment, seated on a snow-white charger who seems to share his master's prowess?

In the concert room, also, these drums have found a worthy place. Lully is said to have been the first to use them in his operas for the *Grande Ecurie* of the French Court during the last half of the seventeenth century.[1] In England they appear in the Handelian Orchestra, and the great master frequently borrowed from the Tower a pair of Kettledrums which had been captured at Malplaquet in 1709. In his *Firework Music* (1749) he used three drums, but the French composer Berlioz has surpassed all, for he has used in the famous music of his Requiem Mass eight pairs of drums and ten players thereupon.

[1] For more about seventeenth-century kettledrums, with examples of their music, see Caldwell Titcomb, "Baroque Court and Military Trumpets and Kettledrums: Technique and Music", *GSJ*, IX, pp. 56–81.

The two drums usually employed are tuned a fourth or fifth apart by a mechanical device which stretches or loosens the skin-head until the required note is obtained; the larger drum has a range of notes from F to c, and the smaller a range from $B\flat$ to f. Drums can, of course, be tuned to other intervals and to notes of a higher or lower pitch according to their size, while the introduction of a third drum extends their usefulness in the orchestra. An interesting paper on the Kettledrum was read by Mr Gordon Cleather before the Musical Association in 1909 and is published in their *Proceedings*.

For the Handel Commemoration of 1784, held in the Great Church at Westminster, two pairs of common Kettledrums, the pair of Double Drums from the Tower, and a pair of Double Bass Drums were used. We are told that "except for their destruction, they had all the effect of the most powerful artillery". So the Abbey is fortunately still preserved to us.

Chapter XIV

Cymbals and Chimes

Praise Him with Simballs, loud Simballes
With instruments were us'd by Jewes;
With Syrons, Crowdes and Virginalls
To sing His praise do not refuse.

SIR WILLIAM LEIGHTON (1613)

AMONG THE ACCOMPANIMENTS of military music included under the French word *Batterie* are those metal sound-producers known as the Cymbals and the Triangle; and though both of them were introduced into our army bands with the other elements of Janissary music during the eighteenth century, yet they have a long history behind them. On the ancient monuments of Assyria the cymbal player is depicted clashing his thin plates of metal with all the impressive vigour of more modern times, and in the British Museum may be seen a pair of bronze cymbals which once did duty at the sacred rites of Egyptian deities.

From these Eastern countries they came to Greece, Etruria and Rome; they were made in various sizes from the large *cymbala* to the little jingles known as *acetabula* or vinegar cups, which, held between thumb and finger of each hand, provided, like the castanets, a rhythmic accompaniment to the dance. But to the Parthians, the Persians, and the Arabians the Cymbals were something more than mere aids to religious fervour or adornments of posturing maidens; they were instruments of war, and their clashing din, mingling with the wild fury of the battlecry, is frequently mentioned by Western writers of classical and medieval times.

In our own country they appear in the illuminated manuscripts of the thirteenth century, and are either flat or hemispherical in shape (Plate 50). Being connected with Jewish ceremonies and with early Christian worship, they are often represented in biblical scenes as in the Chapter-house paintings at Westminster (fifteenth century) and in ecclesiastical carvings.

In the fourteenth-century manuscript (Brit. Mus., 2 B. vii) known as Queen Mary's Psalter they are shown in company with the long Trumpet

187

called Buzine, with which they were connected in the Saracenic armies (Fig. 46).

In the next century the name is written Symbale, and in the seventeenth century Simball, as in the verse from Sir William Leighton's *Teares and Lamentacions of a Sorrowfull Soule*, which stands at the head of this chapter. In that century, too, small cymbals became very popular in France as an accompaniment to dance and song, whilst Gluck, in 1779, introduced them into his opera *Iphigenia in Tauris*, as an appropriate adjunct to the chorus of Scythians. But by this time the army bands had adopted them, and with "dusky Moors" wielding the "clash-pans" with immense effect and *empressement* at the head of the regiment, military music, in the words of Browning, "grew burning bright with fife shriek, cymbal clash and trumpet blast".

Fig. 46 Cymbals and Buzine – 14th cent.
(British Museum)

Of the TRIANGLE much the same may be said. Closely allied to the ancient *sistrum* – for in medieval times three, four, or five small rings were generally strung on the lower bar, and the open corner closed up – it was used by the Romans in dances connected with the orgies of their imported Eastern religions.

In a manuscript of the tenth century, found at St Emmeran by Gerbert and illustrated by him in his work *De Cantu*, etc. the Triangle appears of elaborate outline and with pierced ornamentation without rings; but examples portrayed in fourteenth and fifteenth century works, where it is depicted in the hands of angels and adoring saints, show the lower bar strung with the rings, which doubtless assisted the tinkling sound of the instrument.

In the Janissary bands several triangles were employed, and thus they passed, with other noise-producers, into the military music of the West. The old French name, as given by Machault, was Trepie, and was derived

PLATE 45

1. Portative Organ after Luca Della Robbia, fifteenth century
2. Positive Organ, *c.* 1600

PLATE 46

1

2

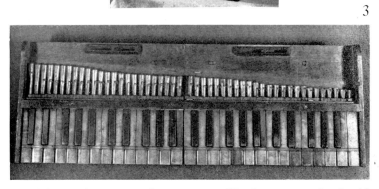

3

1. Bible Regal, seventeenth century. 2. The instrument closed with
keyboard inside. 3. The keyboard and pipes

PLATE 47

Large Regal by John Loosemore, 1650

PLATE 48

From the Luttrell Psalter, fourteenth century, showing the portative organ, the bagpipe, the symphony and the nakers

from the medieval Latin *tripos*, but in old English literature we have failed to find any allusion to the instrument. An illustration, however, from the hands of an English artist of the early fifteenth century will be seen on Plate 53.

We have already remarked that the "tryangel" mentioned by Mr Pepys in his *Diary* was the name of the three-legged stand on which instruments of the Spinet kind usually rested, and has no connection with our present subject.

THE JINGLING JOHNNY (on Plate 50) – the *Chapeau Chinois*, or the Turkish Crescent – we have already mentioned. It appears to have been originally a Pasha's standard, which was borne before the troops and, placed firmly in the ground, formed a rallying point in battle and a centre for the strenuous musicians who encircled it. When in the latter part of the eighteenth century it came with the other Turkish music into Western Europe, it was decorated with little bells and other adornments, but the crescent which crowned its summit was retained. In an old sketch by Cruikshank a foot regiment is shown marching to church with their Jingling Johnny. It has now for many years been laid aside, superseded by the lyre-shaped Glockenspiel or Metal Harmonica, a far worthier instrument of music.

Before we quit these primitive sound-producers, a few words must be said on those noisy contrivances which Dr Burney has described as the Old National Instruments of our island, namely the Poker and Tongs, the Marrow-bones and Cleavers, and the Saltbox and Hurdy-gurdy. Of the last, details have already been given in a previous chapter, but of the rest we may safely say that this sort of national music is no more peculiar to our country than to any other. Man will have noise if he cannot get music, and he will extract it from the simplest materials and those nearest to his hand.

The primitive instruments here named are, however, interesting, because Shakespeare, in his *Midsummer Night's Dream*, puts into the lips of Bottom, turned into an ass, this conceited statement: "I have a reasonable good ear in music; let us have the tongs and the bones."

In a Flemish manuscript of the fourteenth century in the Bodleian Library (Douce 5. 6) we find many such caricatures of Music's Art; for instance, a man is fiddling on a large ladle, whilst his companion accompanies him on the gridiron after the manner of Box and Cox, and a minstrel is portrayed playing with the tongs on a pair of bellows; while on the stall carvings of Lavenham Church, Suffolk, a man is represented using his crutch for the same purpose. In fact, buffoons of all times have invented these drolleries which, by no stretch of the words, could be called national music.

189

In Addison's *Spectator* (Vol. V, No. 570) a tavernkeeper is brought to our notice who played upon the frying-pan and gridiron, and declared that he had laid down the tongs and key because they had become unfashionable. In 1673, in a play performed before the Lord Mayor of London, a droll of Moors was exhibited; they were shown at work in a garden of spices with three pipers, "which, together with the tongs, key, frying-pan, gridiron and saltbox, make very melodious music; which the worse it is performed, the better it is accepted". In the previous year these worthies were described as "kitchen musicians" and their efforts as "confused music". Bonnel Thornton's *Burlesque Ode*, composed in 1763 and set to music by Dr Arne, brings out the latent possibilities of these instruments. For instance, an air accompanied by the saltbox, was sung to the following words:

> In strains more exalted the Saltbox shall join,
> And clattering and battering and clapping combine:
> With a rap and a tap while the hollow side sounds,
> Up and down leaps the flap and with rattling rebounds.

The effect produced was certainly not unlike that of the *crotala* or wooden clappers of more ancient times, of which the use in this country is shown in the Anglo-Saxon Psalter of the early eleventh century at Cambridge (Plate 38), where they are held by Idithun in his right hand. In a ninth-century Book of Prayers, written for Charles the Bald, Heman is depicted with them. In the seventeenth century clappers or bones were commonly called Knicky-knackers, and are represented in Inigo Jones' designs for Court masques.

The Marrow-bones and Cleavers are still a recognized form of ready-music among the butchers, especially for weddings, but are not, as Thornton would have us believe, a relic of the time when our brave ancestors rushed upon their enemies, like the ancient Gauls, clashing their weapons and cleaving them down.

Closely allied to the Cymbals there is an important class of metallic sound-producers which must not be overlooked. Into the history and folklore of BELLS it is impossible and unnecessary here to enter, for in *The Bells of England*, by the late Dr Raven, the subject has been most ably and exhaustively treated. Their use as little appendages to horse-trappings, personal dress, or as handbells dates from times most remote, and several Assyrian bells may be seen in the British Museum. The bas-reliefs show that a clapper was fixed inside as in the modern bells; but in China and Japan the oldest types of bell were without clappers and were struck by a hammer on the outside. An English handbell of the thirteenth or fourteenth century made of riveted iron and formerly bronzed in the same way as the medieval Irish bells is illustrated on Plate 50. It was found at a farmhouse in Chalfont St Giles, Buckinghamshire, and is said to have been originally used to sound the Curfew. Handbells of the twelfth century are depicted in the Glasgow Psalter, where in the lower corner of the illustration on Plate 20 they will be seen accompanied by a Psaltery. The invention of large church bells is generally attributed to Paulinus, Bishop of Nola in the Campagna, about the year A.D. 420, and from his place of residence were derived the medieval Latin names for the larger bells.[1] It is probable, however, that the good Bishop only introduced them, or approved their use in his diocese, for bells of large size were employed for religious purposes in the East long before the Christian era. In 680 Bede speaks of their use in Brittany, and the Chronicler Ingulphus states that in the ninth century the Abbot of Croyland gave six bells to his monastery and a great bell called "Guthlac, which was tuned to the other bells, and produced an admirable harmony, not to be equalled in England". From this celebrated peal may perhaps have started the fondness for ringing and efficiency in the art which have always distinguished our countrymen. An illustration of medieval bell-ringing will be found in a fourteenth-century manuscript in the British Museum (6 E. vi): the bells are properly hung and raised by ropes.

But besides the larger and smaller bells there are the CHYMME-BELLS or Bell-chimes, which appear so frequently in English and Continental illustrations from the eleventh to fifteenth centuries. They are small bells, either of the usual shape or like hemispherical gongs arranged in order, and suspended in a frame over the performer's head or placed on a suitable stand in front of him; on this chime he plays with a single hammer, or with two, one in each hand. The number of bells varies from four or five to eight or nine in the single set; the earliest English example is in an eleventh-century treatise on Music in the Cambridge University Library (Ii. 3. 12) but formerly belonging to the monastery of Christchurch, Canterbury. Here there are eight hemispherical bells struck with one hammer, and the performer is supposed to represent Pythagoras.

In the twelfth-century Psalter of St John's College (Plate 43), seven gongs are depicted, and in the Glasgow University Psalter of the same century there is a double set of eight bell-shaped chimes, with two performers, both holding hammers in each hand. As will be seen from the illustration on

---

[1] This is now thought to be mere folk-etymology. Bells were regularly used in Ireland from the sixth century AD, and throughout the Christian world from the eighth century onwards.

Plate 20, the names of the notes are inscribed on the supporting beam; on the right hand, UT, RE, MI, FA, SOL, LA, MI, and on the left in reverse order UT, RE, MI, FA, SOL, LA, FA – the centre bell, being the octave, is not marked. This corresponds to Guido's system, and on the right the bells sounded c' d' e' f' g' a' $b\natural'$ c''; and on the left c' d' e' f' g' a' $b\flat'$ c''.

In the Belvoir Psalter of about 1275 (Plate 44) there are thirteen similarly shaped bells, but not in use; and in a fourteenth-century Psalter (Lambeth Palace Library, MS. 233) David is shown playing with a hammer in each hand on nine bells arranged in a gable-shaped frame over his head (Plate 51). In an early fifteenth-century manuscript in the British Museum (1E. ix), of which an illustration is given in Plate 53, the instrument is drawn in a smaller form, unless we are to understand that the artist did not wish to introduce more than four bells into his picture, which was sometimes the case. Continental representations are very similar, but in one of the thirteenth-century manuscripts of the *Cantigas de Santa Maria* there is an interesting example in which seven bells are placed in a low frame and, by an attachment to their clappers, are being rung by a seated musician who pulls the cords, which bear labels showing the note of each bell – an early form of chiming apparatus.

As to the old name of this instrument we are not left in doubt, for the author of the *Promptuarium Parvulorum* (1440) gives us as the Latin of the Chymme-belle *Cimbalum*.[1] Bateman also, in his sixteenth-century notes on Bartholomew's treatise *De Proprietatibus Rerum*, tells us that "Cymbales are compassed like a hoope; on the upper compass, under a certain holownes, hangeth half bells, five or seven"; while in a manuscript of the next century (Sloane 1326) "Cymballs or Little Bells" are included among the *striking* instruments. We are told by his biographer, Osbern, that Dunstan, who died in 988, excelled especially in playing on musical instruments, like David, "taking the Psaltery, striking the Lyre, modulating the Organ and touching the Cymbals (*cymbala tangens*)". These last words evidently refer to the bell-chimes struck with hammers, the usual phrase for sounding the Clash-pans being *cymbala quatiens*, "crashing the Cymbals". These Chimes were much used in churches and with the organ, though they were not included in its mechanism, or electrically controlled, as in the present day at Westminster Abbey. Aelred, Abbot of Rievaulx, in Yorkshire, who lived in the twelfth century, exclaims in pious horror: "Why such organs and so many cymbals in the Church? What with the sound of the bellows, the noise of the cymbals,

[1] See Smits van Waesberghe, *Cymbala* (Rome, 1949).

192

and the united strains of the organ pipes, the common folk stand with wondering faces, trembling and amazed."

The association of organ and chime is shown in the Belvoir manuscript already alluded to, and the two are mentioned together in the quotation from the very early fourteenth-century poem by Robert Manning, of Lincolnshire, which prefaces our fourth chapter. In the romance entitled *The Life of Alexander* "orgues and chymbes" are also placed together.

At the Westminster Feast, in 1306, "Le Ménestral avec les cloches" received one mark; and the name there given to the instrument explains an obscure word in the English poem already so frequently quoted, *The Squyr of Lowe Degre*; for amongst the music which contributed to mirth and melody was the "clokarde". This is evidently connected with the French *Cloche* and the German *Glocke*; and, in Agricola's *Musica Instrumentalis* (1528), an illustration, showing ten small bells arranged on a frame, is described as "Glocklein oder Zimbeln". We also find an organ-stop called the *Zimbel* or, as on Henry VIII's regals, "The Cimball", and this we are told by Praetorius, in 1618, was a compound stop or mixture intended to represent the sound of bells. Even to the present day bell effects are generally produced in the organ by the combination of the mixture and the double diapason stops. We presume also that the name Zimbal or Cymbal, given in the later Middle Ages to the Psaltery, and afterwards to the Dulcimer, was so applied because the tone of its wire strings resembled the sound of the Bell-chimes so popular at that period, and from the Psaltery is passed to its keyboard offspring, the Clavicymbal or Harpsichord. In fact, Mersenne, in 1636, describes the carillon of bells provided with a keyboard as a *Clavicymbalum*.

Dr Rimbault in his *History of the Pianoforte*, transcribes a very interesting treatise by Theophilus, a monk who lived at the latter end of the eleventh century, in which he describes the making of these bell cymbals. The little hemispherical gongs were cast in moulds carefully prepared and proportioned, the metal was a mixture of tin and copper, one fifth or sixth being tin. Irregularities in tone or pitch were rectified by filing. Dr Rimbault expresses surprise at the mention of "tuning" cymbals, but Theophilus is treating of those used in the old English "Clokarde", and not the Oriental noise-producers.[1]

Closely allied to the Bell-chimes are the METAL and GLASS HARMONICAS. Grassineau, indeed, in his *Musical Dictionary*, gives the name Cymbal to an instrument constructed of metal bars with a compass of more than three

[1] For an edition and translation, with commentary, see *Theophilus: De Diversis Artibus*, ed. C. R. Dodwell (Nelson, 1961).

octaves. It was struck with two wooden sticks, and was known in England as the *Sticcado Pastorale*. He tells us that the low notes resembled the tone of a Flute and the upper those of a small Flageolet. The instrument which he thus describes was only an improved form of the wooden Harmonica known in previous centuries as the *Strohfiedel, Regale à bois* or *Xylorganum*. The first name is derived from the fact that the strips of wood were laid on straw bands, as they are at the present day. We are not aware of any old English illustration of this instrument, unless a curious drawing in a manuscript of the tenth or eleventh century (Brit. Mus., Harl. 603) is intended for it. The illustration is supposed to represent a scene by the waters of Babylon, and something is hung upon a tree – the English version suggests that it is a "harp", but the Latin Vulgate says *organa nostra*. Perhaps, therefore, the artist intended his production for a panpipe of abnormal size.

At the beginning of the last century the Nail-harmonica or Nail Violin, invented about 1740 by a Russian violinist named Wilde, was introduced into this country as the Semi-luna (Plate 50). It had a semicircular sound-box on the edge of which metal pins were placed; these were set in vibration by means of a bow, and the sound, of the higher notes, at least, was clear and flute-like. The compass usually embraced two or three chromatic octaves, from *f* or *g*.[1]

The type of Harmonica, however, most interesting to English readers is that usually called THE MUSICAL GLASSES. Originally they were merely a set of hemispherical glass bowls, into which water was poured for tuning as well as for playing purposes. The executant, moistening his fingers, rubbed the rims of the glasses in order, thus exiting vibration and bringing forth clear musical notes, which continued to sound until the fingers were removed. An Irishman named Pockrich is said to have first used glasses in this way, and when in 1744 he produced his Harmonica before the English public, it soon became both the fashion and the craze. In 1746 Gluck gave a performance on the musical glasses with orchestral accompaniment at the Little Theatre in the Haymarket. Admirers of Goldsmith will remember how, in his *Vicar of Wakefield* (1761), he makes the town ladies talk of nothing else but "high life, pictures, Shakespeare and the Musical Glasses". Even scientific men were interested in this passing fancy, and Dr Benjamin Franklin improved on the Irishman's instrument by affixing hemispherical glasses of graded sizes on a revolving rod, which was turned by a foot-pedal.

[1] For an example of chamber music employing the Nail-Violin – by a composer most appropriately named Rust – see *Das Erbe Deutscher Musik*, Landschaftsdenkmal Mittel-Deutschland Band 1 (Wolfenbüttel, 1939), pp. 78–90.

There were thirty-seven glasses in the full set with a compass of three octaves from *g*. In order that the performer might easily distinguish the proper tones, the glasses which represented the natural notes of each octave were painted the seven prismatic colours, and the sharps and flats were left white. The fingers catch the glass more easily and bring out the sound more readily, if they are soaked in water and rubbed occasionally with fine chalk. Owing to its wonderful power of expression the "Musical Glasses" received the notice of several celebrated composers; Mozart and Beethoven both wrote compositions for it, and the first great player, Miss Marianne Davies, was famous throughout Europe. It had, unfortunately, a most prejudicial effect upon the player's nerves, as the writer has reason to remember, and in England its use was discarded in the early part of the last century, though in Scotland it was still played by amateurs in 1850. An English specimen of the instrument in a portable form for travelling is shown on Plate 50.

One other example of the Harmonica class deserves, in conclusion, a brief notice. The JEW'S HARP belongs to the number of those universal sound-producers which seem to defy both time and space. The little metal tongue, which, whilst it vibrates across the open cavity of the mouth, emits various tones according as the size of the cavity behind it is altered at the will of the player, appears in New Guinea as a long narrow strip of wood, but its purpose is the same. The *K'ou ch'in* of Pekin, depicted in Chinese books of the twelfth century, is almost identical with the European form, and in an old grave in the province of Mandal, in Norway, a similar instrument of copper finely gilt was discovered. The first printed treatise on musical instruments, written by Sebastian Virdung in 1511, shows the Jew's Harp in exactly the same shape as we have it today; and at the end of the seventeenth century on the lonely island of St Kilda it was the only tuneful solace for weary hours which the inhabitants possessed.

With regard to the name, it appears to have been formerly called the Jew's Trumpe, but had, we believe, no immediate connection with the sons of Israel. The suggestion that the name is a corruption of Jaw's Trumpe, because it is held between the lips, is brilliant, but unfortunately other languages beside our own connect it with Jews and not with jaws, as, for instance, in Germany, where it is known as the Judenharfe. Probably the words are a corruption or transliteration of the Dutch *Jeugdtrompe*, which means a child's trumpet.[1]

[1] The etymology remains obscure, but it is more likely to have some satirical intent; to those determined to mock or hate, the sounds made by an unmusical synagogue offer ample scope for parody. Organologists now prefer to use the term "guimbarde" for the instrument.

The greatest performer ever heard in England was Charles Eulenstein, a native of Württemberg, who, in 1827 and following years, gave concerts in London and Scotland.[1] He used sixteen instruments of various pitches and sizes, and could shift from one to another very quickly, so that the melody was not interrupted; by employing two at a time, he produced the effect of a duet.

The explanation of the sound-producing qualities of the instrument is probably this, that the notes obtainable depend on the natural series of sounds called Harmonics, which appear in the open tones of the Trumpet or in the harmonic notes of the Violin. In the metal vibrator of the Jew's Harp they are all present in combination, but can be separately reinforced by resonators of suitable size, which, in this case, are formed by altering the cavity of the mouth. If the vibrating tongue be made of a different length and pitch, another series of harmonic notes can be obtained as in the Trumpet (from which it takes one of its names), and so, by a multiplication of instruments, diatonic and chromatic melodies are possible. It was undoubtedly called the Jew's *Harp*, from the action of the finger in striking the vibrator.

Among the illuminated manuscripts so small an instrument naturally finds no place, but it is apparently allotted to one of the figures which grace the fourteenth-century Minstrels' Gallery in Exeter Cathedral, and it also appears in the French enamels upon the crozier of William of Wykeham. In both examples the player is treated as angelic, which redeems the Jew's Harp from the stigma put upon it in Scotland, where in the sixteenth century it was connected with a case of witchcraft which caused some unfortunate people great tortures and cost others their lives, though Geilie Duncan, one of the sorcerers who provided the music for the nocturnal dance, "upon the like trump did play the like dance before the King's Majesty" without any ill effect on the royal listener. In old English literature its name does not appear, unless it is hidden under the general title Trompe; but in the *Houlgate*, a Scotch poem of the fifteenth century, the "ributhe" is probably the instrument, for in France it was formerly called the Rebute, though now it is known as the Guimbarde. In the sixteenth century, however, Henry Chettle (*Kind-Hart's Dreame*, 1592) writes: "There is another Jugler, that beeing well skild a dealer in the Jewes Trumpe, takes upon him to bee a dealer in Musicke: especiall good at mending Instruments."

But the little music-maker will, we fear, always remain a mystery, both as to its origin and its nature – a Trump without a blast, a Harp without a string.

---

[1] For more about Eulenstein, see Grove's *Dictionary* (Fifth Edition). His autobiography is worth reading.

PLATE 49

The Tournament, late fourteenth century, showing the clarion and the nakers (Worcester Cathedral)

PLATE 50

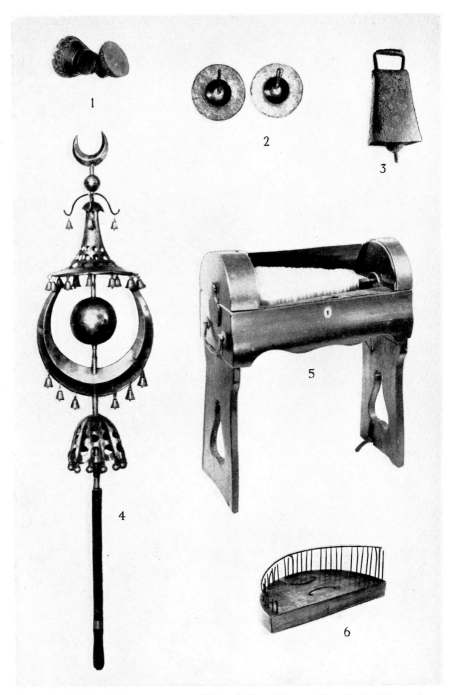

1. Naqqareh, Arabian Drums. 2. Oriental Cymbals. 3. Handbell, thirteenth or fourteenth century. 4. Turkish Crescent or Jingling Johnny, *c.* 1810. 5. Glass Harmonica, eighteenth century. 6. Semi-luna or Nail-violin, *c.* 1800

Chapter XV

The Consort

The modulacion of Musyke is swete and celestiall,
In the sp[h]eris of the planettis makynge sownde armonicall;
If we moder oure Musyke as the trewe tune is,
In hevyn we shall synge OSANNA IN EXCELSIS.

LEKINGFELDE PROVERB (temp. Henry VIII)

IT IS A RECOGNIZED FACT that we are born for society and for the companionship of each other; and what is true of human beings is also characteristic of instruments of music; for although certain instruments may stand forth from their comperes by virtue of some particularly pleasing effect in beauty of tone or depth of feeling, yet it is in the association of their ever-varying sounds that the trained ear of the listener finds its truest delight and the artistic genius of the composer its highest expression.

Hitherto we have treated the musical instruments which were formerly used in our own country as separate units; but in our concluding chapter we will consider them in "consort", allied in that marvellous combination of concerted harmonies which we now call the Orchestra.

It is needless to say that the first efforts of our race in this direction proved anything but a concord of sweet sounds; for not only was harmony, in our technical meaning of the word, unheard of, but the softer tones of lyre and harp were overpowered by the multitude of drums, rattles, gongs, cymbals, and other blatant accompaniments, designed to give rhythm where melody was wanting. But the records which have been left us in stone and colour by the ancient peoples of Sumer and of Egypt clearly show that ages before our Christian era the musical ear had learnt to appreciate the more refined tones of the stringed instruments and to dissociate music from mere noise. In the great Assyrian kingdom, for instance, there were large bands of harps and trigons, sometimes of trigons only, either playing by themselves or supported by the small drum and the clapping of hands. In a few cases the double pipe finds a place amongst them, and for the dance lyre and harp are linked with tambourine and cymbals; but there is no trace of that multiplication of percussion instruments which marks the barbaric orchestras of the African tribes or the Chinese music of Eastern Asia. Under the old-world dynasties of Egypt it was much the same, though the flutes and pipes took a more important part in the Consorts; for we notice that they are frequently depicted in the mural paintings, together with the Oriental pillarless Harp and the Tanboura (or Eastern Lute), accompanying a chorus of singers or a group of dancers. In the sacred music of the temples a harp, a lute, and two vertical flutes were generally employed, the sistrum being kept for special use in the Isis ritual; for the less decorous performances of the Shawazee the double reed-pipe, with a small drum or tambourine, was preferred, as in the present day, while the military music consisted of the straight Trumpet and large Drum. The Jews, on the other hand, banished all Flutes and Pipes from Divine worship; for the ordinary temple band, which is frequently mentioned in the sacred books, consisted of large numbers of Lyres (*Kinnor*), Lutes (*Nebel*), and Timbrels and Tambourines, which were used to accompany the vocal music: while the priestly instruments for ritual purposes were the Straight Trumpet (*Chatzozerah*), the Ram's-horn Trumpet (*Shophar*) and the Cymbals. The pipe, however, was in popular use at all seasons of merriment, taking its place with the lyre, lute, and tabret at feasts and times of public rejoicing; it was also found in the house of weeping, its plaintive tones mingling with the wails of the mourners. In the army the Ram's-horn was employed, the straight Trumpet being blown only by the priests on special occasions, such as the proclamation of the sovereign's accession.

We observe, therefore, in the history of these nations the early recognition of *stringed* instruments as the highest form and true basis of concerted music, and the reservation of certain instruments, such as the pipe and the trumpet, for special purposes and effects, the one giving us the dance orchestra and the other the military band; there is also the gradual elimination of the more noisy sound-producers as the pure tones of melody begin to be appreciated and admired. When we pass, however, to the Greeks and Romans, it is strange to find that this desire for orchestral effect and colouring is almost entirely absent. The Greeks were pre-eminently soloists, a single lyre or cythara accompanying the recitation of their epic poems and giving to them the name of Lyric Poetry; and, although they were in close contact with the many forms of stringed instruments used in Egypt and Asia Minor, yet they refused to admit them within the sacred confines of their national art and always considered them as things foreign to the sons of Hellas. Plato, in his Ideal Republic, reflects the true spirit of the Greek when, in purging his city, he eliminates all flute-makers and instruments with many strings and leaves only the *lyra* and *cythara* for the town, with some kind of pipe for the herdsmen in the country, Apollo's instruments preferred to those of Asiatic Marsyas. The same seems to have been true of the old Minoan civilization as revealed to us by the recent discoveries in Crete.

The Romans, on the other hand, with their fondness for display, loved noise, and large bands of Pipeplayers, with Hornblowers and Trumpeters, produced so great an effect that, in the opinion of the poet Horace, they drowned the chorus of singers they meant to accompany. The *cythara* might serve for mystic ceremonies and the *lyra* for the quietude of home, but the actor, the dancer, the religious devotee, and the weeping mourner must attune their minds and actions to the pipe. It is in the plays of Terence, however, that we first find directions given to the theatre band, probably only a one-man orchestra; for there, pipes of equal or unequal length, of high or low pitch, are required according to the character of the piece: such interesting attempts at musical suggestion we see repeated in the interludes of England's first tragedy, *Gorboduc*.

In this second stage, then, of musical development, as it passed westward, we notice a want of appreciation of concerted music and a greater desire either for solo accompaniment or loud martial effect. And this will help us to understand why, in the early Middle Ages, the Consort existed only in a poor and emaciated form. For the Christian Church objected to the strident tones of Trumpet and Drum, and the pipe was too suggestive of those pagan orgies with which it was so closely connected. So the *lyra* and the *cythara* became the sole accompaniment of religious worship, until the Organistrum and Organ took their place as greater aids to vocal music. With these, too, the Cymbals or Bellchimes were used, the sharp tones of the little gongs emphasizing the plain chant as they were struck; but, save for harp and psaltery, musical instruments were crude and kept to themselves or to their immediate kith and kin, strings with strings and wind with wind. Even at the commencement of the thirteenth century the nine instruments, on which a really competent minstrel should have been able to play, were all *stringed* instruments, except the Pipe and Tabor, which were considered as separate items and dedicated to the dance.

It is true that in illuminated manuscripts and in ecclesiastical carvings we observe a large number of various instruments grouped together, but there is nothing to show that they were so used in actual practice. The artists who produced these medieval illustrations and the sculptures of our churches were imbued with the spirit of the Psalmist, and called on everything, whether string, pipe, or drum, to praise the Lord; and in their grand works of art they surrounded the royal musician and poet with all those forms of musical instruments which could in any way swell the glorious strain. We are not therefore justified in considering such combined forces as representative of the actual orchestras of those days, unless the scenes in which they are depicted are taken from ordinary life or their presence in combination can be supported by the evidence of contemporary literature; and from these two sources of information we gather that, except for the vagaries of wandering minstrels, the instruments were, as a rule, united in certain groups which were kept distinct.[1]

We find that the stringed instruments, including the harp, lute, gittern, citole, psaltery, and the various kinds of viol, were used for accompanying the voice. In this connection they continued for several centuries as a recognized feature of the English Court; for instance, the musicians "for the consort" appearing, according to the *Lord Chamberlain's Records*, at the funeral of James I, were all players on the lute and the viol with the exception of the one singer. A stringed orchestra (*Lautenchor*) of the early seventeenth century is described by Praetorius as consisting of a Clavicymbal or Spinet with Theorboes, Lutes, Bandores, Orpharions, Citterns, and a large Bass Lyra; a Bass Viol too, he says, would not be amiss for a foundation.

Another group was composed of a section of the wind instruments, namely flutes, shawms and other reed-pipes, cornetts, and trombones. The shawms were especially favoured by the later minstrels; in fact, their name became synonymous with that of a wind band. The "Mynstrells" in the musical establishment of Henry VII are identical with "the Shalmes" of his successor; and in the illustration of the banquet and jousts of the preceding century they are frequently depicted in the music gallery playing to the assembled guests. The increase in the size and number of the wind instruments during the sixteenth century added greatly to the importance of these bands, and the "sakbushes and shalmoyes" of Henry VII's reign were

---

[1] The grouping of instruments in accordance with their strictly-defined functions is of the highest importance if we are to understand (and perform correctly) medieval music. See a most important article by Edmund A. Bowles, "Were Musical Instruments used in the Liturgical Service during the Middle Ages?", *GSJ*, X, pp. 40–56, and the ensuing correspondence in subsequent issues of the *Journal*. There can be little doubt that the only instruments used in polyphonic liturgical music during the thirteenth, fourteenth and fifteenth centuries were the organ, organistrum (large hurdy-gurdy) and chime-bells; on occasions of the utmost ceremony, such instruments as cornetts and sackbuts may also have been used to double the voices (*not* to play independent parts), and a certain amount of sacred polyphony was also performed non-liturgically, in consort arrangements of every kind. But so far as the service itself was concerned, the evidence of the documents is overwhelmingly clear. A point too often overlooked is that only trained singers were musically literate; the average medieval instrumentalist, like his jazz colleague of the present day, was quite unable to read elaborate musical notation.

succeeded by the Flutes, Cornetts, Hautboys, and Sackbuts of later sovereigns. Each of these could be played with other kinds of wind instruments or with the corresponding members of their own immediate family, but, as the scale of the Shawms and Sackbuts was limited upwards and that of the Flutes and Cornetts downwards, a better effect was produced by grouping the more useful and resonant members of each family together.

A third section consisted of Trumpets, Clarions, and Drums; and as we have already mentioned, the use of these instruments was restricted to royal and noble purposes and the panoply of war. The following lines from *The Life of St Werberge*, printed by Pynson in 1521, show us the domestic use to which they were put and remind us of the stately days of Queen Elizabeth:

> Certayne at eche cours of servyce in the hall
> Trumpettes blewe up Shalmes and Claryons
> Shewynge theyr melody with toynes musycall.

Here the shawm is added, probably for the "melodye", and the drums omitted, as in the well-known Braunche brass of the fourteenth century.[1] Such were the types of bands in the closing years of the Middle Ages, and we find that Chaucer, when describing the multitude of musicians who appear in his *House of Fame*, separates them into three distinct groups, the first consisting of stringed minstrels, the second of pipers (including players on flute, shawm, bagpipe and other reed instruments) and the third of those who sounded the trompe, beme and clarion – the men of brass.

In after centuries these groups were known as "noises", though the word did not necessarily cast unworthy reflections on the performers. In the *History of John Newchurche* (1597) we read "there was a noise of musicians that played all the way before her"; and Sneak's noise, which delighted Sir John Falstaff at the Boar's Head in Eastcheap, was what our fathers would have more politely called a Quadrille Band. Although "a noise of Trumpets" was a technical term for the gaily bedizened musicians and the fanfares they played, yet Milton, in his *Hymn on the Nativity*, speaks of a "stringed noise" and describes it as "sweet as never was by mortal finger strook". An Elizabethan Stringed Consort, painted on panels at Gilling Castle, Yorkshire, is shown in Plates 55, 56.

In the sixteenth century the various groups of instruments were still kept apart. The orchestra for the interludes in *Gorboduc* (1561) was a large one, but it was divided into five sections, viz. Violins, Cornetts, Flutes, Haut-

---

[1] See footnote to p. 118.

boys, and Drums and Fifes, each section playing separately. In *Sophonisba* (1606) the four *entr'actes* were rendered by Cornetts and Organs, by Organs mixed with Recorders, by Organs, Viols and voices, and by a Bass Lute and Treble Viol; while, at the obsequies of Charles III of Lorraine in 1608, described by Jacquot in his history of the music of that province (1882), one chorus of singers was accompanied by Lutes, Guittarons and Spanish Viols, and another by Cornetts, Sackbuts and Bass Shawms (*gros haulxbois*).

Now such combinations as we have been describing were also called Consorts; if they consisted solely of the members of one family of instruments, such as the Viols, or the Lutes, or the Recorders, or the Shawms, they were termed "whole consorts"; if members of different families were united, a "broken consort" was the result. This is clearly shown by an entry in the *Lord Chamberlain's Records* under the year 1660, when Henry Hawes, a viol player, was admitted to a place in the "*broken* consort", and we learn that this consort was the King's "Private Music for lutes, violls and voices", consisting of six singers, three lutenists, two violinists and eight viol players. Lord Bacon, in his *Sylva Sylvarum* (Cent. III, 278), says: "In that Musicke, which we call Broken Musicke, or Consort Musicke; Some Consort of Instruments are sweeter than others; (A Thing not sufficiently yet observed:) As the Irish Harpe, and Base Viall agree well: The Recorder and stringed Musick agree well: Organs and the Voice agree well; &c. But the Virginalls and the Lute; Or the Welch-Harpe, and Irish-Harpe; Or the Voice and Pipes alone, agree not so well; But for the Melioration of Musicke, there is yet much left (in this Point of Exquisite Consorts) to try and enquire." A combination of strings and wind in broken consort is seen in an early fifteenth-century manuscript of English work (Brit. Mus., Harl. 2838), where a Viol and a Recorder are playing together at a banquet.

Praetorius' allusion to these Broken Consorts is interesting: he writes, "The English give the name Consort to what is very appropriate to a grouping of instruments (*consortio*), when several persons with various instruments, such as a Clavicymbal or a large Spinet, a large Lyra, a Double Harp, Lutes, Theorboes, Bandores, Penorcons, Citterns, Bass Viol, a little Treble Fiddle, a Transverse Flute or a Recorder, sometimes also a soft Trombone or a Racket, all together in a Company or Society play with very quiet, soft and sweet accord and harmonize with one another in pleasing symphony."

Albert Dürer's engravings of the allegorical triumph of the Emperor Maximilian (1512) provide us with interesting details of various consorts, for in the procession are representative groups of musicians. The cavalcade is headed by mounted fifers and drummers; the music of the church consists of a choir accompanied by cornett and sackbut (trombone); lutes and rybebes (viols da gamba) are typical of chamber music; cromornes, shawms and trombones of the wind band; the regal and the positive organ occupy a car to themselves, being the only keyboard instruments shown. The group in the next car, described as "Music of sweet melody", depicts a tabor and pipe, several shawms, two viols (fiddle and rybebe), and treble and bass lutes. Behind them are the jesters and fools with pipe and Jew's harp; then a Burgundian mounted band, playing on shawms and trombones, followed by the Imperial trumpets and kettledrums also on horseback. The whole

Fig. 47 A Consort (Spenser's *Shephearde's Calendar*, 1579)

procession is closed by a car representing country music, a herdsman playing on a reed-pipe surrounded by his vinous companions.

An early combination, popular on the Continent, was the use of the transverse flute with the lute and other strings, and that it was adopted in this country is seen from an engraving in Spenser's *Shephearde's Calendar* (1579), reproduced in Fig. 47, where four ladies are portrayed playing on the harp, the viol, the lute, and the transverse flute. In the large painting now in the National Portrait Gallery, representing scenes in the life of Sir Henry Unton, the masque which is being performed at his marriage is accompanied by six players on the treble "violon", a bass viol, lute, cittern, transverse flute and probably the bandore, though only the neck of the instrument is visible (Plate 54). The performers are seated at a table on which their music is placed, and the whole scene reminds us of Morley's and Rosseter's settings of popular melodies and dances issued as consort lessons at the close of the Elizabethan age;[1] the painting was executed about the year 1596, probably by the famous Court painter, Gheeraerts, a Dutchman resident in England, who had already painted Sir Henry's portrait; but, instead of the continental cross-flute, he should perhaps have introduced the English vertical flute or recorder, which is required for the mean or tenor part.

The instrumental resources then at the command of English musicians may be inferred from a list of instruments at Hengrave Hall, Suffolk, according to the inventory made in the year 1602–3. They consisted of six viols, six violins (probably in both cases two trebles, two means and two basses), seven recorders, four cornetts and a mute cornett, four lutes (one treble, two means and one great bass), a bandore, a cittern, two sackbuts, three hautbois, a curtall (bassoon), a lysarden (probably a serpent), two flutes, a pair of little virginals, a pair of double virginals, "a wind instrument like a virginall" (probably a regal), and a pair of great organs. The music included two "lewting books", many song books, five books with pavines, galliards, measures and country dances, five books of levaultoes and corantoes, and five books with pavines and galliards "for the consort". In the chamber where the musicians played were "one long bord with ii tressels, one long joyned form, and one playne forme" with hangings of "blewe and yellow saye complete".

One of the most interesting allusions to "broken music" is found in the well-known passage which Shakespeare has penned in the final act of his play *King Henry V*; according to the dramatist, Katharine's sweet voice, intermingling her native French with the English words she found so difficult to learn, reminds her royal lover of the "broken music" with its blending of strange sounds: " 'Therefore Queen of all, Katharine, break thy mind to me in broken English: wilt thou have me?' 'Dat is, as it shall please de roy mon père.' "

Such music, to an extent unknown before, except in the bygone days of Assyria and Egypt, having become the fashion, we read of some curious combinations in the orchestras which accompanied the seventeenth-century masques. In Campion's masque at Lord Hay's marriage (1607) there were two groups of players – one with mean and bass lutes, a bandore, two treble violins, a virginal and a double sackbut; the other with nine violins and three lutes. In another masque presented by Queen Anne, consort of James I,

---

[1] See footnote to p. 21. The unidentified painter of the Unton mural is undoubtedly correct in showing a violin and a tenor flute among the six consort instruments; note, too, the "back-handed" playing of the bass viol, designed to produce a specially soft and gentle tone.

at Christmas in 1610, there were twelve lutes and a flute, twelve violencas (violins, etc.), with eighteen hautbois and sackbuts. In *Silenus* (1613) a pipe and tabor, a treble and two bass violins, two sackbuts, a mandora, and a tenor cornett appeared; but the Restoration placed the organization of the orchestra on a more definite footing, and for the play presented before Charles II at Windsor in 1674 there were thirty-nine violins (including violas and violoncellos), three bass viols, two theorboes, four gittars, four recorders, two harpsicalls (harpsichords) with four trumpeters and a kettle-drummer.

And so the orchestra grew. "Whole consorts" still existed, as shown by Matthew Locke's *Compositions for Broken and Whole Consorts*, issued in 1672, the whole consort consisting of three viols and the broken consort of the same instruments with theorboes and harpsichord added.[1] Moreover, in the Fancies for viols (beloved of Mace and Britton) which were the predecessors of the string quartet, in the music for the recorders, and in the bands of hautboys and bassoons, the instruments of one particular family were frequently played together to the exclusion of others. But in "broken music" composers saw the consort *par excellence*, and Sebastian Bach, while utilizing the older forms of instrumental combination, sought and found in this sphere effects of tone-colour unknown before; with his horns, trumpets and reeds of dainty sound, so enriching its capabilities as to foreshadow that glorious masterpiece of Music's Art, the Orchestral Symphony.

Of the Waits, the last survivors of the old Minstrels, we have already spoken. Their "noise", too, has disappeared, but in the church bands of the early part of the last century they made an effort which, with judicious management, might have kept them with us still as adjuncts to Divine worship. Abuses, no doubt, existed. A possible carouse is suggested by the entry in the accounts of certain churchwardens "for beare when the new bassoon come". Many also will recollect Thomas Hardy's vivid description in *Life's Little Ironies* of the fateful occasion on which the church band, overcome by much fiddling at a Christmas dance on the previous night, played the "Devil among the Tailors" in mistake for the evening hymn on the following Sabbath, and made the cobwebs in the roof shiver like ghosts as the leader shouted out, "Top couples cross hands, and when I make the fiddle squeak with the bow, every man kiss his partner under the mistletoe." It was, alas! their death song; such absent-mindedness could not be tolerated. But are not abuses – less open perhaps, yet probably more reprehensible – known

---

[1] No such printed collection by Locke is known to exist. Galpin was perhaps referring to Locke's *Little Consort of three parts . . . for viols or violins. . . . To be performed either alone or with theorbo's and harpsecord*, published by Playford in 1656.

even among our modern surpliced choirs? And ought we not to recollect that the vagaries of these village musicians arose rather as a result of the spirit of the age in which they lived than from a desire for irreverence or wilful villainy? Certain it is that few laboured so hard to make the Sunday worship acceptable and attractive as did these homely minstrels – old men and children ably supported by young men and maidens. In many of the West Country churches the bands were still playing sixty years ago; at Selworthy it disappeared in 1871. But to the writer there was given the opportunity of hearing probably the last of these old institutions, which at Winterborne Abbas, a remote Dorset parish, continued to play until about fifteen years ago. It consisted of only three instrumentalists – a thatcher, a shepherd, and a farm labourer – who performed on the clarinet, the flute, and the violoncello; but they were men worthy of their parts, who could not brook the introduction of the inevitable harmonium. A full description of their doings and the music which they played has been given in the *Musical News* (1893) and the *Antiquary* (1906).

From details which we have gathered of similar bands, we find that the instruments generally favoured were the violin, violoncello (called the bass viol), flute, clarinet, and bassoon; but we have also observed the tenor violin (the viola), the hautboy, which was sometimes called the Vox Humana (though that name was more properly given to the tenor instrument), the trombone (a bit of the old sackbut), the serpent, bass horn, and keyed bugle (sole survivals of the medieval cornetts). In a few parishes in the Midlands even the megaphone, under the name of the "Vamphorn", was pressed into the service, its long tube and spreading bell reinforcing the natural strength of the voice in a far more effective way than the commoner practice of singing through the hands.

To what cause did these old players attribute the disappearance of their bands? Certainly not to their own delinquencies. No; it was to the introduction of the clarinets; it was, in fact, the breaking of the old consort which broke them up. "Yes," said one of these vanished minstrels, "they should ha' stuck to strings. Your brass-man is brass, well and good; your reed-man is reed, well and good; your percussion-man is percussion, good again. But I don't care who hears me say it, nothing will speak to your heart with the sweetness of the man of strings." Was this lingering affection for stringed music, after all but the call of the blood? The call of those far-off days, when to the quivering chords of the Crot the British bards chanted our country's fame, and Saxon minstrels swept the trembling strings of their Harps as with prophetic fire they sang the glories of an England yet to be.

THE REVIVAL OF THE FITTEST

I AM no skilful vocalist;
   I can't control my *mezza gola*;
I have but an indifferent fist
   (Or foot) upon the Pianola.

But there are instruments, I own,
   That fire me with a fond ambition
To master for their names alone
   Apart from their august tradition.

They are the Fipple-Flute, a word
   Suggestive of seraphic screeches;
The Poliphant comes next, and third
   The Humstrum – aren't they perfect peaches?

About their tone I cannot say
   Much that would carry clear conviction,
For, till I read of them today.
   I knew them not in fact or fiction.

As yet I am, alas! without
   Instruction in the art of fippling,
Though something may be found about
   It in the works of LEAR or KIPLING.

And possibly I may unearth
   In LECKY or in LAURENCE OLIPHANT
Some facts to remedy my dearth
   Of knowledge bearing on the Poliphant.

But, now their pictures I have seen
   In GALPIN'S learned dissertation,
So far as in me lies I mean
   To bring about their restoration.

Yet since I cannot learn all three
   And time is ever onward humming,
My few remaining years shall be
   Devoted wholly to humstrumming.

That, when my bones to rest are laid,
   Upon my tomb it may be written:
"He was the very last who played
   Upon the Humstrum in Great Britain."

By permission of the Proprietors of "Punch".

APPENDICES

1 · Abbreviations of Musical Staff Notation

2 · The Ullard "Harp"

ALTHOUGH rather beyond the scope of the present work, an additional note on the true character of the so-called Harp sculptured on the ninth-century cross standing in the old churchyard of Ullard, Co. Kilkenny, may prove interesting. Since 1840, when Edward Bunting published an engraving of it in his *Ancient Music of Ireland* and stated that it was the first specimen of a harp without a fore-pillar hitherto discovered out of Egypt, conjecture and imagination as to its real nature have been allowed free play. The writer therefore considered it a duty, before completing the chapter on the Rote and Harp, to visit Ullard in order to inspect personally this much-debated example. The cross is made of granite of very unequal substance and in parts much worn by age; it is 12 ft 6 in. in height, but the middle section of the shaft has been lost and is replaced with concrete. The head has as its central figure the crucified Christ, while on the right arm is carved the Sacrifice of Isaac, and on the left the Royal Psalmist playing on the instrument in question.

In the year 1834 Sir Samuel Fergusson sent a sketch of it to his friend Dr Petrie, and in an accompanying letter wrote as follows: "I protest it is a true copy, but if it is a harp he plays, how could the strings be fastened, as they would seem to be, on such a frame?" In 1836 Bunting secured a drawing of it from Mr E. V. Alcock, son of the Rector of Ullard, which he afterwards published in his book with the remark already quoted; and Engel (*Musical Instruments*, 1874), Grattan Flood (*The Harp*, 1905) and others have reproduced the illustration or alluded to it as though correct. O'Neill (*Sculptured Crosses*, 1857) apparently had some doubt about it, and solved it to his own satisfaction by representing it as an ordinary triangular harp, which it is not. Miss Panum, in the Magazine of the International Musical Society (1905), depicts her idea of what it should be, but it is evident that she did not see the original.

A close inspection of the actual carving, together with a series of photographs (one of which is given on Plate 1) and rubbings, shows that Bunting was misled by the drawing sent to him: there is a distinct fore-pillar supporting the frame of the instrument. The head stands out, as usual, with greater prominence, for it was often carved and decorated; but from its right-hand corner a raised line passes directly downward and joins on to the lower end. When standing immediately beneath the sculpture and looking upwards, the swell of the once more-definitely raised front pillar (8 in. long in the original carving) can be unmistakably traced.

In fact, the instrument is a large quadrangular Crot or Cruit with six strings as described on page 7, and it must not be confounded with the later Irish Harp of triangular shape. A similar instrument appears on an ancient cross now in the graveyard of Duiske Abbey, Graignamanagh, three miles from Ullard, to which our attention was drawn by the well-known local antiquary, Mr P. O'Leary. At Castledermot a like quadrangular Cruit is depicted, as shown in Miss Stoke's *High Crosses of Castledermot and Durrow*: at Kells and Clonmacnoise it is also to be seen, and in Scotland on the Great Cross at Iona, known as St Martin's Cross.

The Ullard instrument is therefore no unique example as has been generally supposed, but represents the common type of large Cruit used by the Irish minstrels from the seventh to the tenth centuries, when it was superseded by the triangular Harp.

....

3·Single and Double Regals

So many explanations have been given of the meaning of the words "Single" and "Double" as applied in the sixteenth century to the smaller Organs and also to the Virginals, that we have deferred a review of the subject until, in an additional note, we could deal with it in detail.

The terms are, first of all, peculiar to the English language, though it was the custom formerly in Germany to describe the various-sized organs as Whole, Half, and Quarter instruments according to their pitch and depth of tone.

One of the earliest suggestions made was that they referred to the number of bellows, a "single" Regal having one (as in the Portative Organ) and a "double" Regal two. It is hardly necessary to say that facts do not support this theory; for not only are the bellows of Single Regals described in a way and in a position which necessarily imply two (for the air-reservoir was not used in the sixteenth century), but "single" *Virginals* required no bellows at all.

A second theory, held by Dr Rimbault, was that "single" Regals had but one row of pipes, while "double" Regals had, it is presumed, two or more rows. But what shall we say of Henry VIII's Single Regals – three with two stops of pipes, one with three stops, two with six half-stops, one with seven half-stops and one with four whole-stops!

Yet another opinion, supported by the late Sir George Grove and Mr A. J. Hipkins, is that Single Regals and Single Virginals had one keyboard or manual, and that Double Regals and Double Virginals had two. This is certainly more plausible, but unfortunately no specimen of a two-manual Portable Organ (for such were the Regals) exists, nor is it described by writers of the sixteenth to eighteenth centuries as existing in their day; and

PLATE 51

Chime-bells, fourteenth century

PLATE 52

Musical instruments of the thirteenth century: psaltery, harp, trumpet, viol, rybybe, symphony, crowd and organ moreover no example of a two-manual Virginal or Clavicymbal appears until the close of the sixteenth century, when, as stated by the Dutch musician Van Blankenburg (b. 1654), it was first introduced by Hans Ruckers, the famous Flemish maker. Neither Virdung (1511) nor Praetorius (1618–20) give any illustration or suggestion of a two-manual Virginal, but Mersenne in 1636 says that on the Clavicymbal there were sometimes two rows of keys. The earliest known instance of such an instrument is one made by Hans Ruckers and dated 1590; and even so, the explanation of the words "single" and "double" must apply equally to the Regals as to the Virginals, and we have no proof at all of the use of a two-manual Regal.

In the year 1547 King Henry VIII died possessed of five Double Regals, two of them with two stops only; on the supposition that these were two-manual instruments, there would be but one stop to each manual! Moreover, these Regals were "standing upon a foot covered with fustian of Naples, garnished with red ribbon; the same foot being the case for the same Regals"; so this two-manual Organ could be packed away into a stuff-covered case!

It must also be remembered that even on what were termed the Great Organs two manuals were very uncommon in England during the sixteenth century, and probably unknown for the most part of the time. The churches had their "Grete Organs" and their "Little Organs", but they were distinct instruments and occupied different positions in the building. The first instance which we have of the term "double organ" applied to a combination of a Great Organ and a Positive (or Choir Organ) is to be found in the records of Worcester Cathedral: "A.D. 1613. All the materials and workmanship of the new double organ in the Cathedral Church of Worcester to Thomas Dallam, organ-maker, came to 211$^{li.}$"; and as Dallam had seven years before built an instrument for King's College Chapel, Cambridge, consisting of a "Greate" and a "Chayre" organ, no doubt that at Worcester was similarly constructed. From that date the words "single" and "double", as applied to organs and harpsichords, certainly mean a one-manual or a two-manual instrument. Matthew Locke, for instance, in his *Melothesia* (1673), has an organ piece for "Chaire organ and Greate organ" described as "for a double organ"; Henry Purcell wrote a Voluntary for a Double Organ, viz. a great and little organ; and so with several of Dr Blow's organ compositions still among the manuscripts in the British Museum;[1] but surely we are not entitled to take terms which relate to the combination of Positive and Great Organs and

[1] See Watkins Shaw's edition of Blow's complete organ works (Schott, 1958), and the editions of organ music by Locke and Purcell published by Stainer & Bell and Novello.

give them the same meaning when applied to the small Portable Organ in use in a previous century.

What, then, is the solution? We believe that the words refer to the compass and pitch of the instrument, as do the German terms already quoted. The recognized musical scale in England during the sixteenth century was based on the old Guidonian septenaries and embraced a chromatic compass from G on the lowest line of the Bass stave to e in the top space of the Treble stave. Playford, in his *Introduction to the Skill of Music* (1661), tells us that the usual compass employed by Morley and other composers at the close of the Elizabethan era was confined within these limits; but, he adds, "there are many Notes used, both above and below, and do exceed this Compass, both in Vocal and Instrumental Musick, which ought not to be omitted"; and "those below Gamut in the Bassus are called double Notes. I have therefore expressed them with double Letters". We have the same use of the word "double" in Anthony Duddington's contract for an organ to be supplied to the Church of All Hallows, Barking, in the year 1519, given in full by Dr Rimbault in his *History of the Organ*. The downward compass of the instrument is stated to be "dowble Ce fa ut" or, as we should write it in England, CC, though in Germany it would be written C. Now an analysis of the illustrations of keyboard instruments given by Virdung in 1511 shows that, allowing for the "short octave", the compass of the Organ and the Clavicymbal was from G (gamut) on the lowest line of the Bass stave to g above the top line of the Treble stave (the Portative Organ having the like, but an octave higher), and of the Positive from G on the Bass line also to the d above the Treble stave; while the Virginal, the Clavicytherium and the Clavichord extended from the F below the Bass (though without F sharp) to g above the Treble. But from the contract, just mentioned, we know that in this country the compass of the Organ descended to the C below the Bass stave or CC, and Clavicymbals or Virginals of the first half of the sixteenth century are still in existence with keys reaching not only to CC but to GG, a fourth lower.

A Single Regal, therefore, and a Single Virginal were instruments of a limited compass descending only to single C or to single G (Gamut), whereas Double Regals and Double Virginals were larger, descending to double C or to double G.

This explanation will, we believe, meet all the requirements of the sixteenth-century keyboard instruments; it allows for several rows of pipes in a Single Regal (as in the Single Positive shown on Plate 45), and makes it easy for Double Regals (such as the Bible Regal on Plate 46) to be packed into a decorated case. We have, moreover, an interesting corroboration of this meaning of the words by Praetorius; for he informs us that in England the Fagotto (Bassoon), descending to single *G* (gamut), was called the Single Courtal, and that reaching double *C* the Double Courtal.

......

4·The Musical Instruments of King Henry VIII

From an Inventory of the Guarderobes, etc., 1547
(Brit. Mus., Harl. 1419)

Stuffe and Implements at GREENWICHE.

In the Kynges priuey Chambre.
f. 54. One paier of Regalles with the case.

In the Kynges Withdrawing Chambre.
f. 56. One faire Instrument being Regalles and Virgynalles.

In the Kynges Gallery.
f. 57*b*. A paier of Virgynalles.

In the Closet over the Waterstewe.
f. 59. A Horne of Iverey.

At WESTMINSTER.

In the Study nexte tholde Bellechambre.
f. 155*b*. An Antique horne garnisshed with Siluer guilte with a Bawdrike likewise garnisshed.
f. 156*b*. ii hornes copper guilte enameled grene and redde.

Instruments at Westminster in the charge of
Philipp Van Wilder

DOUBLE REGALLES

f. 200. FIRSTE a paire of double Regalles with twoo Stoppes of pipes couered in purple vellat all over enbrawdered with Venice gold and damaske pirles havinge the Kinges Armes and badges likewise enbrawdered standinge uppon a foote couered with fustian of Naples and garnisshed with redd ribon the same foote beinge the Case for the same Regalles.

Item. A paire of double Regalles with twoo Stoppes of pipes couered with purple vellat all over enbrawdered with Venice golde and damaske pirles havinge the Kinges Armes and badges likewise enbrawdered standinge upon the Case of the same couered with fustian of Naples.

Item. A paire of double Regalles of latten with iii Stoppes of pipes couered with purple vellat enbrawdered all over with damaske pirles and Venice golde and the Cover thereof the inner parte couered with crimeson vellat likewise enbrawdered with damaske pirles havinge a stele Glasse in the same and the Kinges Armes and Quene Janes Armes likewise enbrawdered with a couer the pipes couered with crimeson vellat likewise enbrawdered having a rose crowned uppon the same standinge uppon a foote of wainscott painted in Rabeske woorke wherein liethe the Bellowes.

Item. A paire of double Regalles with viii halfe Stoppes and one hole stoppe of pipes, of woodde gilte siluered and painted with Rabeske woorke and histories havinge the Kinges Armes with a gartire supported by his graces beastes painted and gilt uppon the trimmer of the same standinge uppon a foote of woode beinge painted wherein liethe the Bellowes.

Item. A paire of double Regalles with iii stoppes of pipes, of woode vernisshed yellowe and painted with anticke woorke hauinge the Kinges Armes and Quene Janes armes with twoo playinge uppon a lute and a harpe and twoo singinge painted uppon the same standinge uppon a foote of wainscott painted yellowe with anticke woorkes wherein liethe the Bellowes: the same hath but two stoppes of pipes and thother Stoppe is but a Cimball.

SINGLE REGALLES

Item. One paire of single Regalles with iii stoppes of pipes, of woodde vernisshed yellowe standinge uppon a frame of woode withe iii pillors: it hathe but one Stoppe pipe of tinne one Regall of Tinne and a Cimball.

f. 201. – Item. One paire of single Regalles with twoo Stoppes of pipes, of woode vernisshed yellowe and painted with blacke Rabeske woorke standinge uppon a foote of wainscott the Bellowes liynge in the same: it hathe but one Stoppe of pipes of woode with a Cimball of Tinne and the Regall of papire.

Item. Twoo paire of single Regalles euerie of them with vi halfe stoppes of brase pipes, of woode gilte and painted and hauinge the Kinges Armes within a gartier and badges painted uppon the Bellowes standinge uppon a foote of woodde like a Cheste painted blacke.

Item. V small single Regalles twoo of them beinge in Cases of Timbre couered with leather and thother iii in cases of Timbre not couered.

Item. One paire of single Regalles with twoo Stoppes of pipes of timbre and one Stoppe of pipes of Tinne, of woode painted with blacke Rabeske woorke and vernisshed standinge uppon a foote of wainscott wherein liethe the Bellowes: the same hathe but one Stoppe of pipes of woode the Regall of papire and hathe a Cimball.

Item. One paire of single Regalles with iiii Stoppes of pipes, of woode vernisshed yellowe and painted with blacke anticke woorke standinge uppon a foote of wainscott the Bellowes lieing in the same: it hathe but one Stoppe of pipes of woode a Cimball of Tinne and a Regall.

Item. One paire of single Regalles with twoo stoppes of pipes couered with grene vellat and garnisshed on the foreparte with a narrow fringe of Venice golde standinge uppon a foote of wainscott painted grene with the Bellowes liinge in the same havinge a Cimball.

Item. One paire of single Regalles with vii halfe Stoppes of pipes, of woode vernisshed yellowe and painted with blacke Rabeske woorke with a foote of wainscott unpainted wherein liethe the Bellowes: the saide vii stoppes are but vii Registers diuided in three Stoppes with a Cimball.

VIRGYNALLES

Item. An Instrumente with a single Virgynall and single Regall withe a Stoppe of timbre pipes, of woode vernisshed grene and redde.

Item. An Instrumente with a double Virgynall and a double Regall with iii Stoppes of pipes, of woode painted with grene Rabeske woorke with a foote of wainscott and the Bellowes lyinge in the same.

Item. An Instrumente that goethe with a whele without playinge uppon, of woode vernisshed yellowe and painted blewe with vi round plates of siluer pounced with anticke garnisshed with an edge of copper and guilte.

Item. Twoo paire of double Virgynalles thone couered with blacke Leather and the lidde lined with grene bridges Satten and thother couered with redde leather.

Item. A paire of double Virgynalles couered with blacke Leather partelie siluered the lidde lined with grene bridges satten.

Item. A paire of double Virgynalles of Cipres in a case of wainscot.

Item. A paire of single Virgynalles couered with redde leather and the lidde with grene bridges Satten.

Item. Twoo paire of single Virgynalles thone of them havinge keies of Ivorie and thother of Boxe with twoo Cases to them of redde leather partelie gilte and lined with blacke vellat.

Item. A paire of single Virgynalles couered with grene bridges Satten with iii Tilles in them.

f. 202. – Item. Twoo paire of single Virgynalles couered with blacke Leather.

Item. One paire of single Virgynalles couered with redde Leather.

Item. A paire of single Virgynalles with pipes underneth and in a case of timbre couered in blacke Leather.

Item. A paire of single Virgynalles couered with redde leather partelie guilte.

INSTRUMENTS OF SOUNDRIE KINDES

Item. A paire of Claricordes couered with gilte leather.

Item. A paire of Claricordes couered with leather siluered.

Item. xix Vialles greate and small with iii cases of woodde couered with blacke leather to the same.

Item. Foure Gitterons with iiii cases to them: they are caulled Spanishe Vialles.

Item. Twoo Gitteron pipes of Ivorie tipped with siluer and gilte: they are caulled Cornettes.

Item. xiiii Gitteronne pipes of woodde in a bagge of Leather: they are caulled Cornettes.

Item. A Gitteron and a Lute beinge in a Case Cheste fashion of Timbre couered with leather.

Item. xxiii Lutes with xxiii Cases to them.

Item. v Cases with Flutes and in euerie of iiii of the saide Cases iiii flutes and in the vth three Flutes.

Item. One Case furnisshed with xv Flutes in it.

Item. One Case with tenne flutes in it: the same are caulled pilgrim Staves and the same case furnisshed conteinethe butt vi hole pipes.

Item. One case with vii Flutes in hitt.

Item. v Flutes of Iuorie tipped with golde enameled blacke with a Case of purple vellat garnisshed at both thendes with Siluer and guilte: the same Case furnisshed conteinethe but iiii hole pipes.

Item. Foure Flutes of Iuorie tipped with golde in a Case couered with grene vellat.

Item. One case with vii Crumhornes in it.

Item. One case with vi recorders of Boxe in it.

Item. viii Recorders greate and smale in a Case couered with blacke Leather and lined with clothe.

f. 203. – Item. Twoo base Recorders of waulnuttre, one of them tipped with Siluer: the same are butt redde woodde.

Item. Foure Recorders made of okin bowes.

Item. vi Recorders of Iuorie in a case of blacke vellat.

Item. One greate base Recorder of woode in a case of woode.

Item. Foure Recorders of waulnuttre in a case couered with blacke vellat.

Item. ix Recorders of woode in a case of woode.

Item. A Pipe for a Taberde in a Case of blacke leather.

Item. viii Shalmes in iii Cases couered with leather.

Item. A case with vii Shalmes in it: the same case furnisshed conteineth but v whole pipes caulled pilgrim Staves.

Item. A case with a Shalme of Boxe in it.

Item. One Shalme of woode.

Item. A Baggepipe with pipes of Iuorie, the bagge couered with purple vellat.

f. 204b. – FYRSTE one newe paire of double Virginalles couered with blacke leather with smale roses printed and gilte upon it the lidde lined with grene satten and garnisshed upon with redde silke Ribonne lozenge wise.

Item. Another newe paire of double Virginalles vernisshed yellowe and painted all ouer with redde rabeske woorke the lidde beinge lined with purple serrconet and havinge the Kinges armes painted and guilte in the middes of hit.

Item. A little paire of Virginalles single couered with redde leather in a Case of woode couered with blacke lether.

Item. Twoo faire paire of newe longe Virginalles made harpe fasshion of Cipres with keies of Iuorie havinge the Kinges armes crowned and supported by his graces beastes within a gartier guilte standinge ouer the saide keies with twoo caeses to them couered with blacke leather the inner partes of the liddes to the saide caeses beinge of wallnuttre with sondrie antickes of white woode wroughte in the same.

f. 205. – Item. A Case couered with crimeson vellat hauinge locke and all other garnisshements to the same of Siluer gilte with viii recorders of Iuerie in the same Case the twoo bases garnisshed with Siluer and guilte.

Item. One case of blacke leather with viii recorders of boxe.

Item. A case of white woode with ix recorders of boxe in the same.

Item. A case couered with blacke lether with vii recorders of woode in it.

Item. A little case couered with blacke leather with iiii recorders of Iuerie in it.

Item. One flute and vi phiphes of blacke Ibonie tipped withe Siluer thone of the phiphes lackinge a tippinge at one ende in a bagge of redde leather.

Item. iii Flutes of glasse and one of woode painted like glasse in a Case of blacke leather.

Item. iii Flutes of woode in a case of blacke leather.

Item. iiii Flutes in a redde leather bagge.

Item. A case with iiii Crumhornes in it.

Item. Another case with vii Crumhornes in it.

Item. v shorte Instruments caulled Dulceuses in v seuerall cases to them couered with blacke leather.

Item. viii Dulceuses couered with blacke leather, some of them havinge tippinges of Siluer.

Item. iiii bagge pipes with pipes of Iuerie.

Item. A litle Venice lute with a case to the same.

Item. Sondrie bookes and skrolles of songes and ballattes.

Item. An olde chest couered with blacke fustian of Naples.

Item. A chest collored redde with vi Vialles hauinge the Kinges Armes.

At HAMPTON COURTE

In the Priuey Chambre

f. 243*b*. One payre of portatives with the Kynges and Quene Janes Armes.

In the next bedchambre

f. 245*b*. A paire of Virgynalles the case couered with blacke Lether.

In the long Galorie

f. 247. A paire of Regalles in a case couered with crimson vellat.

Seven paires of Virginalles in cases of printed lether.

A paire of Virginalles facioned like a harp.

f. 247*b*. A case of printed lether with vii crokhornes of Iuorie.

In another Chambre

f. 248. One paire of portatives couered with crimeson Satten and em-brawdered with passumynt of golde and Siluer standing upon a square table of wainscotte.

In the Quenes Galorie

f. 249*b*. Paire of Regalles in a case of lether.

At WYNSORE

f. 315. One doble Regall with doble pipes painted and gilte with Antique

PLATE 53

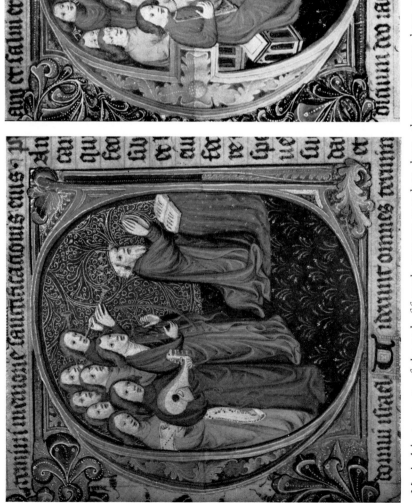

Musical instruments of the early fifteenth century: mandore, harp, shawm, trumpet, harp, psaltery, triangle, clarion and chime-bells

PLATE 54

A Consort for the Masque at Sir Henry Unton's Marriage, sixteenth century. Treble violon, flute, cittern, bandore(?), lute and bass viol. On one side a drum

PLATE 55

A Stringed Consort, *c.* 1585. (*Above*) Small Bass Viola and Cittern. (*Below*) Treble Violon and Bandore

PLATE 56

1. A Stringed Consort, *c.* 1585. Meane Violon and Lute
2. A Musical Water Party, *c.* 1780, by Zoffany

woorke with a greate Rose painted and gilte uppon the foreparte of the foote thereof.

At THE MORE

Soundrie parcelles

f. 340. One olde paire of Regalles broken in peces.

f. 340b. Two paires of olde Virginalles.

At NEWHALL

f. 362. A paire of faire greate Organes in the Chappell with a curten afore them of lynnen clothe staynd redd and blewe paned.

A paire of Virginalles verye olde and broken.

One olde Lute.

At NOTYNGHAM CASTELL

f. 367. An olde paire of Organes.

The Guarderobe of THE ROBES

HORNES

f. 408b. A Horne of Brasse garnisshed with nedle worke with a Bawdricke of Stole worke.

Item. A Horne of Saintte Cornelis couered with grene vellat.

Item. A Horne garnisshed with Siluer with a grene Coursse sett with Bullions of Siluer.

Item. A litle White Horne garnisshed with golde, the Bawdrick of blacke Corssey: the saide Bawdrick tied together with a buckle of golde and euerie ende the Corsse a Tape of golde with a paire of couples of silke and golde.

Item. A horne couered with grene satten garnisshed with siluer the Bawdericke of grene silke and Venice golde.

Item. One blacke horne garnisshed with siluer and guilte with a Bawdricke of redde Corssey.

Item. Three white hornes garnisshed with Siluer their Bawdrickes of silke.

Item. One white horne slewed with silver and guilte.

Item. A great blacke base horne slewed with siluer.

Item. A horne of brasse guilte.

Item. A great white horne graven with Antique wourk garnisshed with siluer and guilte with a bawdrick of grene vellat with buckles and studdes of siluer and guilte and a coller of Stole worke with turret buckle and pendaunt siluer and guilte.

Item. iii blacke hornes garnisshed with siluer and guilte two havinge Cheines of siluer guilte.

Item. One white horne garnisshed with siluer guilte with a Cheine of siluer guilte.

At SAYNT JAMES HOUSE •

f. 445. A paire of Organes standinge in the Chapple.

At WESTMINSTER

In the lytle Studye

f. 473. An antique horne garnisshed with siluer gilte with a Bawdricke likewise garnisshed.

An Inuentory taken at WESTMINSTER, 1550

f. 762. One case of Cornettes of v couered with blacke leather and a locke and a keye to it.

....

5·Some Illustrations of Musical Instruments in Manuscripts, Carvings and Paintings from the Eighth to the Eighteenth Century

(*British Examples Only*)

FOR the following list the MSS of English, Scotch and Irish workmanship at the British Museum, Lambeth Palace Library, the Bodleian Library, Cambridge University Library, the Advocates' Library (Edinburgh) and many of the college libraries have been collated. The fantastic representations of early instruments which are generally found in connection with the spurious letter of St Jerome to Dardanus, and are exhibited by English artists in MSS Tib. C. vi and Peterhouse 189, have been purposely omitted; for they appear to have been derived from some common Continental source, as similar illustrations occur in the Angers Psalter (ninth century), Boulogne Psalter No. 20 and Paris 7211 (tenth century), Munich 14523 (eleventh century) and Virdung's and Gerbert's reproductions from old manuscripts. It is interesting, however, to observe in connection with the opinion expressed in Chapter I, that in these delineations the Triangular Harp does not appear, the Cithara being always drawn as a Rote or Crot.

The MSS and carvings, from which illustrations have been taken for the present work, are marked with an asterisk.

Abbreviations

Add. (Additional MSS)	British Museum
Antiquaries	The Society of Antiquaries, London (Lindesey Psalter).
All Souls	All Souls College, Oxford
Ar. (Arundel)	British Museum
Aug. (Augustus)	British Museum
Belvoir	Reading Psalter, Belvoir Castle
Bodl.	Bodleian Library, Oxford
Cam.	University Library, Cambridge
Claud. (Claudius)	British Museum
Cleop. (Cleopatra)	British Museum
Corp. Chr.	Corpus Christi College, Cambridge
Douce	Bodleian Library, Oxford
Durham	Cathedral Library
Edin.	Advocates' Library, Edinburgh
Exeter Coll.	Exeter College, Oxford (Bohun Psalter).
Glasgow	University Library
Gorleston	Gorleston Psalter (Facsimile by S. C. Cockrell).
Harl. (Harley)	British Museum
Julius	British Museum
Junius	Bodleian Library.
Kings (James' Catalogue)	King's College, Cambridge.
Lamb.	Lambeth Palace Library.
Lans. (Lansdowne)	British Museum
Litlington	Missal, Westminster Abbey.
Luttrell	Psalter, British Museum
Nero	British Museum
Paris	National Library
Peterborough	Psalter, Mus. Royal, Brussels (Facsimile by Van den Gheyn).
Peterhouse	Peterhouse, Cambridge
Queens	Queens' College, Cambridge.
Royal	British Museum
St John's	St John's College, Cambridge
Sloane	British Museum.

Tib. (Tiberius)   British Museum.
Trinity   Trinity College, Cambridge.
Vesp. (Vespasian)   British Museum.
Vit. (Vitellius)   British Museum

The examples of carvings and paintings are selected from well-known buildings such as cathedrals, abbeys and large parish churches.

Bagpipe. MSS 13*th Cent.* Royal 2 B. vi, Add. 24686, Royal Roll 14 B. v.
    14*th Cent.* Harl. 6563, Nero D. ii, Royal 2 B. vii,* Ar. 83, Lamb. 233, Gorleston,* Peterborough, Luttrell.*
    15*th Cent.* Royal 17 C. xxxviii.
    CARVINGS. 14*th Cent.* Exeter, Beverley.
    15*th Cent.* Melrose, Malvern, Ripon, Boston, Hull, Manchester, Christchurch (Hants), Beverley, Westminster.
Bandore. MSS 17*th Cent.* Harl. 2027.
Bassoon. See Curtall.
Bells. MSS 11*th Cent.* Cam. Ii. 3. 12.
    12*th Cent.* Glasgow, U. 3. 2.*
    13*th Cent.* Add. 21926, Royal 2 A. xxii, Royal 13 B. viii (Irish), Add. 15253, Lans. 431, Queens 17, Trinity B. 10. 24, Douce, 366, Lamb. 233,* Peterborough, Luttrell, All Souls vii, Edin. 18. 8. 17 and Rusk. Bib.
    14*th Cent.* Ar. 83, Royal 6 E. vi, Harl. 6563, Cam. Kk. 6. 14.
    15*th Cent.* Royal 1 E. ix.*
    CARVINGS 12*th Cent.* Barfreston (?).
Buzine. See Trumpet (straight).
Chimes. See Bells.
Citole. CARVINGS 14*th Cent.* Worcester, Exeter,* Hereford, Lynn (St Margaret's).
    15*th Cent.* Beverley, *Malvern, Shrewsbury (St Mary's).
Cittern. MSS 17*th Cent.* Harl. 2027. See also Citole.
Clappers. MSS 11*th Cent.* Cam. Ff. 1. 23.*
    14*th Cent.* Peterborough.
Clarion. See Trumpet (folded).
Clavichord. CARVINGS 15*th Cent.* Shrewsbury (St Mary's).*
Clavicymbal. CARVINGS 15*th Cent.* Manchester.*
Cornett (curved). MSS 11*th Cent.* Cam. Ff. 1. 23,* Tib. B. v, Paris 11550, Harl. 630, Tib. C. vi.
    12*th Cent.* St John's B. 18.*
    13*th Cent.* Lans. 431, Royal 2 B. vi.

14*th Cent.* Lamb. 233, Trinity B. 11. 27.

15*th Cent.* Cam. Dd. 8. 18.

17*th Cent.* Harl. 2034.

CARVINGS 12*th Cent.* Canterbury (Crypt).*

15*th Cent.* Ware (Herts).

Cornett (straight). MSS 13*th Cent.* Royal Roll 14 B. v.

Crowd (Crwth). MSS 11*th Cent.* Cam. Ff. 1. 23.*

13*th Cent.* Add. 35166.*

14*th Cent.* Trinity B. 10. 2.

16*th Cent.* Add. 15036.

CARVINGS 12*th Cent.* Church Island (Kerry).

14*th Cent.* Worcester.

15*th Cent.* Shrewsbury (St Mary's*), Westminster (Chapter Ho. paintings).

Cruit or Crot. See Rote.

Curtall. MSS 17*th Cent.* Harl. 2027 and 2034.

Cymbals. MSS 13*th Cent.* Lans. 431, Add. 35166.

14*th Cent.* Royal 2 B. vii,* Royal 6 E. vi, Trinity B. 10. 2.

CARVINGS 14*th Cent.* Exeter.

15*th Cent.* Westminster (Ch. Ho. paintings).

Drum. MSS 12*th Cent.* Lans. 383, St John's B. 18.*

13*th Cent.* Edin. Rusk. Bib.

14*th Cent.* Royal 10 E. iv, Trinity B. 11. 27.

15*th Cent.* Harl. 2838.

16*th Cent.* Aug. A. iii.*

17*th Cent.* Harl. 2027.

CARVINGS 15*th Cent.* Ely, Boston.

16*th Cent.* Westminster. See also Pipe and Tabor.

Dulcimer. MSS 16*th Cent.* Royal 2 A. xvi.

17*th Cent.* Harl. 2027.

CARVINGS 15*th Cent.* Manchester.*

Fife. MSS 16*th Cent.* Aug. A. iii.*

Flute (vertical). MSS 14*th Cent.* Royal 2 B. vii.*

Flute (transverse). MSS 17*th Cent.* Harl. 2027.

Gittern. MSS 13*th Cent.* Douce 366.

14*th Cent.* Royal 2 B. vii, Ar. 83,* Royal 6 E. vi, All Souls vii,* Gorleston, Peterborough.

CARVINGS 13*th Cent.* Lincoln.

14*th Cent.* Exeter.

15*th Cent.* Beverley.

Guitar. See Gittern.

Harp. MSS 10*th Cent.* Junius xi (Bodleian).*

    11*th Cent.* Tib. C. vi, Ar. 60, Claud. B. iv, Harl. 603, Cam. Ff. 1. 23,* Corp. Chr. Parker 391,* Bodl. 352, Paris 11550.

    12*th Cent.* Lans. 383, Trinity B. 2. 3, Glasgow U. 3. 2.*

    13*th Cent.* Vesp. A. i (inserted leaf), Lans. 431, Ar. 157, Cleop. C. xi, Royal 2 A. xxii, Add. 24686, Lans. 420, Add. 35166,* Harl. 745, Add. 16975, Belvoir, Antiquaries, Kings 35, Bodl. Auct. D. 4. 17.

    14*th Cent.* Nero D. ii, Royal 10 E. iv, Royal 2 B. vii, Ar. 83, Harl. 6563, Harl. 273, Royal 19 B. xv, Add. 28681, Royal 15 D. ii, Sloane, 2466, All Souls vii, Exeter Coll., Gorleston, Litlington, Peterborough, Luttrell, Edin. 18. 8. 10.

    15*th Cent.* Royal 1 E. ix,* Harl. 2838, Julius F. vii, Lamb. 59, Bedford Psalter.

    16*th Cent.* Royal 2 A. xvi.

    17*th Cent.* Harl. 2027, Add. 17784, Add. 14905.

    18*th Cent.* Add. 15025 (Welsh).

    CARVINGS 9*th Cent.* Audbar (Forfar).

    10*th Cent.* Nigg (Ross).

    11*th Cent.* Monifieth (Forfar), Dupplin (Perth), Dublin (Nat. Mus.).

    12*th Cent.* Canterbury, Ely, Barfreston, Ardmore (Waterford).

    13*th Cent.* Lincoln, Iona.

    14*th Cent.* Exeter, Keills (Argyll), Dublin (Nat. Mus.)

    15*th Cent.* Manchester, Beverley, Malvern (window), Westminster, Jerpoint (Kilkenny).

Harpsicall (Harpsichord). MSS 17*th Cent.* Harl. 2027. See also Clavicymbal.

Hautboy. MSS 17*th Cent.* Harl. 2027 and 2934. See also Pipe (single).

Horns. MSS 8*th Cent* Vesp. A. i,* Nero D. iv.

    10*th Cent.* Harl. 603.

    11*th Cent.* Tib. C. vi, Add. 24199, Cleop. C. viii, Tib. B. v, Bodl. 352.

    12*th Cent* Lans. 383, Nero C. iv.

    13*th Cent.* Ar. 157, Cleop. C. xi, Royal 14 B. v, Add. 35166, Royal 13 B. viii (Irish), Bodl. Auct. D. 4. 17.

    14*th Cent.* Sloane 3544, Royal 10 E. iv,* Harl. 6563, Harl. 273, Trin. B. 10. 2,* Lamb. 233, Edin. 18. 6. 5, Gorleston, Luttrell.

    15*th Cent.* Tib. A. vii, Harl. 2838.

    CARVINGS 11*th Cent.* Durrow (King's Co.)

    14*th Cent.* Worcester, Ely.

    16*th Cent.* Cirencester.

Jew's Harp. MSS 17*th Cent.* Harl. 2027.

   CARVINGS 14*th Cent.* Exeter (Mins. Gall.).

Kettledrums. See Nakers.

Kit. MSS 17*th Cent.* Harl. 2027.

Lute. MSS 15*th Cent.* Harl. 2838.*

   17*th Cent.* Add. 17784, Add. 29372–29377.

   CARVINGS 15*th Cent.* Manchester, Beverley (St Mary's), Malvern (window),
     Westminster (Ch. Ho. paintings).

   16*th Cent.* Cirencester.

   17*th Cent.* Harl. 2027.

Lutina. See Mandore.

Lyre. MSS 11*th Cent.* Add. 24199, Cleop. C. viii, Tib. B. v, Bodl. 352.

Mandore. MSS 14*th Cent.* (late). Litlington.*

   15*th Cent.* Royal 1 E. ix.*

   CARVINGS 15*th Cent.* Chester, Westminster (Ch. Ho. paintings), Beverley.

Monochord. MSS 11*th Cent.* Cam. Ii. 3. 12.

   12*th Cent.* St John's B. 18.*

Nakers. MSS 14*th Cent.* Luttrell,* Litlington.

   CARVINGS 14*th Cent.* Worcester.*

   15*th Cent.* Beverley, Duston (Northants).

Organ. MSS 12*th Cent.* St John's B. 18.*

   13*th Cent.* Add. 21926, Add. 15253, Add. 35166,* Belvoir,* Bodl. Auct.
     D. 4. 17.

   14*th Cent.* Royal 2 B. vii, Ar. 83, Harl. 6563, All Souls vii, Trinity B. 10. 2,*
     Gorleston,* Peterborough,* Luttrell.

   15*th Cent.* Tib. A. vii, Lamb. 69.

   17*th Cent.* Harl. 2027.

   CARVINGS 14*th Cent.* Beverley (Percy Tomb), Exeter.

   15*th Cent.* Manchester,* Boston, Beverley, Westminster (Ch. Ho. paint-
     ings).

   16*th Cent.* Cirencester.

Organistrum. MSS 12*th Cent.* Glasgow U. 3. 2.*

   13*th Cent.* Lans. 431, Add. 21926, Add. 35166,* Antiquaries,* Belvoir,
     Bodl. Auct. D. 4. 17.

   14*th Cent.* Sloane 3544,* Harl. 6563, Trinity B. 10. 2, Luttrell,* Litlington.

   17*th Cent.* Harl. 2027.

   CARVINGS 13*th Cent.* Peterborough.

   15*th Cent.* Manchester, Beverley.

   16*th Cent.* Cirencester.

Panpipes. MSS 10*th Cent.* Harl. 603.

    11*th Cent.* Cam. Ff. 1. 23,* Paris 11550.

    12*th Cent.* St John's B. 18,* Glasgow, U. 3. 2.*

    13*th Cent.* Lans. 420.

    15*th Cent.* Julius F. vii.

    CARVINGS 12*th Cent.* Barfreston.* 13*th Cent.* Bristol.

Pipe (single). MSS 11*th Cent.* Harl. 603.

    13*th Cent.* Royal 2 B. vi, Add. 21926, Douce 366.

    14*th Cent.* Royal 2 B. vii,* Royal 6 E. vi, Lamb. 233,* Gorleston, Luttrell.

    15*th Cent.* Royal 1 E. ix,* Royal 17 C. xxxviii, Julius F. vii, Harl. 2838, Royal 19 C. vi.

    CARVINGS 10*th Cent.* Monasterboice (Louth).

    11*th Cent.* Durrow (King's County).

    12*th Cent.* Canterbury, Barfreston, Ely.

    14*th Cent.* Exeter, Lynn (St Margaret's).

    15*th Cent.* Manchester, Beverley,* Malvern (window).

    16*th Cent.* Cirencester.

Pipe (double). MSS 11*th Cent.* Cleop. C. viii, Add. 24199, Harl. 603.

    14*th Cent.* Royal 10 E. iv,* Royal 2 B. vii, Harl. 6563, Luttrell,* Litlington.

    CARVINGS 10*th Cent.* Clonmacnoise (King's County).

    11*th Cent.* Ardchattan (Argyll).

    13*th Cent.* Winchester, Lincoln.

    15*th Cent.* Hull.

    16*th Cent.* Cirencester.

Pipe and Tabor. MSS 13*th Cent.* Harl. 7640, Royal 14 B. v.

    14*th Cent.* Royal 2 B. vii, Harl, 6563, Royal 10 E. iv,* Ar. 83, Lamb. 233, Luttrell, Exeter Coll.

    16*th Cent.* Royal 2 A. xvi.

    CARVINGS 13*th Cent.* Lincoln, Exeter.

    14*th Cent.* Ely.

    15*th Cent.* Manchester, Beverley, New College (Oxford), Shrewsbury (St Mary's).

    16*th Cent.* Cirencester, Durham Castle.

Poliphant. MSS 17*th Cent.* Harl. 2034.

Psaltery. MSS 11*th Cent.* Tib. C. vi,* Bodl. 352.*

    12*th Cent.* Glasgow U. 3. 2,* St John's B. 18.*

    13*th Cent.* Lans. 431, Lans. 420, Ar. 157, Add. 21926, Add. 35166,* Add. 16975, Royal 13 B. viii (Irish), Antiquaries, Bodl. Auct. D. 4. 17.

14*th Cent.* Royal 2 B. vii, Harl. 6563, Edin. 18. 6. 5, Gorleston, Peterborough, Luttrell.

15*th Cent.* Royal 1 E. ix,* Tib. A. vii.

17*th Cent.* Harl. 2027.

CARVINGS 13*th Cent.* Peterborough.

14*th Cent.* Ely, Beverley, Shrewsbury (St Mary's).

15*th Cent.* Manchester, Westminster (Ch. Ho. paintings).

Rebec. MSS 11*th Cent.* Tib. C. vi, Paris 11550, Bodl. 352.*

12*th Cent.* Lans. 383, Glasgow U. 3. 2,* St John's B. 18,* Trin. B. 2. 3.

13*th Cent.* Lans. 420, Ar. 157, Add. 35166,* Antiquaries.

14*th Cent.* Trin. B. 10. 2, Luttrell.

15*th Cent.* Tib. A. vii, Cam. Dd. 8. 18.

CARVINGS 12*th Cent.* Canterbury (crypt),* Ely, Barfreston.

14*th Cent.* Exeter (W. front).

15*th Cent.* Westminster (Ch. Ho. paintings).

Recorder. MSS 12*th Cent.* Glasgow U. 3. 2.*

13*th Cent.* Douce 366.*

15*th Cent.* Harl. 2838.

CARVINGS 13*th Cent.* Chichester.

15*th Cent.* Boston, Manchester, Beverley (St Mary's).

16*th Cent.* Cirencester (double).*

Regals. See Organ.

Rote (Crot). MSS 8*th Cent.* Vesp. A. i,* Durham B. 2. 30.

9*th Cent.* Vit. F. xi (Irish).

11*th Cent.* Claud B. iv, Harl. 603, Bodl. 352,* Cam. Ff. 1. 23,* Paris 11550. 13*th Cent.* Add. 35166.

CARVINGS 8*th Cent.* Castledermot* (Kildare).

9*th Cent.* Ullard (Kilkenny),* Castledermot (South Cross).

10*th Cent.* Clonmacnoise (King's Co.).

11*th Cent.* Durrow (King's Co.).

Rybybe (Oval). MSS 13*th Cent.* Lans. 431, Add. 24686, Royal 14 B. v, Peterhouse 44, Trin. B. 3. 12, Trin. O. 9. 13, Douce 366, Edin. Rusk. Bib., Bodl. Auct. D. 4. 17.

14*th Cent.* Royal 2 B. vii, Harl. 6563, Add. 28681, All Souls vii,* Trin. B. 10. 2, Trin. R. 7. 3.

CARVINGS 12*th Cent.* Barfreston.*

13*th Cent.* Bristol.

15*th Cent.* Manchester (square).

16*th Cent.* Cirencester.

R

Symphony. See Organistrum.

Shawm. See Pipe (single).

Tabor. See Drum, and Pipe and Tabor.

Tambourine. See Timbrel.

Theorboe. MSS 17th Cent. Harl. 2034.

Timbrel. MSS 14th Cent. Royal 2 B. vii, Harl. 6553,* Edin. 18. 6. 5, Gorleston, Peterborough, Luttrell.

    CARVINGS 13th Cent. Chichester.

    14th Cent. Exeter.

    15th Cent. Beverley.

    16th Cent. Cirencester.

Triangle. MSS 15th Cent. Royal 1 E. ix.*

    17th Cent. Harl. 2027.

Trumpet (straight). MSS 13th Cent. Add. 21926, Add. 24686, Add. 35166,* Douce 366, Belvoir, Royal 14 B. v.

    14th Cent. Royal 15 D. ii, Royal 10 E. iv, Royal 2 B. vii,* Ar. 83, Royal 19 B. xv, Lamb. 233, All Souls vii,* Edin. 18. 6. 5, Gorleston, Peterborough, Luttrell.

    15th Cent. Royal 1 E. ix,* Lamb. 6, Bedford Psalter, Harl. 2278.

    16th Cent. Royal 2 A. xvi.

    CARVINGS 13th Cent. Lincoln.

    14th Cent. Exeter, Lynn (St Margaret's).

    15th Cent. Westminster (Ch. Ho.).

Trumpet (bent or folded). MSS 15th Cent. Royal 1 E. ix,* Harl. Roll. 7353,* Lamb. 6.*

    17th Cent. Add. 35324, Harl. 2027 and 2034.

    CARVINGS 14th Cent. Worcester.*

    15th Cent. Manchester.

Trumpet Marine. MSS 17th Cent. Harl. 2027 and 2034.

Vielle. See Rybybe and Viol.

Viol (incurved). MSS 12th Cent. Trin. O. 4. 7,* Glasgow U. 3. 2,* Nero C. iv.

    13th Cent. Lans. 431, Lans. 420, Ar. 157, Harl. 7640, Add. 21926, Add. 35166,* Add. 16975, Douce 366, Antiquaries.

    14th Cent. Ar. 83, Royal 6 E. vi, Add. 28681, Lamb. 233, Gorleston, Exeter Coll.

    15th Cent. Harl. 2838.

    17th Cent. Add. 17784, Harl. 2027.

    CARVINGS 13th Cent. Winchester, Lincoln, Beverley, Peterborough.

    14th Cent. Hereford, Lynn (St Margaret's).

15th Cent. Beverley, Westminster (Ch. Ho. paintings).
Wayte. See Hautboy.

References to continental examples occurring in the British Museum Manuscripts will be found in Mr A. Hughes-Hughes' excellent *Catalogue of the Manuscript Music*, Vol III, 1909.

....

6·The Classification of Instruments of Music

To M. Victor Mahillon, of Brussels, is due the credit of the first systematic and scientific method of grouping Musical Instruments, and his classification is set out in the well-known catalogue of the museum of the Brussels Conservatoire of Music. For the tripartite division into strings, wind and percussion, adopted by earlier writers, is incomplete, while the common sub-division of the wind instruments into wood and brass is very superficial, the material used in their construction being of secondary importance.

The following classification, drawn up by the writer in the first instance for the International Music Exhibition, held at the Crystal Palace, London, in 1900, is less intricate than M. Mahillon's, to whose valuable work and research the fullest acknowledgment is due. Its effectiveness for museum purposes has been proved in the catalogue of the Musikhistoriska Museum at Stockholm, and in that of the famous collection formed by Mrs J. Crosby Brown and presented by her to the Metropolitan Museum of New York; in this case, however, an inverse order of the classes was preferred, starting with the stringed instruments and working down to the more primitive Sonorous Substances as in the chapters of this book.

It only remains for our own country to create a collection as typical as these, and as illustrative of the evolution and development of musical instruments as those of Brussels, Berlin, Leipzig, Copenhagen and Paris.

To the subjoined scheme the names of some characteristic types in each division or section are added in the footnotes.

Classification

CLASS A: SONOROUS SUBSTANCES

I Without a keyboard $\begin{cases} \text{A Rhythmic (1)} \\ \text{B Tonal (2)} \end{cases}$

II With a keyboard (3)

III With automatic mechanism (4)

CLASS B: VIBRATING MEMBRANES

I Without a keyboard $\begin{cases} \text{A Rhythmic (5)} \\ \text{B Tonal (6)} \end{cases}$

II With a keyboard (7)

III With automatic mechanism (8)

CLASS C: WIND INSTRUMENTS

I Without a keyboard:

A. Flutes $\begin{cases} \text{i Vertical or Beaked (9)} \\ \text{ii Transverse (10)} \end{cases}$

B. Reeds $\begin{cases} \text{i Beating} \begin{cases} a \text{ Single} \begin{cases} \text{*with cylindrical tube (11)} \\ \text{**with conical tube (12)} \end{cases} \\ b \text{ Double} \begin{cases} \text{*with cylindrical tube (13)} \\ \text{**with conical tube (14)} \end{cases} \\ c \text{ Combined with air-reservoir (15)} \end{cases} \\ \text{ii Free (16)} \end{cases}$

C Cup mouthpieces $\begin{cases} \text{i with conical tube (17)} \\ \text{ii with cylindrical tube (18)} \end{cases}$

II With a keyboard:

A Flutes, Beating and Retreating Reeds (19)

B Free Reeds (20).

III With automatic mechanism (21)

CLASS D: STRINGED INSTRUMENTS

I Without a keyboard $\begin{cases} \text{i Air-vibrated (22)} \\ \text{ii Plucked} \begin{cases} a \text{ without a neck (23)} \\ b \text{ with a neck (24)} \end{cases} \\ \text{iii Struck (25)} \\ \text{iv Bowed (26)} \end{cases}$

II With a keyboard $\begin{cases} \text{i Air-vibrated (27)} \\ \text{ii Plucked (28)} \\ \text{iii Struck (29)} \\ \text{iv Bowed (30)} \end{cases}$

III With automatic mechanism (31)

N.B. – The *Classes* are distinguished by small capitals; the *Divisions* by Roman numerals; the *Groups* by large Roman capitals; the *Sections* by small Roman numerals; the *Sub-sections* by small italic letters; the *Branches* by asterisk marks. *Families* (Treble, Alto, Tenor, Bass, etc.) should be placed together in successive order.

Characteristic Examples

1. Cymbals, Castanets, Rattles, Gongs, Triangle.
2. African Marimba and Zanze, Xylophone, Bells, Jew's Harp, Nail Violin, Musical Glasses.
3. Keyed Harmonica, Carillons.
4. Clock Chimes, Musical Box.
5. Side and Bass Drums, Tambourine, Tom-toms.
6. Kettledrums, Onion Flute, Indian Nyastaranga.
7. Not yet in use.
8. Drums attached to self-acting Organs; Phonograph, Gramophone.
9. Arabian Nay, Bulgarian Kaval, Panpipes, Recorder, Flageolet.
10. Nose Flutes, Indian Murali, "German" Flute.
11. Syrian Arghool, Egyptian Zummarah, Hornpipe, Clarinet.
12. Saxophone.
13. Chinese Kwantzu, Japanese Hitschiriki, Krumhorn, Racket.
14. Arabian Zamr, Shawm, Oboe, Bassoon.
15. Indian Zitty, Platerspiel, Bagpipe, Musette.
16. Malay Kronee, Burmese Phan, Chinese Cheng, Mouth Harmonica, Concertina.
17. Bugle, Horn, Cornett, Cornet, Saxhorn.
18. Trumpet, Trombone.
19. Pipe Organs.
20. Harmonium, Reed Organs.
21. Barrel Organs, Orguinettes.
22. Aeolian Harp, Chinese Kite-bows, Air Violin.
23. Musical Bows, Lyre, Rote, Harp, Psaltery.
24. Guitar, Cittern, Lute, Mandoline.
25. Persian Santir, Dulcimer, Keyed Cittern, Provençal Tambourin.
26. Indian Ravanastrom, Burmese Thro, Arabian Rebab, Crowd, Viol, Violin, Hurdy-gurdy.
27. French Aero-clavicorde.
28. Virginal, Spinet, Harpsichord.
29. Clavichord, Pianoforte.
30. Nuremberg Geigenwerk, Arched Viall, Claviola.
31. Barrel Piano, Pianolas, etc.

If it should be thought that the incorporation of *all* forms of stringed instruments or of wind instruments, etc., under a single class renders the collection cumbersome and confused, the classification given above can be carried out in *geographical* departments, taking the types found in Europe, Asia, Africa, Oceania and America (native races), with a system of cross-references as so admirably set forth in the cases and catalogues of the Crosby Brown Collection (Metropolitan Museum of Art, New York).

In 1914 the above classification was elaborated by Professors von Hornbostel and Sachs. The four *Classes* are preserved and called Idiophones, Membranophones, Aerophones and Chordophones, the order of the two last being reversed. These *Classes*, denoted by figures, are divided into *Sub-Classes* marked by double figures, the *Class* number being to the left. *Sub-Classes* are again divided into *Orders*, denoted by three figures, the *Class* number and *Sub-Class* number to the left. *Sub-Orders* are marked by a figure standing to the right, and smaller divisions in the same way.

This somewhat intricate system with its multiplied nomenclature has not been generally accepted.

INDEX

A page reference followed by f *indicates a figure (illustration) on the page; followed by* n *a footnote. Plate numbers are in bold type and are followed by the number of the page they face or follow.*